PLATO'S *PHAEDO*

PLATO'S *PHAEDO*

DAVID BOSTOCK

CLARENDON PRESS · OXFORD

This book has been printed digitally and produced in a standard specification
in order to ensure its continuing availability

OXFORD
UNIVERSITY PRESS

Great Clarendon Street, Oxford OX2 6DP

Oxford University Press is a department of the University of Oxford.
It furthers the University's objective of excellence in research, scholarship,
and education by publishing worldwide in

Oxford New York

Auckland Bangkok Buenos Aires Cape Town Chennai
Dar es Salaam Delhi Hong Kong Istanbul Karachi Kolkata
Kuala Lumpur Madrid Melbourne Mexico City Mumbai Nairobi
São Paulo Shanghai Singapore Taipei Tokyo Toronto

Oxford is a registered trade mark of Oxford University Press
in the UK and in certain other countries

Published in the United States
by Oxford University Press Inc., New York

ISBN 0-19-824918-7

PREFACE

THIS book stems from a course of lectures designed for under-graduates at Oxford who were studying the *Phaedo* as their first introduction to philosophy. It therefore concentrates entirely on the philosophical interest of the dialogue, and has nothing to say of its considerable literary merits and dramatic power. It should be comprehensible to readers who have no background in philosophy, and it aims to avoid unnecessary technical devices and specialized terminology. On the other hand, it does treat the arguments of the text in considerable detail, and may be tough going at times. But philosophy is not easy, and there is no merit in pretending that it is.

Although the lectures were delivered to an audience who were studying the dialogue in the original Greek, when preparing them for publication I have deliberately not presupposed any knowledge of Greek, and have given a full explanation of those few passages where the translation of Greek words or phrases is both disputed and important to the argument. (On other occasions I have sometimes inserted a Greek gloss on my English vocabulary, to stir a chord in those who do know the language. But those who do not should simply ignore this.) It was therefore necessary to choose some translation to work from, and I have chosen the translation by David Gallop, in his contribution to the Clarendon Plato series (D. Gallop, *Plato: Phaedo*, Oxford 1975). This is an accurate translation and should be readily available. Gallop's commentary is also very full, and contains many useful discussions (though sometimes over-technical). But there are many trans-lations available, and it should be possible to use this book in conjunction with any that gives the standard page and section numbering in the margin.[1] Readers using other translations should simply bear in mind that my quotations may not fit their texts word for word.

---

[1] My line references are to the Greek text by Burnet, in the series of Oxford Classical Texts (Oxford, 1900). They may not exactly fit the lines of an English translation, but it should be easy to allow for any discrepancy.

When discussing interpretations of Plato's text, I have drawn freely from the scholarly literature on the *Phaedo*, but I have not burdened my discussion with references to it. I here apologize to all the many scholars whose ideas I have used without acknowl-, edgement. The suggestions for further reading at the end of the book do not go very far towards putting this right, as no such list of suggestions is helpful unless it is kept short and therefore very selective. The reader who wishes to trace my sources may usually do so by consulting Gallop's notes on the relevant passages, where interpretations that I discuss or advocate will generally be found attributed to their proper authors. There are very few places where I could claim a suggested interpretation as my own.

Plato is, and always has been, an author who fascinates me. Unfortunately the book may not succeed in conveying that impression to the reader, since it is mainly concerned to evaluate the arguments that Plato advances, and so it inevitably pays more attention to their faults than to their merits. It is worth making two general comments on this, before we come to the details. First, I am confident that Plato would himself approve the attempt to unravel the complexities of his arguments and lay bare the awkward tensions in his theories. He said himself that 'friendly refutations' form a major part of the study of philosophy,[2] and surely he was right. It is important not to let arguments pass unexamined—whether accepting them in the assurance that they come from a revered authority, or rejecting them simply because they do not fit one's own preconceptions. This is especially so when the arguments concern a claim so perennially attractive as the claim that the soul is immortal. That claim, the major thesis of the dialogue, I do not pretend to have refuted. But we should be in a better position to reflect upon it when the problems of Plato's most sustained attempt to argue for it are clearly seen. Second, we should bear in mind that Plato was the first person even to raise the question of the soul's immortality as a *philosophical* problem, i.e. as a problem for rational discussion rather than for religious— or anti-religious—dogma. Indeed there are many other important philosophical issues, both in the *Phaedo* and elsewhere, where it is absolutely clear that the credit for first raising the problem belongs to Plato. We should recognize that it requires genius to raise

---

[2] The phrase is from *Letter VII*, 344b, whose authenticity is disputed. But the idea is prominent also in much of *Republic* vii.

problems no less than to resolve them, and in this respect Plato was certainly a genius. What would have happened to philosophy if Plato had never lived? At least this much is obvious: it would be a long way behind where it now is.

Merton College, Oxford   DAVID BOSTOCK
April 1985

CONTENTS

I

INTRODUCTION

A. CHRONOLOGY

WHEN considering any philosophical work, ancient or modern, one will naturally wish to compare it with other works by the same author. The comparison may shed light on obscure passages, allow us to adjudicate between rival interpretations, and provide further elucidation of otherwise puzzling doctrines. However, there are risks in this procedure, for it cannot be assumed that an author never changes his opinions, and even where he still maintains the same opinion it still cannot be assumed that it is always that same opinion he is trying to express. He will, after all, have plenty of opinions, and one must beware of presuming that a similarity of language always indicates the same thought. Roughly speaking, it is reasonable to expect similar views in works composed at about the same time, but where two treatments differ widely in date one should be specially wary of the assumption that they must each be trying to say the same thing.

Unfortunately, with most ancient authors we do not know the dates of their various works, and Plato is no exception. There is, however, a fair measure of scholarly consensus on the general outline of the chronology of Plato's writings, and this will suffice for our purposes. Three main periods are distinguished—early, middle, and late—and the dialogues are distributed as shown in the table on the next page.[1] Although there are many more works in the early period, most of them are short. (Apart from placing the *Apology* first, I have listed these early dialogues simply in order of length, running from the *Crito* at 9 pages[2] to the *Euthydemus* at 36, the *Protagoras* at 53, and the *Gorgias* at 80.) By contrast, the middle and the late period each contain one very long work, the *Republic* and the *Laws* respectively, and the rest are

---

[1] I have omitted several short dialogues whose authenticity has been doubted, often with good reason (*Hipparchus, Amatores, Theages, Menexenus, Alcibiades I & II, Minos, Epinomis*).

[2] i.e., the pages in the edition of Stephanus (1578), which is always used when referring to Plato's text.

Early	*Middle*	*Late*
Apology	Phaedo	Parmenides
Crito	Symposium	Theaetetus
Ion	Republic	Sophist
Hippias minor	Phaedrus	Politicus
Euthyphro	Timaeus	Philebus
Lysis	(and Critias) ⎤ → ?	Laws
Laches	? ←—[Cratylus	
Charmides		
Hippias major		
Meno		
Euthydemus		
Protagoras		
Gorgias		

mostly of what seems to be the 'regulation' length of between 50 and 60 pages.[3] As a result, the total outputs of the middle and late periods (as listed) are about the same, and each is about twice the total output of the early period.

Within the early period there is no agreement on how the individual dialogues are to be ordered. It has often been held that the *Apology* (which is not, strictly, a dialogue) was the first thing that Plato wrote, but there is really no evidence for this (perfectly reasonable) conjecture. What one can say with confidence is that the *Apology* is certainly earlier than any of the other dialogues that will here be concerning us. The *Meno* and the *Gorgias* are usually thought to be towards the end of the early period, for reasons which I mention later (pp. 8–9).

Within the middle period it is admitted that there is no firm ground for saying which of the *Phaedo* and the *Symposium* comes before the other, though I think a majority vote would put the *Phaedo* first. On all accounts they are near-contemporaries, and it is also universally agreed that both come before the *Republic*,

---

[3] Our dialogue, the *Phaedo*, is a trifle on the long side at 61 pages. Other exceptions are that the *Parmenides* at 40 pages is unusually short, and the *Theaetetus* at 68 pages unusually long. The *Timaeus* (88 pages) is notably long, but it is hardly a dialogue. Its sequel the *Critias* (15 pages) is only an unfinished fragment.

which in turn comes before the *Phaedrus*. There is some dispute about the *Timaeus* (and *Critias*) and the *Cratylus*. Traditionally the *Timaeus* was thought to be a late dialogue, but more recently there has been a move to place it in the middle period, after the *Republic*. By contrast, the *Cratylus* was often classed as early, though I think the arguments for a post-*Republic* date are now finding general acceptance. Since neither of these dialogues is particularly relevant to the concerns of the *Phaedo*, we need not enter into these disputes.[4]

Within the late period, there is general agreement that the *Parmenides* and *Theaetetus* go together at the start, and some have regarded them as ending the middle period rather than beginning the late period. The *Sophist* and the *Politicus* are also agreed to have been written in that order, and to precede the *Philebus*. Although the *Laws* always used to be reckoned as Plato's last work, the argument for this is not actually very convincing. But again for our purposes we can leave this problem on one side.

I do not intend to examine the various reasons that scholars have had for dating the dialogues in this way. (They rely on changes of literary style, and to some extent on cross-references between the dialogues and on changes of doctrine from one dialogue to another.) From our point of view the most important points are that the *Meno* comes before the *Phaedo*, and the *Republic* comes fairly soon after it, while the *Symposium* is about contemporary. On these points there is no scholarly disagreement at all. So I here leave this question of the ordering of Plato's dialogues, and turn instead to a few remarks on how it relates to Plato's life.

Socrates was condemned to death in 399 BC, at which time Plato was nearing the age of thirty. (He was born probably in 428/7 BC.) The *Apology*, of course, purports to be the speech—or rather, speeches—that Socrates delivered at his trial, and so cannot have been written before then. It seems probable (though not certain) that it was written fairly shortly after. If we are right to suppose that the *Apology* begins Plato's writings, it will then follow that he

---

[4] My own ordering would be: *Republic* x, *Cratylus*, *Timaeus*. The *Phaedrus* could have been written before *Republic* x, but after *Republic* ii–ix; equally, it could have been very much later. All we can be quite sure of is that it precedes the *Sophist*.

started writing at about the age of thirty. In any case, it can hardly have been before then. All the early dialogues contain Socrates as chief speaker, and it does not seem at all likely that any of them were written while Socrates was still alive, and still conducting his own dialogues. So whether or not the *Apology* begins the series, we can still be confident that the series itself does not begin until after Socrates' death.

Now we are told that Plato first visited Sicily at about the age of forty, and that he there made the acquaintance of some Pythagoreans, in particular Archytas of Tarentum.[5] The *Phaedo*, as we shall see (p. 11), fairly clearly acknowledges a Pythagorean background, in a way that no other dialogue does. To this we may add that the *Symposium* seems to be dateable to after 385 BC, since it contains an anachronistic reference to the way the Spartans split up the territory of Mantinea in that year (*Symposium* 193a). In 385, Plato was forty-two or forty-three, so this is a couple of years after his first visit to Sicily. Finally, we are told that he founded his school at the Academy 'soon after' that visit.[6] Putting these points together, it is fair to conjecture that Plato's visit to Sicily at the age of forty coincides with the break between the early and the middle dialogues. There is ample time for the composition of the early dialogues before then, and the *Phaedo* can plausibly be put soon afterwards, while the Pythagoreans were still fresh in Plato's mind. The *Symposium* then comes a little later. Neither of these dialogues seems to have been written with the needs of the new Academy in view, whereas the long *Republic*, which comes next, is certainly connected with the Academy's concerns: it shows a notable interest in the rule and function of education.

If all this is right, then when Plato wrote the *Phaedo* Socrates had been dead for some fifteen years. In the interim Plato had written a number of other philosophical works, and had acquired sufficient stature as a thinker to be able to found the first 'university'. He had come a long way from the young man who had once sat at Socrates' feet and been fired by his enthusiasm for philosophy. Of course it does not follow that the influence of Socrates was now negligible, but it would no doubt have been modified by other influences, and there had been plenty of time for it to be shaped and fashioned in a distinctive way by Plato's

---

[5] Cicero, *De Republica* i. 16.
[6] Diogenes Laertius iii. 20.

own reflections. So I now leave matters of pure chronology for a few remarks on this head.

B. BACKGROUND

(i) *Socrates*

Plato's impetus to philosophize clearly came from Socrates, and since he was nearly thirty when Socrates died he could have been listening to Socrates' way of philosophizing for ten years or even twenty before then. 'Listening' is the right word, for Socrates wrote nothing. Moreover, he did not offer instruction by holding classes or giving lectures, which was the normal practice of the so-called Sophists, who undertook to educate the young for a fee. Instead, Socrates simply walked about Athens and struck up conversations with whoever he happened to meet. He would ask some innocent-seeming question, probe the answer a little so as to bring to light a deeper question, and then settle to a rigorous examination of the answers he was offered. But it all took the form of a conversation.

This approach to philosophy evidently caught Plato's liking, and it probably underlies Plato's choice of the dialogue form for his own writings. With only two notable exceptions, the early *Apology* and the middle-to-late *Timaeus*, Plato wrote only dialogues. If you had asked Plato why he adopted this particular literary form, he might perhaps have replied that the chief thing about philosophy is that one must *argue*. Philosophy deals with questions on which opinions tend to conflict, and which cannot easily be settled just by gathering evidence. So to get at the truth of the matter one has to argue it out. It is easy enough simply to state an opinion. Moreover, at Athens public speaking was very much a regular feature, and there was plenty of interest in the rhetorically effective ways of presenting an opinion and winning over an audience. But rhetoric is no friend of truth. Skilfully used it will hide the weak points of a case by a distracting irrelevance or an emotional appeal; it will use fine words for doubtful occasions, neat antitheses for quite misleading contrasts; and above all the vigorous flow of the speech will carry the audience on with a momentum that gives no time for proper reflection. The main trouble, as Plato saw it, is that the orator cannot be stopped and questioned every other sentence, and so he never does have to argue in the philosophical sense of the word: step by step, and with each step properly examined before we proceed to the next. In order to reach the *truth* on these difficult issues what is required is serious questioning and honest answers, careful deduction of conclusions from explicitly stated premisses, and plenty of opportunity for objections to be put and considered. That, one might say, was characteristic of Socrates' own method of philosophizing, and that was what Plato too was trying to capture in his dialogue form. No doubt the early dialogues do give us a reasonably accurate picture of Socrates' methods.

As for Socrates' beliefs, that is a large question which it would take us too long to go into. But I shall just briefly mention a couple of points that are of some relevance to the *Phaedo*. The first is that the early dialogues portray Socrates as preoccupied with questions of *ethics*. As he saw it, the chief and most pressing problem, to which all else is subordinate, is to know how one ought to live. Now there were, of course, some very traditional answers available. For example, a standard list of Greek virtues would be: one must be just (δίκαιος), wise (σοφός), courageous (ἀνδρεῖος), moderate or self-controlled (σώφρων), and god-fearing (ὅσιος). There were also some rather untraditional answers being put about by the Sophists, but Socrates always professed his allegiance to the traditional virtues. Nevertheless he evidently did not find the usual list very helpful, not because he thought it was wrong but because he did not find it sufficiently *clear*. What exactly is *meant* by 'justice', 'courage', and so on? So a typical Socratic conversation would be devoted to a 'what is *X*?' question—what is justice, courage, moderation, and so on—and he used to make it clear that he did not want a list of examples or cases of *X*, but an account of the one thing common to all those examples. Most people seemed to think they knew well enough, but on a little investigation their answers all turned out to be inadequate, and it soon became clear that it was really very difficult to find a proper account of what, e.g., justice is. I shall have more to say about Socrates' pursuit of 'what is *X*?' questions when we come to consider the theory of forms in the *Phaedo*. For the moment it is enough to say that the theory of forms emphatically asserts the existence of those things that Socrates was so anxious to define—justice, beauty, goodness, and so forth—and asserts that these 'forms' exist even though they are never perfectly exemplified in this world. But the theory of forms is a topic for later discussion, and I say no more of it now. The other point that I shall mention at this stage is that Socrates evidently regarded his philosophical worries over what exactly the virtues are as something with genuinely practical implications. He thought that if we do not really know what, say, justice is, then we can hardly be just: you must know how you ought to live before you can set about trying to live like that. Moreover, this concern for living in the right way he described as a concern for his *soul* (and he thought that everyone should share this concern). While he did not, so far as we know, hold any particular views about the nature of the soul, he did take it as obvious that the most important thing about a man is his soul. So the thing one should be most concerned about is the care of one's soul (ἐπιμέλεια τῆς ψυχῆς), and that he took to be the same thing as being concerned to live rightly, and that in turn he took to be the same thing as knowing how one ought to live, i.e. knowing what the virtues are. So he saw a direct connection between looking after your soul and seeking to answer those difficult 'what is *X*?' questions. This is clearly a connection that we also find in the *Phaedo* (though rather differently drawn).

In these brief remarks about what *Socrates* used to do and say I have been relying entirely on the evidence of *Plato's* early dialogues, for that is just about the only worthwhile evidence we have on Socrates' philosophy. This appears to assume that in his early dialogues Plato was writing history, that is, simply recording various conversations in which the actual Socrates took part. But actually I do not believe that at all. Nor do I even believe the weaker thesis that, while it will be Plato's part to have fashioned and structured the conversation, still every substantial point made by his character Socrates is a faithful reproduction of something that the actual Socrates did once say. So I had better say a little of the relation between what we may call Plato's Socrates—that is, the character Socrates in Plato's dialogues—and the actual Socrates.

Some people (notably Burnet and A. E. Taylor) have held the extreme historicist thesis that absolutely everything that Plato's Socrates says the actual Socrates said too. But this view is far too extreme. I think everyone will now agree that it is obviously out of question for the late dialogues, and scarcely more defensible for the middle dialogues. I give just one example, because of its relevance to the *Phaedo*. In the *Phaedo* the soul is regarded as a single and undivided entity, whereas later in the *Republic* it is argued to be a compound of three parts. On the historicist thesis the explanation can only be that Socrates himself held both these views, and must have held the *Phaedo*'s view at the time of his death, and the *Republic*'s view at some earlier time. (If he had held the *Republic*'s view when the conversation allegedly recorded in the *Phaedo* took place, he would inevitably have brought it in: it is by no means irrelevant to the *Phaedo*'s arguments.) But this explanation must be the wrong way round, for the *Republic*'s view is clearly the more thoughtful of the two, and no one who had reached that view could revert to the more naïve view of the *Phaedo* without considerable qualifications. The true explanation is obviously that it was Plato, and not Socrates, who worked out the view that the soul has three parts, and the arguments for that view which are given in the *Republic*. When he wrote the *Phaedo*, Plato had not yet reached that more sophisticated view, and that is why the *Phaedo* shows no knowledge of it. But in later dialogues it is the tripartite view of the soul that is retained (*Phaedrus* 246 ff., *Timaeus* 69–72). Here is a clear example, then, of a theory which is put into the mouth of Plato's Socrates, but cannot be due to Socrates himself. The extreme historicist thesis can at best be held to apply to the early dialogues: it makes nonsense of the middle and the late dialogues.

There is in fact quite a marked difference of approach between the early and the middle dialogues, which one can put in broad terms like this. Nearly all the early dialogues are formally *inconclusive*. They ask for a definition of some virtue, or they raise some question such as 'can virtue be taught?', and they end without an answer to the question raised. The dialogue will canvas various answers, but in the end all answers will be rejected. (Often one can see which of the various answers Plato thought most interesting, and sometimes it is tempting to read between the lines, and find an answer that he may be interpreted as recommending; but the formal structure remains an inconclusive one.) For this reason, the dialogues are often called 'elenctic', as they mostly consist of suggestions and their refutations (ἔλεγχος = refutation). There are some exceptions to this generalization: for example, the *Meno* puts forward the doctrine of recollection for the first time, which the *Phaedo* will enlarge upon, and the *Gorgias* has some quite positive things to say about morality. But by and large 'elenctic' is the right title for these early dialogues. By contrast, the middle dialogues are much more positive: in the *Phaedo*, *Symposium*, and *Republic* Plato is clearly putting forward and arguing for some quite positive views. The two main claims of the *Phaedo* are the immortality of the soul and the theory of forms; the *Symposium* is very informative on love and beauty; and the *Republic* is full of positive proposals, on the definition of 'justice' and other virtues, on how states ought to be governed, on the proper place of women, on education, and so on. It seems to me that *none* of these positive doctrines is genuinely Socratic; in particular, neither the theory of forms nor the immortality of the soul should be credited to the historical Socrates.

While many would agree with me about the theory of forms, the question of the immortality of the soul is more controversial. It has often seemed difficult to believe that Plato simply *invented* the idea that Socrates spent his last day on earth trying to prove the immortality of the soul. But I do not myself see this as very much of a difficulty; after all, we know that he was quite capable of inventing other things for Socrates to do and say. Nor need I deny that Socrates *discussed* the question of immortality on his last day, but if he did he was surely much more tentative in his view than the *Phaedo* says.

The clearest evidence for this is the contrast between the *Phaedo* and the *Apology* on this topic, for in the *Apology* Socrates is very clearly represented as taking an agnostic stance. As he says towards the end:

Death is one of two things. *Either* it is annihilation, and the dead have no consciousness of anything, *or*—as we are told—it is really a change—a migration of the soul from this place to another. (40d–e, tr. Tredennick.)

He goes on to point out that *both* these possibilities have their good points: there is much to be said for oblivion, and much to be said also for meeting with those who have died and talking with them. But his main point is that we simply do not know what happens after death. Thus his final word is:

Now it is time that we were going, I to die and you to live. But which of us has the happier prospect is unknown to anyone but God. (42a.)

But perhaps the most forthright passage is rather earlier:

> To be afraid of death is only another form of thinking that one is wise when one is not; it is to think that one knows what one does not know . . . If I were to claim to be wiser than my neighbour in any respect, it would be in this—that not possessing any real knowledge of what comes after death, I am also conscious that I do not possess it. (29a–b.)

It is true that there is not an outright contradiction between the *Apology* and the *Phaedo* on this topic. In the *Apology* Socrates' main claim is that he does not know, and in the *Phaedo* he never does claim strictly to know. But in the *Phaedo* he certainly does have a definite view, he is entirely confident in it, and he offers plenty of arguments for it. These arguments are presented as depending on the theory of forms, so they would not have been available to the historical Socrates. Because of this dependence Plato does admit that they cannot be regarded as providing an irrefragable proof, since the theory of forms is a premiss that has not itself been proved. But no one can doubt that Plato himself believed wholeheartedly in this premiss, and that is why the dialogue is so full of confidence. However, the historical Socrates did not, and he—I imagine—was perfectly well aware that he could give no good argument on the question, one way or the other. That is why he no doubt was, as the *Apology* portrays him, determinedly agnostic. Though he may of course have considered the possibility that the soul is immortal, I do not think he can have committed himself to it. (It is worth remarking that the doctrine seems to have played no part in his ethical views, though Plato certainly did see it as having ethical consequences.) The confidence in immortality that we find in the *Phaedo*, and the arguments there offered for it, should therefore be ascribed to Plato himself and not to Socrates.[7]

To generalize, then, it seems to me that the positive theories put forward for the first time in the middle dialogues are not inherited from Socrates but must be credited to Plato himself. Doubtless Plato saw them as in some way growing out of a concern with Socrates' problems—I shall later indicate how the theory of forms may have grown out of a concern with 'what is *X*?' questions (pp. 96–8)—but they are not themselves Socratic views. It is natural to

---

[7] For another divergence between the *Apology* and the *Phaedo*, which I think has a similar explanation, see p. 136, n.2.

suppose that in the early dialogues Plato began by putting into Socrates' mouth only the kinds of views and the kinds of arguments that Socrates himself might have used. But Plato was a philosopher in his own right, and would soon be having new ideas of his own. Even in the very early dialogues (whichever they are) there is doubtless some material which is Plato's own contribution, and I imagine that this increased as he wrote more. It would not be surprising if after some time he could not have said himself which of the things he attributes to his character Socrates were genuinely Socrates' own views, and perhaps he really did feel that, for example, the theory of forms was already 'implicit' in the kind of way that Socrates himself thought. But we need not agree with him.

Tentatively, then, I ascribe to Socrates himself the concern with morality (equated with the concern for one's soul), and the focussing on 'what is *X*?' questions about morality, for these are both pervasive themes in the early dialogues. But the particular arguments are offered in those dialogues are just as likely to be due to Plato as to Socrates.

(ii) *The Pythagoreans*

As well as Socrates in the background there are also others, and notably the Pythagoreans. Indeed, Plato seems rather to go out of his way to give the *Phaedo* a Pythagorean setting. It is narrated to one Echecrates, who lived at the small town of Phlius in the Peloponnese (about ten miles south of Sicyon). We are told that Phlius was a centre of Pythagorean philosophy, and that Echecrates was himself a Pythagorean who had once been a pupil of the greatest Pythagorean in mainland Greece at this time, namely Philolaus.[8] Philolaus had migrated from Sicily to Thebes, and Thebes was also the home of the two chief interlocutors in our dialogue, Simmias and Cebes. The text explicitly mentions that they had learnt something from Philolaus (61d); so they too would be familiar with Pythagorean ideas. What significance should we see in this? It is tempting to suppose that Plato is wishing to acknowledge a debt to the Pythagoreans, and perhaps in particular to his new friend Archytas of Tarentum (represented in the dialogue by Philolaus). If the chronology given earlier (p. 4) is right, he had recently been visiting them, and may here be

[8] Diogenes Laertius viii. 46.

obliquely expressing his thanks. But if so, what for? What did he think he had learnt from them?

A necessary preliminary to answering that question would be to determine what doctrines the Pythagoreans themselves held, but on that point all is confusion. Though it is clear that many people in the fifth century and later were called 'Pythagoreans', the evidence on what doctrine or doctrines were characteristic of this school is both obscure and unreliable. (For example, there are a few dark fragments purporting to be from Philolaus' pen, but their authenticity is often doubted.) The best we can say is that at least these three ideas count as Pythagorean: (i) that the soul is immortal, and periodically reincarnated from one animal body to another;[9] (ii) in some quite obscure way 'things are numbers'; (iii) the notion of 'harmony' is very important.

Now Plato did not need to visit any Pythagoreans to get the idea that the soul is immortal and periodically reincarnated. In his own writings, he first looks favourably on this idea in the *Meno* (81a–b), where he credits it to 'priests and priestesses of the sort who make it their business to be able to account for the functions which they perform', goes on to remark that you can find the idea in Pindar and other poets, and proceeds to quote Pindar on the topic. (In our own dialogue the idea is simply called an 'ancient doctrine', 70c5–6.) It is clear that in the *Meno* he is a bit tentative about this theory; so it would be reasonable to suppose that his Pythagorean contacts bolstered his conviction and gave him a much firmer belief. But what is not clear is how they did it. Did Plato take some (or perhaps all) of his *arguments* for immortality from his Pythagorean friends? The suggestion seems to me very unlikely, but the truth is that we do not know: there is no record of any Pythagorean *argument* for immortality, except that Pythagoras himself claimed to remember previous incarnations (and so did Empedocles).[10]

A suggestion one might perhaps consider is that the Pythagoreans somehow gave Plato the idea of the theory of forms, and at the same time provided a connection between that and the immortality of the soul. Could the obscure doctrine that 'things are numbers' have played a part in the formation of the theory of forms? Again we have to say that we do not know, because we have no clear

---

[9] And perhaps sometimes to vegetable bodies (Cf. Empedocles, fr. 117 DK)
[10] Diogenes Laertius viii. 4–5.

evidence on what this doctrine meant, but the indications are that it was highly muddled and really very silly. For example we are told of one Eurytus, a disciple of Philolaus and known to Archytas of Tarentum, that he would find how many coloured pebbles were needed to outline a picture of a man and then call that *number* 'the definition of man'.[11] Anyone who had thought about the problems of definition, as Plato certainly had, would clearly dismiss this as puerile. A slightly better connection between things and numbers is one that approaches closer to the notion of 'harmony': Pythagoras himself is reputed to have discovered that concordant musical intervals are created by strings whose lengths are in simple numerical proportions (e.g. 1 : 2 for the octave, 2 : 3 for the fifth, and so on).[12] Though there are some passages in much later dialogues of Plato which seem to pick up and develop this idea (especially in the *Philebus*), it does not seem to play any role in the theory of forms that we find in the *Phaedo*. On the whole, then, I remain rather sceptical of the suggestion that the mysterious doctrine that 'things are numbers' is the key to Plato's theory of forms.

The most that one can reasonably conjecture is I think this. The Pythagoreans evidently had a peculiar reverence for numbers, and some of them (including Plato's friend Archytas) were in fact mathematicians of some note. It may be, then, that contact with the Pythagoreans led Plato to pay more attention to the notion of number than he had done before, and to raise in his own mind the question of what kind of a thing a number is. This may be relevant to the development of his theory of forms, for at least the *Republic* connects forms very closely with number and mathematics, though the connection is not prominent in the *Phaedo*. In addition it is worth nothing that the recollection argument had first appeared in the *Meno* (80–86c) in connection with our knowledge of mathematical truths, though again this is not how it is presented in the *Phaedo*. The recollection argument, of course, is one of the *Phaedo*'s crucial links between the theory of forms and the immortality of the soul. Perhaps, then, in Plato's own mind there is a closer tie between forms and numbers, and between recollection and mathematics, than would appear from the way the

Phaedo presents things, and this mathematical side to his thinking may owe something to Pythagorean influences. But the Pythagoreans surely stimulated Plato to think for himself: there is no reason at all to suppose that they had already reached his conclusions. I shall later have more to say on how numbers and mathematics fit into the theory of forms and the theory of recollection, so I leave further elaboration until then. For the moment I simply ' repeat that there is no proper evidence to show that the Pythagoreans had anything to do with it. There is equally no proper evidence bearing on another possible Pythagorean influence, the suggestion that the soul is a 'harmony'. But that too can be left until we come to it.

(iii) *Others*

There are various other suggestions about what led Plato to his theory of forms. One which is perhaps worth mentioning is Aristotle's view that he was impressed by Heraclitus' well-known thesis that 'everything is in flux' (πάντα ῥεῖ):

After the systems we have named came the philosophy of Plato. Having in his youth first become familiar with Cratylus and with the Heraclitean doctrines (that all sensible things are ever in a state of flux and there is no knowledge about them), these views he held even in later years. Socrates, however, was busying himself about ethical matters and neglecting the world of nature as a whole but seeking the universal in these ethical matters, and fixed thought for the first time on definitions; Plato accepted his teaching, but held that the problem applied not to sensible things but to entities of another kind—for this reason, that the common definition could not be a definition of any sensible thing, as they were always changing. Things of this other sort, then, he called Forms . . . (*Metaphysics* 987a29–b8, tr. Ross.)

On this account, then, the theory arises by combining the two views that sensible things are constantly changing and that what a Socratic definition defines must be unchanging. Certainly the *Phaedo* does claim that all sensible things are constantly changing, though one may doubt whether it gives this as a *reason* for saying that there are forms. (It does indeed figure as a reason later, in the *Timaeus*, but I think that by then the theory of forms has itself altered considerably.) It may also be mentioned that while Aristotle cites the Socratic search for definitions as the foil to

Heraclitean flux, others have seen rather the influence of Parmenides, who insisted that what genuinely is cannot change. But again that seems to me to be a rather later influence. After these remarks about the background to Plato's thinking, let us now come to the *Phaedo* itself.

C. PRELIMINARIES (61b–63e)

(i) *Prospectus*

The dialogue can be regarded as dividing into two main parts, separated by an interlude, and furnished with an introduction and conclusion. In more detail, the main divisions are:

Introduction	(i)	of the Dialogue (57a–59c)
57a–63e	(ii)	of the Scene (59c–61b)
	(iii)	of the Theme (61b–63e)
Part I	(i)	Socrates' Defence (63e–69e)
64a–84b	(ii)	The Cyclical Argument (69e–72d)
	(iii)	The Recollection Argument (72e–77d)
	(iv)	The Affinity Argument (77e–80b)
	(v)	The Defence Elaborated (80c–84b)
Interlude	(i)	Simmias' Objection (84c–86e)
84c–95e	(ii)	Cebes' Objection (86e–88b)
	(iii)	Remarks on Argument (88c–91c)
	(iv)	Reply to Simmias (91c–95a)
	(v)	Recapitulation of Cebes (95a–e)
Part II	(i)	Explanations and Hypotheses (95e–102a)
95e–107b	(ii)	The Final Argument (102a–107b)
Conclusion	(i)	The Myth (107c–114c)
107c–118a	(ii)	Socrates' Death (115a–118a)

This table of contents contains six sections of argument directly about immortality: the cyclical argument, the recollection argument, and the affinity argument in Part I; the reply to Simmias in the Interlude; and both sections of Part II, which together form a continuous argument. Most of my discussion will be devoted to these six sections. But before I start on this, I make some general remarks on the soul, so that we can begin with some idea of *what* it is that we are trying to prove immortal, and these remarks will draw mainly on Socrates' Defence, and its Elaboration, with a few asides on the Myth. I shall also add at the end a short retrospective discussion of the theory of forms and its role in the dialogue as a whole.

Before I begin on this programme, I shall insert here a few
observations on the last section of the Introduction, for this little
discussion of suicide raises a point of some interest.

(ii) *Suicide (61b–63e)*

One may observe that the main theme of the dialogue—the
immortality of the soul—is slipped in unobtrusively and then at
once submerged in a puzzle about suicide. To begin with, no one
questions the immortality assumption, and the first point raised is
how it could be reasonable to combine this with the usual and
traditional prohibition on suicide.

As a matter of fact, one does not need to believe in immortality
to find the ban on suicide puzzling. Even if you hold that death is
the end, you may still find it difficult to say what is wrong with
suicide. After all, there is nothing very surprising in the thought
that some unfortunate people live such wretched lives that their
life is not worth living, and they would, therefore, be better off
dead. In that case, why should they not be permitted to do away
with themselves? The way the point arises for Socrates is rather
different. He too believes that some people would be better off
dead, namely the philosophers, but of course this is not because
their lives are especially wretched but because great rewards await
them when they are dead. That is why he takes the trouble to ask
whether Evenus is a philosopher, for if he were not there would be
no reason to say that death would be a benefit to him. (Curiously,
he receives the answer 'yes'. But it seems doubtful that Evenus did
practise what Socrates calls philosophy—of which more anon.)
But anyway, the problem arises for anyone who thinks, for
whatever reason, that some people would be better off dead.

It is clear that the problem comes from combining the two theses

(i) Some people are better off dead.
(ii) No one should kill himself.

Unfortunately the sentence in which Socrates actually poses the
problem (at 62a) is somewhat ambiguous, but since Gallop spends
some time dissecting various alternative ways of construing it, and
since it really makes no difference to the problem just how this
sentence is construed, I shall treat the point very brusquely. As I
read it, the sentence may be paraphrased:

You will perhaps be surprised if this rule alone is unqualified, namely that it never turns out that there are some people, on some occasions, for whom it is better to be dead than alive (though there are such qualifications to other general rules); but if there are some who would be better off dead, you will perhaps be surprised if they are not permitted to do themselves a good turn, but must await some other benefactor.[13]

That is: it would be surprising if (i) were false, and no one were ever better off dead; but granted that (i) is true, it then seems surprising that (ii) is true, i.e. that no one should commit suicide, not even those who would benefit by it. In fact all the company are agreed that (i) is true, and I think we too may agree with it. Can we, then, agree that (ii) is true as well? The company do seem to accept it, though with a small qualification: at 62c6–8 it is suggested that when Socrates drinks the hemlock that *will* be suicide, but will also be permitted, because it is a 'necessity sent by God'. But clearly the exception is a very special case, and the company do accept the traditional doctrine that suicide is always wrong in all ordinary cases. We might not feel so bound by traditional doctrine, and we might therefore evade the problem entirely by denying (ii). But Socrates and company do not take this course, and they have to face the problem.

Let us first ask why there is a problem here at all. After all, (i) and (ii) are not themselves contradictory, so why should they not both be true? In order to obtain a contradiction we need to add a third premiss

(iii) If anyone ought to do something, then doing it is good for him.

(Hence: if anyone ought not to kill himself, then not killing himself is good for him. But by (ii) everyone ought not to kill himself, whereas by (i) not killing oneself is not good for some people.) Anyone who wishes to accept both (i) and (ii) must therefore deny (iii). But (iii) must certainly be true if the *reason* why one ought to do something is always that it is good for one. So if we are to deny (iii), we must find some *other reason* for why one ought to do this or that. Putting it in more grandiose terms, we must find some other basis for morality than self-interest. To illustrate, suppose

[13] I take τοῦτο in a2 to look forward to the rule stated in the very next lines, that life is always better than death. (Gallop is quite wrong to object that this rule is 'completely unstated'.) I take ὥσπερ καὶ τἄλλα in a4 to mean 'as in the case of other general rules (sc. about what is better than what)'.

we took the view that there are *two* reasons why you ought to do things, one that it is good for you, and the other that it is good for others. It will then follow that if you ought not to commit suicide, then *either* it must be good for you if you do not commit suicide, *or* it must be good for others. And perhaps the second alternative will cover some relevant cases. For example, if Socrates is right, then it would no doubt have been good for him if he had committed suicide some years ago. But it would not have been good for others: his friends would have been deprived of his company, and the Athenians generally would have been deprived of the 'gadfly' that they needed (*Apology*, 30e). Consequently we can still maintain that he was right not to have committed suicide, even though it would have been in his own interest to do so.

It may properly be objected that although this suggestion does widen the basis for morality, it does not widen it enough to justify the traditional ban on suicide. On the present suggestion, if there are people who themselves would be better off if they were dead, *and* whose death would not make others worse off, then there is no reason why these people should not commit suicide, and they are permitted to do it. (Indeed the present suggestion apparently entails that these people ought to commit suicide.) This does not seem to accord with the traditional prohibition. So let us now drop this suggestion, which anyway was introduced only for illustration, and see what suggestions Socrates makes himself. My point has been that in order to reconcile (i) and (ii) one must suggest some other basis for morality than simple self-interest.

Socrates' first idea is a non-starter, just because it has no implications about the basis of morality. His point probably is the (Orphic and Pythagorean) doctrine that our souls are *imprisoned* in our bodies while we are alive.[14] But even if they are, that has no tendency to explain why the way we ought to act is not always in our own interests. So I see no useful lead in this suggestion, and since Socrates himself immediately drops it, so shall I.

The second idea is that we are the gods' possessions. This looks more promising, because the analogy that Socrates goes on to make between divine and human shepherds (or slave-owners) at once brings in the thought that the gods have wishes about the behaviour of their flock, and so suggests the principle needed:

---

[14] ἔν τινι φρουρᾷ (62 b3). The Greek could mean 'in a kind of prison' or 'in a kind of guardhouse' (as if on sentry-duty). The same criticism applies in either case.

what we ought to do is not necessarily what is in our own interest, but may rather be what the gods want us to do. However, the problem is merely postponed, because we can now raise this question: since the gods are clearly construed as benevolent gods, why is it not the case that what they want us to do always is what is most in our own interests? If so, we are simply back where we started. A possible answer reverts to my illustrative suggestion earlier: it would be quite natural to suppose that what the gods want is what is best for their flock *as a whole*, which may not be the same as what is best for any one member of it, considered individually. (What is in *my* best interests may at the same time be against the interests of others.) But again, the objection I raised earlier still applies. Although this is—in my view—an improvement on a purely self-interested basis for morality, it still does not seem enough to justify the near-absolute prohibition of suicide that is part of the traditional morality. There may surely be cases in which it would be better both for me and for the flock as a whole that I should be dead (e.g. if I were very old, incurably ill, and a burden to others).

Well, we could continue this debate a little. It might be suggested that the gods do not want us to commit suicide either for some other reason which we do not know of, or perhaps for no reason at all. But the latter is surely an untenable position, for it seems not to be fitting to the nature of the gods that they should want things for no reason at all. Moreover, once we admit this, it must follow that the introduction of the gods was after all irrelevant. If the reason why we ought to do something is that the gods want us to, and the reason why they want us to do it is such and such, then we can simply cut out the mention of the gods altogether: the reason why we ought to do it can be given simply as such and such. In other words, if the gods must have a reason for wanting whatever they do want, then the mere fact that the gods do want us to do something cannot ever be the final answer to the question why we ought to do it, so morality cannot, in the end, be founded on theology. (A similar argument to this same conclusion had in fact been given by Plato himself, in an earlier dialogue, the *Euthyphro* (7a–11b).)

Where does all this leave us? Well, first, it is certainly *consistent* to hold both that some people would be better off dead and that no one ought ever to commit suicide, but in that case one cannot also hold that the sole basis of morality is self-interest.[15] Socrates suggests introducing what the gods want as an alternative basis for morality, but on investigation that turns out to be merely postponing the problem. The fact that God wants us to do something can never be the final answer to why we ought to do it, unless God can want things for no reason at all. So we still require a different basis for morality if we are to justify the prohibition of suicide, and so far we have not found one. Of course it is *consistent* to say 'no one ought ever to commit suicide, but I do not know why', but it is hardly a satisfying position.

With that, I leave this issue, and move on to the main topic of the dialogue.

[15] We shall see (pp. 32–5) that in fact Plato *does* seem to take self-interest as the sole basis of morality.

II

THE SOUL AND IMMORTALITY
(63e–69e; 80c–84b)

A. PRELIMINARIES

THE introductory section of the dialogue is brought to an end by the little exchange with Crito at 63d–e, and the main discussion begins at 63e8 with Socrates offering a further 'defence'. Like the defence that he offered at his trial it is intended to justify the way he has lived, but more particularly it is intended as a justification of his present attitude in the face of death. His main theme is that the true philosopher has been *practising* for death all his life. As he develops this theme we begin to learn what he takes a 'true philosopher' to be, and what he thinks is actually going to happen to him at his death. Throughout this part of the dialogue the immortality of the soul is simply assumed—of course, the rest of the dialogue will be devoted to proving it—and we may regard the discussion here as mainly an exposition of *what* has to be proved. In particular, I shall concentrate on the question of what exactly it is that Socrates calls a 'soul' and takes to be immortal.

He begins by defining death as the separation of soul and body, and the state of being dead as the state in which soul and body exist separately from one another (64c4–8). The second part of this definition is somewhat careless, for there is obviously no reason to insist that a man's body must go on existing all the time that he is dead (as is later recognized, e.g. at 80b–c). Those who are sceptical of immortality will evidently say the same of the soul. Setting this aside, another point worth observing is that the definition is somewhat vague about *what* it is that can be said to die or be dead. For the most part Socrates speaks of a *person* dying or being dead, meaning thereby that his soul and body have separated. But on one occasion he also speaks of a *body* dying (106e6), which we can understand as a matter of that body being separated from its soul, and three times he speaks of a *soul* dying or being dead (77d2–4, 84b2, 88a6), which is presumably to be taken in the same way. Death as separation, then, can easily be understood as applicable to persons and to bodies and to souls. But this last usage is somewhat awkward, for in the Final Argument Socrates will claim that souls 'do not admit death'. (His position, obviously, is that souls can be separated from bodies, but cannot be destroyed. Perhaps he should have admitted that the word 'death' has other meanings than that which is here assigned to it.) But for the present these problems are hardly serious, and I turn instead to the much more fundamental problem that underlies this definition: what is meant by a 'soul', and in particular a soul 'separated from the body'?

One must of course begin with the observation that the Greek word ψυχή (*psyche*) is not very well translated by the English word 'soul'. I shall continue to use 'soul' as a purely conventional translation, but the English word has several unfortunate associations. (For example, it is often reserved for use in religious contexts, which is by no means the case with the Greek word. In more idiomatic speech 'soul' is often associated with emotion and feeling, in opposition to reason or intellect, but again there is no hint of this with the Greek.) What, then does the Greek word mean?

B. ACTIVITIES OF THE SOUL

The Greek word has *many* meanings. At its widest it simply connotes life, in a very general sense. For example the living and the non-living are contrasted in Greek as the things with soul and without soul (τὰ ἔμψυχα and τὰ ἄψυχα), and in this dichotomy it is by no means unusual to count plants as things with soul, just because they can reasonably be called living things. Thus Aristotle, who explicitly recognizes a variety of different kinds of soul, has what he calls the 'nutritive' soul (τὸ φυτικον) as his lowest kind, and this is the kind of soul that plants have. His point is that they exhibit life by taking in nourishment and so growing, and because this is something that only living things can do there must be a corresponding kind of soul responsible for their doing it. All ordinary[1] living things have this 'nutritive' soul, but many will also have other kinds of soul in addition. For example, animals typically have 'locomotive' souls, which just means that they also exhibit life by moving around, and so on.

---

[1] For Aristotle, the stars are alive, and they have 'locomotive' souls but no 'nutritive' souls. God is a living thing with neither of these kinds of soul.

The general principle behind Aristotle's approach is clearly to begin by classifying the different kinds of activity that living things exhibit, and in virtue of which we class them as living, and then to associate a different kind of soul with each. It will be best if we too begin with this line of approach, listing some of the activities that can be credited to souls, so that we can sidestep the awkward question of what kind of a thing the soul *is*, and concentrate rather on what it *does*. (Equally, I shall begin by being somewhat careless over the question whether it is quite right to say that the soul itself *does* this or that, or whether we ought strictly to say that it is the person who does these things, by virtue of the soul that he has. I shall take up later the question of the relation between the person and his soul.)

First, then, we should note that 'soul' may be invoked to account for any activity typical of living things, including those more or less biological activities that human beings share with even very 'lowly' living things, for example nutrition and growth, reproduction, locomotion, and so on. But without attempting any more detailed list here, I shall pass straight on to what we may call *conscious* activities, for consciousness seems to us a very important ingredient in the typical activities of men (and higher animals), and most distinctive of their life-style. Within this general area there are still a wide variety of activities which can usefully be distinguished.

(i) *Perception* is perhaps the most simple form of conscious activity, as when one feels hot or cold, or hears a loud bang, or sees a blue sky. But it should be noted that we also speak of perception when much more sophisticated activities are concerned, for example seeing that the approaching bus is a No. 7. One cannot have this kind of perception without (in this example) some knowledge of what buses are, and of the significance of this way of classifying them; so altogether more complex mental apparatus is involved. Along with simple perceptions one might include feeling pain, which seems just a special kind of perception. In a different direction, many have sought to assimilate *memory* to perception, and one might also wish to add the peculiar phenomena of dreaming, hallucinating, and so forth.

(ii) Perception very often leads to action because we have *goals*, or *desires*, e.g. the avoidance of pain. Desires again range from very simple kinds, such as hunger or thirst, which are quite naturally called 'bodily', to much more sophisticated kinds. Consider, for example, the differences between wanting a drink, wanting to watch television, wanting to be prime minister, wanting to know who put the drawing-pin on the chair, wanting to understand differential equations, and so on and on indefinitely. Clearly there is scope for all manner of classifications of different kinds of desire. Along with desires we might mention the enjoyment or pleasure one may get from satisfying a desire (or in other ways), and the unpleasantness of pain or hunger, or again of continuing to be baffled by differential equations.

(iii) Desires are in some ways similar, and in other ways dissimilar, to *emotions* such as fear, love, hatred, compassion, and so on. Some emotions (such as fear or embarrassment) are typically short-lived states, involving special kinds of feelings, and often with marked physical manifestations (e.g. sweating, blushing). Others are long-lasting states of mind with no such accompaniments, and shade off towards those states of mind or dispositions which we count as part of a man's character. (Compare pride, which is sometimes counted as an emotion, and humility, which usually is not, with for example meanness or generosity.) Along with the emotions we might perhaps mention moods such as boredom, hilarity, depression, exhilaration, and so on.

(iv) Most perceptions, desires, and emotions inevitably presuppose *knowledge* of some kind, or at least *belief*. Some beliefs arise fairly directly from perception ('this is water'), some are based on past perception and memory ('water satisfies thirst'), some are due to reasoning of various kinds ('Drinking-water is colourless. This water is dark green. So it probably isn't fit to drink'). *Reason*, again, may be classified into various forms. In one aspect (just hinted at), reason is often thought of as controlling our desires and emotions, and therefore directing our actions. But in another aspect it may be seen as operating 'itself by itself', as when we work out a sum simply because we want to know the answer, and with no intention to act on it. This is often called 'theoretical reason', contrasted with 'practical reason', and I shall have more to say about it as we proceed, since it is clearly important to the *Phaedo*.

This little catalogue of conscious activities (and states) makes no claim to completeness, but does illustrate the wide variety of forms of consciousness: we are typically conscious of almost all the activities and states just listed, and since the soul is specially connected with consciousness they can all be credited to the soul. (On the face of it, they could almost all occur unconsciously too; whether they should then be attributed to the soul is perhaps a matter for debate, which I shall not enter into.)

C. THE DISEMBODIED SOUL (63e–68c; 80c–84b)

When it is claimed that a man's soul is immortal, or anyway that it goes on existing in separation from the body, this claim implies that some at least of these (or similar) activities continue in the separated state. Perhaps this is not strictly necessary. One might be able to make sense of a theory according to which when the soul was separated from the body it remained *dormant*, and nothing at all happened in it. But clearly Plato's theory is not of this kind. He holds that the separated soul does indeed remain conscious and active. What kinds of activities, then, does he think do continue in the separated state?

When one reads Socrates' Defence, one is inevitably given the impression that the only activities of the soul that can survive separation are the activities of the true philosopher. The philosopher, we find, averts his attention from such pleasures as food and drink and sex (64d4–7), and does not desire material possessions (64d8–e6). Such desires concern the body, and such pleasures come by way of the body, whereas the philosopher has no concern with things bodily. The implication apparently is that since in the separated state there is no body, these desires and pleasures cannot then occur. Next we find that the philosopher despises perception and the use of his bodily senses, eyes and ears and so on (65a9–b7). They are merely a hindrance to what he is interested in, and they too, one presumes, will not occur when there is no body. Similarly, the body distracts him by needing to be looked after, by filling him with irrelevant lusts and desires, and with fears (and presumably other emotions) (66b7–c5). Again the point seems to be that when the body falls away, these desires and emotions will fall away with it, and in the separated state there will be no such things. What the philosopher *is* concerned with is called 'reasoning' (τὸ λογίζεσθαι, 65c2) and described as reaching out for the forms 'by pure intellect alone' (εἰλικρινὴς διάνοια, αὐτὴ καθ᾽ αὑτήν, 66a2). Pursuing this goal, the philosopher is already separating his soul from his body as much as he can, and in that way practising for the complete separation that death will bring. We must presumably infer that pure reasoning will continue into the separated state, but nothing else will.

Before proceeding, I should add a few notes on what we have had so far. First, we are not here offered any very good explanation of why the philosopher despises his senses (65a9–b7). It is claimed that they are not accurate or clear, but no argument is offered for this, and it is anyway not much of a ground for rejecting them as a source of knowledge. But as we read on it becomes clear that the real complaint about them is not that what they tell us is inaccurate, but that what they tell us about—the physical world—is something that is of no interest. For the philosopher's concern is with forms, and forms are not to be grasped by the senses anyway, but by pure intellect. There is no explanation at this point of how one can pursue an intellectual enquiry into anything if one cannot at least *start* from information supplied by the senses, and indeed this would seem to be a difficult problem. For centuries philosophers have supposed that all knowledge must begin with experience, for what other starting point is there? But Plato clearly does not agree. We shall come later (ch. VIII) to the alternative method that he proposes. I shall also postpone any discussion of the forms, the objects which the proposed method is to investigate, until we have seen more of Plato's views about them.

A second point worth making here is that Plato is not saying, as a first reading might suggest, that while it is the soul that engages in reasoning it is the *body* that perceives, desires, fears, and so on. If that were his view, it would be difficult to explain how the body's doing these things could so upset the soul, or why getting rid of these desires & emotions should count as purifying the soul. (It would also be difficult to explain the different view of the disembodied soul that we shall meet shortly.) Rather, it is the soul that actually does these things, but it does them when it is in a body, and because of the body it is in. Thus when it sees it sees through the eyes of the body, and will no longer see when it has no body to furnish eyes. Similarly when it wants food it does so because of the feeling which it gets from the body's empty stomach, which again is a feeling it will be free of when it has no body. Generally, while it is in a body it will be sensible of what happens in that body, and this sensibility will inevitably give rise to perceptions, desires, and emotions of all kinds. They happen in the soul, but they would not happen if there were no body for the soul to be sensible of.[2]

This brings me back to the main point that I wish to make. Although there is no direct statement in the *Phaedo* that it is *only* the faculty of pure reason that survives into the disembodied state, that must surely be the implication of Socrates' Defence. The philosopher is described as one who attempts to separate his soul from his body as much as he can, and in effect what this comes to is that he concentrates all his efforts on pure reasoning and pays as little attention as possible to the perceptions, desires, and emotions which arise only because he has a body. This is said to be practising for death, which is the complete separation of soul from body. It must surely follow that in death the soul has no such perceptions, desires, and emotions; it rejoices always in pure reason and nothing else.

But it is now time to look at some of the *other* activities which are elsewhere credited to disembodied souls. We have not completely described even the state of the dead philosopher, for we have omitted to mention that he will be happy, and will enjoy the society of other gods and (possibly) other men (63b–c, 69e, 81a). But with ordinary non-philosophers our description has been way off target, for it seems that they practise pure reason no more after their deaths than before. Rather, they *fear* Hades (81c11), they *retain* their desires for things bodily (81e1), and they keep their characters as virtuous or vicious, social or anti-social, mild or cruel, temperate or gluttonous, and so forth (81e–82b). If we may add the evidence of the closing myth, they also retain a *memory* of their past lives (108b), and can meaningfully be punished and rewarded (133d–e). Dead souls can *appeal* to one another, *persuade* one another, *forgive* one another, and so on (114a–b). In these passages it appears that disembodied souls are capable of pretty well all those conscious activities that embodied souls are capable of: they can perceive (though presumably without eyes), they can feel pain (though without nerves), they can be frightened (though without adrenalin), etc. I do not wish to imply that this

---

[2] In 94b–d it does appear to be the *body* which has desires and emotions and not the soul, but the passage is in any case a surprising one. I shall comment further on it when we reach it (pp. 131–3).

picture is self-contradictory—I do not think it is—but certainly it seems rather less plausible than the more economical picture we had first.

It may be suggested that Plato does offer some explanation of how this could be so: when a non-philosopher dies, he suggests that the soul is not after all *completely* separated from the body, but remains 'interspersed with a corporeal element' (81c4). But this is surely not an explanation that we should take seriously (and its application to ghosts is presumably humorous). If we do take it seriously, then it will imply that the non-philosopher's soul is in life extended throughout his body, and retains this shape after death, with some material particles somehow 'clinging' to it. We can then contrast this with the spatial language which is sometimes used of the philosopher's soul, which is said to 'assemble and gather itself together, away from every part of the body, alone by itself' (67c8, cf. 80e5). The philosopher's soul is perhaps squeezed into a tight ball, so dense that there are no gaps or chinks where a material particle might be embedded, and so smooth of surface that none can stick to it. The theory can then be tested by accurate weighing of bodies just before and just after death: we expect to find that a non-philosopher's body suffers some weight loss at death, while a philosopher's body does not. But obviously this interpretation of the *Phaedo* is absurd. It treats the soul as if it were made of some quasi-material stuff, and just the kind of thing that might be blown apart by the wind, especially if you happened to die in a storm (77e1). It is not what Plato means to suggest at all, and when he spoke of a soul being 'interspersed with a corporeal element' he obviously meant to be understood as speaking figuratively. His point was just that the soul retains its desires for things bodily.

The belief in a reasonably 'full' mental life after death is common, and from Homer onwards (*Odyssey* xi) all those who have pictured it have pictured the souls of the dead as having the shape of human bodies, and as doing just the kind of things that ordinary living human beings do. Upon reflection one has to admit that this picture is not to be taken literally, but we continue to use it because we do not know any better picture to substitute for it. Plato is no exception. He has no explanation of how disembodied souls can continue with very much the same range of conscious activities as living humans have, but he evidently believes that they do, and so he pictures them as if they were living human beings.

We do him an injustice if we think he took the picture seriously.

The *Phaedo*, then, contains two distinct views of life after death. One, which is very much a philosopher's view, and is applied to the philosopher's death, supposes that at death all those aspects of conscious activity which depend upon the soul's awareness of its body will fall away, and as a result the disembodied soul will be capable of pure reasoning but nothing else. The other, which is the more usual religious view, and is applied to other deaths, supposes that pretty well all the conscious activities of ordinary living human beings will persist into the disembodied state. The two are reconciled by a religious doctrine, which Plato took over from Orphics or Pythagoreans, a doctrine of sin, purgatory, reincarnation, and eventual purification and release from 'the wheel of rebirth'. In more detail, the doctrine is that when you die then you are punished for your sins either by a longish period in purgatory (as in the Myth), or by a brisk reincarnation in a less pleasant form of life (as in the elaboration to Socrates' Defence), or by first one and then the other, which seems to be Plato's standard version (as in the myth of the *Republic*). So the object is to live a life that avoids sin—or, if one such life is not enough, then sufficiently many (usually three, according to the myth of the *Phaedrus*). This is 'purification' (κάθαρσις), and will release you from the wheel of rebirth and admit you to bliss everlasting. To obtain our reconciliation, all we have to do is to adapt this religious doctrine. We take bliss everlasting to be the philosophic afterlife, in which the soul pursues pure reason and nothing else, and we take the life of purification to be the philosophic life, in which the body and all its works are held in contempt, and all energies are concentrated on the life of pure reason. The point here is that pure reason can be pursued in complete independence from all things bodily, and it is therefore the most admirable feature of the soul. (As Aristotle was to stress later, it is also the feature in which human beings most differ from other animals.) It will then follow as a corollary that sin must be equated with paying attention to bodily things. If killing others, injuring others, and behaving violently towards one's parents, are to count as sins (114a), that must be because they are cases of paying attention to bodily things, for the scheme now requires that that and nothing else be the criterion of sin.

Now that we have the full doctrine before us, a point that may be observed in parenthesis is that Socrates' Defence is misexpressed. Socrates says simply that he has spent his whole life practising for death, but he does not mean that he has been practising for what happens to all men whey they die. On the contrary, he has been practising for a very special kind of death, the death that admits you to bliss everlasting. That is not, however, a very serious criticism. It is more important to consider the implications which this scheme has for morality, implications which Plato himself points to in 68c5–69d2.

D. IMPLICATIONS FOR MORALITY (68c5–69d2)

Socrates begins with the claim that what is commonly called bravery (ἀνδρεία) belongs especially to philosophers, and what is commonly called temperance (σωφροσύνη)[3] belongs only to them (68c). Both these claims may be questioned, because Socrates seems to have misidentified what are commonly called bravery and temperance. Bravery he takes to be simply a matter of fearlessness in the face of death (68d), and no doubt it is fair to claim that the philosopher does have this characteristic. But in fact we commonly think that there are many other situations in which bravery may be displayed, e.g. by standing up to physical or mental torture, by being prepared to risk life or health or goods in a noble cause, or simply by being calm or cheerful in conditions of pain or adversity. (Plato had discussed the question 'what is bravery?' in the Laches, and he there saw a much wider range for it.) There seems to be no special reason why the philosopher should display these other sorts of bravery as well. With temperance the objection is rather different. We can grant Plato that what is commonly called temperance concerns those kinds of desires that he calls 'bodily', but ordinarily temperance is taken to require moderation or well-orderedness in the pursuit of these desires (ἔχειν κοσμίως περὶ αὐτάς), and not scorning them altogether (ἔχειν ὀλιγωρώς) (68c8–10). The philosopher, it seems, is a single-minded ascetic who suppresses all his bodily desires, and this is not what is ordinarily called temperance (or moderation, or self-control) at all.[4] (Nor is there any reason to suppose that only philosophers

---

[3] σωφροσύνη is a notoriously untranslatable word. It combines the notions of temperance, moderation, and self-control, and often shades off into meaning just 'good sense'.

[4] Aristotle would regard it as a vice opposed to temperance, which he calls ἀναισθησία (E N 1107b6–8)

have it: misers and power-seekers may have it too, as our text appears to recognize at 82c5–8).

Socrates goes on to say that there is something strange and illogical (ἄτοπον, 68d3; ἀδύνατον, 68e3) about ordinary bravery and ordinary temperance. Ordinarily, he says, a man is 'brave through fear'—fear of something he regards as worse than death, perhaps shame, or dishonour. Similarly the ordinary temperate man is 'temperate through being overcome by pleasures', insofar as he abstains from pursuing some pleasures only because he desires others. (For example, he abstains from drinking too much tonight because he wants the 'pleasure' of a clear head tomorrow.) There is actually nothing strange or illogical about this, but it is made to seem strange when the claim that the brave man is brave 'through fear' (of greater evils) is re-expressed as the claim that he is brave 'through cowardice' (68d12), and similarly when the claim that the temperate man is temperate through his desire for other pleasures is put as his being *overcome* by these other pleasures, and hence as his being temperate 'through intemperance'. So apparently these virtues are 'caused' by their opposite vices.[5] But both these extensions are illegitimate.

Intemperance is not a matter of being led by *any* desire—e.g. by the desire for health—but rather of giving in to *immoderate* desires, and especially immoderate bodily desires, when one ought not to. Similarly, cowardice is not a matter of being led by *any* fear. Plato himself earlier specified the relevant fear as specifically the fear of death, and on this account being led by fear of shame or dishonour would not be cowardly. But anyway Plato's simple characterization obviously will not do. Suppose I am thirsty, but abstain from drinking the weedkiller through fear of death, and instead go off to get a drink of water. Surely that is not a case of cowardice? Perhaps a better suggestion might be this: just as intemperance is giving in to *immoderate* desires, so perhaps cowardice is giving in to *unworthy* fears, when one ought not to.[6] The ordinary temperate man, according to Plato, resists his immoderate (bodily) desires only because he has other desires too that he wants to satisfy, but there is no reason why these other

[5] This theme, the causation of something by its opposite, will play a prominent role later (Ch. VII).

[6] But are courage and cowardice always concerned with fears? Neither the child who cries when he is mildly hurt, nor the child who bites back his tears when he is badly hurt, need be afraid of anything.

desires should also be immoderate bodily desires. Similarly the
ordinary brave man may resist his unworthy fears only through
fear of something else, but again that other fear need not be an
unworthy one. Some distinctions such as these are certainly
required, for otherwise, if we adopt Socrates' way of talking, every
rational action whatever will be done through cowardice and
through intemperance. If it is a rational action, there will be some
purpose that the agent is trying to achieve, and we can always say
that he acts out of a desire for the pleasure of achieving that
purpose, and out of a fear that unless he so acts it will not be
achieved. This applies even to the philosopher: he wants the
pleasure of philosophizing and fears to be deprived of it. But
Socrates would not like us to conclude that he is therefore
intemperate and cowardly.

Although we can in this way remove the 'illogicality' that Plato
professed to find in the ordinary man's behaviour, we have not
touched the main complaint that he has against it, namely that its
motivation is purely hedonistic: it consists in trading off one
pleasure against another, and has as its object just the all-round
maximization of pleasure (69a6 ff.). Clearly he is thinking here of
more or less bodily pleasures; at any rate he is certainly excepting
the pleasure of philosophy. But it would appear that once we add
that into the account, the position of the philosopher is not
essentially different. He is equally bent on maximizing pleasure,
we might say, and his life differs from others only because he
enjoys philosophy (or 'wisdom', φρόνησις) much more than
anything else. So he obtains his greatest pleasure by putting all his
energies into philosophy and paying no heed to the things of the
body, but for all that it still seems to be pleasure that he is
pursuing. Perhaps, indeed, he is pursuing it more efficiently than
others, because he is also taking into account the fact that his way
of life will lead swiftly to bliss everlasting, while other ways will
not. His hedonism, therefore, takes the longer view, and is very
much better thought out. But is it not still hedonism?

Perhaps some light would be shed on this if we could follow out
the contrast between 'what is commonly called' a virtue and the
corresponding 'true virtue', for Plato evidently intends such a
contrast, but seems to lose sight of it. One expects him to say that
whereas ordinary bravery consists in overcoming the fear of death

with the help of some other and countervailing fear, the 'true bravery' which is characteristic of the philosopher consists in his not having the fear of death in the first place. Equally the philosopher's 'true temperance' will consist in his not having the temptation to indulge in bodily desires, whereas ordinary temperate men do have such temptations but overcome them (when they are immoderate) with the help of other desires. I think, indeed, that this is what he means to say about true temperance and true bravery at 69b8–c3. Can we extend this idea to explain in the same way the notion of 'true justice' (δικαιοσύνη), and the generalization to 'all true virtue' (καὶ συλλήβδην ἀληθής ἀρετή, 69b3)?[7] If so, then the thought will be that ordinary men are tempted away from virtue because of their interest in things bodily, and consequently if they do continue to act virtuously it can only be by resisting these temptations with the help of some countervailing 'temptation'. By contrast, the true philosopher never is tempted away from virtue in the first place.[8] Plato is claiming, then, that the *only* reason why men are tempted from the path of virtue is that they pay too much attention to the body and all its works. But once a man sees that the only valuable thing is wisdom, and devotes himself single-mindedly to this, then all vicious temptations will fall away and his conduct will automatically be virtuous. That is what counts as 'true virtue'. (Admittedly this interpretation goes somewhat beyond anything that is to be found in our text. The very obscure characterization of 'true virtue' as a matter of recognizing that wisdom is the only 'right coin' (69a9–10) is a decidedly inadequate way of making the point I am here attributing to Plato.)

Supposing that that is Plato's doctrine, then he is doubly wrong: there are *other* temptations from the path of virtue than those which stem from the body, and the single-minded pursuit of wisdom will *not* preserve one from them. Indeed if we pursue wisdom in so devoted a fashion that this pursuit governs our every action, then there will be many virtues that we will lack. Plato has made out a case for saying that our single-minded philosopher will

---

[7] Gallop translates 'and, in short, true goodness', using 'goodness' (instead of the more usual 'virtue') for ἀρετή. Evidently, a generalization to *all* true goodness-or-virtue is intended.

[8] In Aristotle's language, ordinary men can at best attain 'self-control' (ἐγκρατεία), which Aristotle ranks below 'virtue'.

have a kind of courage, and that he will have a kind of temperance (though his 'courage' seems limited to one particular situation, and his 'temperance'—which seems more the asceticism of a fanatic— is far removed from the ordinary virtue). But consider now some virtues that he will *not* have. We can, in fact, begin with justice: why should it be supposed that one whose whole ambition is the pursuit of 'wisdom' should treat others justly and fairly? How would that help him in his one overriding pursuit? Why, indeed, should he be kind, considerate, loyal, merciful, generous, helpful, forgiving, and so on? How would that assist his intellectual enquiry? The answer must be that it would not. The demands of *other people* are just as unwelcome distractions to him as are the demands of his own body, and he will withdraw from them as much as he can. Yet morality, as we think of it, is primarily a matter of how one behaves towards others. The virtues of courage and temperance are in fact untypical, and are often distinguished as 'self-regarding' virtues, since they *can* perfectly well be manifested in actions which do not affect other people. But most virtues are 'other-regarding', and essentially concern one's behaviour to others. These virtues it seems that our philosopher will lack altogether. At any rate the temptation to act only with his own ends in view is a temptation he will certainly have, and apparently he will see no reason to resist it.

In short, the morality which our 'true philosopher' lays claim to is thoroughly egocentric. Perhaps it need not be classed as a kind of hedonism. At any rate, our dialogue lays no stress on the *pleasure* to be got from the pursuit of wisdom, though this is something that Plato does stress elsewhere (notably *Republic* ix, 580d–588a). Perhaps we could say that so far as the *Phaedo* is concerned wisdom is to be pursued for its own sake, and irrespective of any enjoyment that its pursuit may bring. But still, the philosopher clearly pursues *his own* wisdom.[9] That is the one thing he wants, and the one thing that will get him where he wants to be, off the cycle of reincarnation and away to bliss everlasting.

---

[9] One could imagine a modification of Plato's doctrine, in which the pursuit of wisdom was recognized to be a co-operative endeavour, and the object was to make as much wisdom as possible available to the human race. There would still be objections to be raised to this view, though they would not be quite the same objections. But anyway, this would be quite a drastic modification to the religious doctrine of sin, purification, and release from the wheel of rebirth, which was our starting-point. That religious doctrine was always egocentric.

To this one overriding ambition *everything* else is sub-ordinate, not only the demands of his own body but also all sympathy for others, all concern for justice, and in short practically everything that we consider important to morality. For this to be at all acceptable as an account of 'true virtue', it would have to be argued that a concern for others is in fact needed as a prerequisite for the efficient pursuit of one's own intellectual goals, and Plato does indeed try to argue in this way in his *Republic*. I cannot discuss that argument here, but I think it is obvious that the proposition to be argued for is, at least on the face of it, very implausible.

After this digression on morality, let us return to our proper subject, the soul.

E. THE SOUL AND THE PERSON

We have seen that so far as the ordinary person is concerned, Plato's view is that in its disembodied state the soul retains pretty much the same range of conscious activities as the person enjoyed when alive, including many which we naturally think of as due to the happenings in the body. Of course the soul will no longer be performing its function of animating a body—neither such unconscious functions as keeping the heart beating nor such (normally) conscious functions as moving the limbs—but a very good range of its activities will survive. Moreover, the dead soul is thought of as keeping the memory of its life on earth, much the same desires, skills, character, and dispositions, and most of what we regard as contributing to a man's personality. It is therefore very reasonable to say that we can regard what survives as still *the same soul*, and indeed to identify the soul with the person and count it as the continuing existence of that *same person*. When I die, *I* do not cease to exist, and what survives still counts as *me*, though now I have lost my body much as in life I might lose a limb.

But what happens when my soul is reincarnated in a new body? In what sense does that new body have the *same* soul as I had? What makes it the same? Certainly no new child will be born already equipped with my memories, my knowledge, my character, and so on. It may be tempting to imagine that the new child has a soul made from the same lump of 'soul-stuff' as mine was, in the kind of way in which the same lump of gold may be moulded into first one shape and then another. But the difficulty here is that souls are supposed to be *immaterial* things, and the notion of an immaterial stuff does not seem to make much sense. When we conceive the soul as capable of existing in isolation from matter, we are conceiving it as a centre of consciousness, and there seems to be no sense in which the new-born child will have the same consciousness as I now have.

One might perhaps make some headway with the idea of a latent propensity for certain activities. For example, if I am good at mental arithmetic, perhaps my soul will easily (re)acquire this skill when it is next incarnated, though obviously it will not be born with it. We may extend this idea to other features of my personality. Those who believe in reincarnation have often wished to say that memory too is carried over in a latent form, though in this case it will practically always remain latent, and never come to the surface. (There are just a few cases of people who claim to remember a previous life, but they form an infinitesimal proportion of mankind.) Since the idea of a permanently latent memory is somewhat suspect, one might take it as part of the theory of reincarnation that the memories will come to the surface again when the soul is next discarnate, and in that state a soul will enjoy memories of all its previous lives—or, if that seems too over-whelming, at least of its fairly recent lives. (Memories may fade with time, but for discarnate souls the time-span will be very long.) However it must be admitted that this is not how Plato himself seems to envisage it.

The reason why memory seems so important in this issue is that nothing else seems adequate to ensure the *identity* of an immaterial centre of consciousness over time. A soul at one time may surely have all the same ambitions, skills, character, and personality as some *other* soul did earlier, and the two need not on this account be the same soul. Unfortunately, the same may be argued to be true of memory as well: though it does not in fact seem to happen, there is surely nothing *impossible* in the suggestion that two souls which are indeed different souls should nevertheless each seem to remember doing exactly the same things. You may reply that only one of them can be genuinely remembering, and the other must be suffering from a delusion of some kind, but then you are faced with the difficulty of distinguishing between genuine and apparent memory in a way which does not presuppose that we can already attach some content to the idea of being the same soul. Since the issues here become very complicated, I shall have to leave this question unresolved.

For the sake of argument, let us suppose that the question is satisfactorily settled, and that we can make adequate sense of the idea that the same soul may occupy now one body and now another, with periods of discarnate existence in between. I shall leave aside the further question of whether we have any reason to think that this theory is true, or whether on the contrary it has been upset by facts which Plato knew nothing of (such as the age of the earth and the growth of population). For there is still a further philosophical question which needs raising, namely as to the relation between the soul and the person. On Plato's theory, an ordinary living person is a combination of soul and body, and at his death that combination is destroyed. Must not that be the destruction of him, the person? Perhaps, indeed, his soul will live on earth again in another body, but that is surely not the same as to say that *he* will live again. I think it would be generally agreed that if, when I die, your brain is transplanted into my body and the heart is started up again and the body made to live once more, then that may be another life for that body, but it will not be another life for *me*. Assuming the liaison between brain and consciousness that we normally do assume, the resulting person would have your consciousness and my body. But I am not to be identified with my body, and though the body may live again it does not follow that I shall. Why should we not say exactly the same thing about the soul?

The answer is implicit in the example I have just introduced. If your brain is transplanted into my body, and as a result your memories, your mental capacities, your character and personality change from one body to another, then indeed the resulting person is not I. But surely it *is* you? We are familiar with the idea that you might have a kidney-transplant or a heart-transplant, and this seems merely to be the extreme case of a whole-body-transplant. As one might say, where your consciousness is, there also are you. Generally, if a person is a combination of a soul, conceived as a centre of consciousness, and a body, then the soul is the dominant partner so far as the identity of that person is concerned. Admittedly, we have seen that there are problems in understanding

the notion of 'same consciousness', problems which are partly
sidestepped in my example by bringing in the brain, and assuming
that if we have the same brain then we shall have the same
consciousness. But if these problems can be favourably resolved,
then it does not seem unreasonable to identify the person with his
consciousness.

But now notice that it is crucial to this theory that being the
same soul should be a matter of continuity of consciousness, for if
we adopt any other account of being the same soul it will no longer
be reasonable to identify the person with his soul. For example,
suppose we think of a soul merely as a kind of animating agent that
makes a body live, and not specially connected with consciousness,
much as an engine may 'animate' a car. The same engine may be
transferred from one car to another—cars of very different shapes
and sizes, and very different performance on the road—and there
is no temptation to say that these cars are all really 'the same car',
just because they have the same engine. (On the contrary, a car
may be given a new engine and still remain the same car.)
Similarly for souls. If what now animates me will one day animate
an astronaut, but there is no continuity of consciousness between
me and that astronaut, then it is quite unreasonable to regard his
life as another life for *me*. I am not my 'animating agent' on this
view, and *I* shall never be an astronaut.

With these points in mind, let us consider Plato's own version of
the theory of reincarnation. When I die, then since I am an
ordinary person who has not spent his life withdrawing from all
things bodily, it will be reasonable to say that I do survive into the
disembodied state. For in the case of ordinary persons Plato does
provide as much continuity of consciousness as one could ask
between the embodied and the disembodied soul. But the
difficulty comes when we consider the next transition back to the
embodied state, for here Plato seems to provide no continuity of
consciousness at all. Indeed he envisages my soul returning to
earth to inhabit a donkey, a hawk, or an ant, and it is impossible to
see how the consciousness of such a creature could still be *my*
consciousness. (When Apuleius told how he was transformed into
a donkey, he convinced us that the donkey was indeed he by
allowing it to retain his memories, his desires, and his personality.
That made it a very unusual donkey.) Perhaps one can find some

sense in which it is still my soul that will be animating these later creatures, but in that case I am not my soul, and though my soul may be immortal I am not.

In the case of ordinary people, then, it is the transition from the disembodied state back to the next embodied state which creates the greatest problem, but this problem at least does not arise for the 'true philosopher'. When he dies, his soul never does return for a further earthly life. But here we have another problem: does *enough* of his soul survive death for it to be reasonable to say that *he* survives? At a first glance, it appears that the answer must be 'no', for the only thing about him that persists beyond his death is his capacity for abstract reasoning, reasoning which does not in any way depend on what he has learnt through his body. This appears to be so small a part of his total personality that it is unreasonable to identify it with him, and difficult to say in what sense it can even be identified with his soul. Are we to suppose that at least his soul will remember its experiences on earth, even though it has no use for such memories? Since Plato gives us no information on such points, it seems rash to speculate. But perhaps we can just say this: during his life the philosopher has as it were 'identified himself' with his capacity for pure reasoning, insofar as that is the only thing he has been interested in, and that may make it seem reasonable to say that *he* survives. On the other hand, my own consciousness of myself as distinct from others seems not to play any role in the kind of abstract reasoning that Plato envisages, so perhaps it should be regarded as one of those things that the philosopher loses at death. But in that case what survives is not even self-conscious, and if so then it surely cannot be identified with the person it has survived from.

Of course Plato speaks, throughout the *Phaedo*, in terms of personal survival. Socrates says 'Cheer up! This is not the end of *me. I* am going from here to a better place.' It would surely be less comforting if he had said 'This is, after all, the end of me, but some bits of me will still survive: my bones will last for a little while yet, and my reasoning capacity will be disporting itself elsewhere.' But although it is clearly a personal survival that Plato envisages, we can only say that he has not really seen the problems that this involves.

Since Plato seems never to have abandoned the doctrine of

reincarnation, he can never have seen the problem of personal survival properly. But it is connected, as we observed, with the question of *how much* of the soul is supposed to survive death, and on this he certainly did have further thoughts. Indeed the *Republic* poses the question more sharply by explicitly distinguishing three different parts which together make up the whole soul. The 'top' part is the reasoning part (τὸ λογιστικόν), and this both pursues theoretical reasoning (about forms) and has the job of controlling the desires. The 'bottom' part is called the desiring part (τὸ ἐπιθυμητικόν), and this is responsible for the bodily desires and for such longer-term desires as spring from the bodily desires, such as the love of money. In the *Republic* there is less emphasis on the role of the body in prompting these desires, and more emphasis on the point that the desires are themselves desires of the soul. Finally, the 'middle' part is called the spirited part (τo θυμοειδες), and to some extent it seems to represent emotions, such as anger or self-reproach, while to some extent it seems to be the seat of another kind of desire, the desire for honour and glory and success in public life. It is accounted a 'natural ally' of the reasoning part. There are some problems with the precise delimitation of the functions of these three parts, which I do not intend to go into, but one must applaud Plato's recognition that the soul is not after all such a simple and unitary thing as the *Phaedo* seems sometimes to suggest.

Like the *Phaedo*, the *Republic* also argues that the soul is immortal, but seems curiously undecided as to how much of it is immortal. The argument itself (which is quite unlike any argument in the *Phaedo*) speaks simply of 'the soul', and appears to apply to the whole soul (608d–610e). But then there is a passage—reminiscent of the Affinity Argument in the *Phaedo*—which suggests that since the soul is immortal it cannot really be composite, but must merely appear composite because of its association with the body (611b–612a). However, the question is not further explored there, and it seems that Plato continued to remain uncertain over it. The three parts of the soul reappear in the *Phaedrus* (likened to a charioteer controlling a white horse and a black horse), and in the *Timaeus* (located in the head, the breast, and the belly, respectively). In the *Phaedrus* it certainly seems to be implied that the compound of all three parts is immortal, but in the *Timaeus* we are clearly told that only the reasoning part is immortal.

Viewed in terms of the later doctrine of parts, the *Phaedo's* position is that only the reasoning part is, strictly speaking, immortal. The other parts will standardly survive from one incarnation to the next, but they can be made to wither away by living a suitably philosophic life, and when that happens the reasoning part is freed from the wheel of rebirth and never comes back to earth again. (But then the question arises: how did the soul acquire those other unwanted parts in the first place? Perhaps the *Phaedrus* reflects Plato's uneasiness over this question.) Ideally, we should of course hope to determine how much of the soul is immortal by seeing what is *proved* to be immortal by the arguments for immortality, and this brings me at last to a consideration of those arguments.

Briefly, the Cyclical Argument, which comes first, tells us little of the nature of the soul, but aims to show that the cycle of death and rebirth must go on for ever. (So, if it were valid, it would show that not even philosophers can escape reincarnation.) The other arguments have nothing to say about reincarnation, but they are more informative on the nature of the immortal soul. The Recollection Argument aims to show that the reasoning part of the soul did exist before birth, thus making it plausible to hold that it will also exist after death, and the Affinity Argument too concerns the reasoning part of the soul—reason both as pursuing knowledge of the forms and as controlling the desires— arguing (rather weakly) that it is not the kind of thing that can perish. But the Interlude then shows up the weakness of this argument, and so leads us on to the Final Argument, which however, considers the soul in a rather different way, namely as the cause of life. The Interlude is also important for its attempt to defeat an objection of principle. Like most of what I have said so far, the bulk of the *Phaedo* simply assumes that the soul is at least the kind of thing that it would make sense to suppose may exist without a body, though it is a genuine question whether it does so exist. But Simmias' suggestion that the soul is a 'harmony' calls this assumption into dispute; so it does not in the end go undefended.

From this brief review, let us now turn to the detail of these arguments.

III

THE CYCLICAL ARGUMENT
(69e–72d)

AT 69e7 Cebes states the main problem of the dialogue: he is happy to accept the definition of dying as the separating of soul and body, but asks to be shown that when the soul does separate from the body it is not destroyed but continues to exist with some 'power and wisdom'. The point about souls retaining 'power and wisdom' when they are separated is not pursued in the present argument, but we shall take it up later (pp. 116–17). For the moment Socrates is content to rephrase the question simply as the question whether, when men die, their souls do go on existing in Hades (70c4–5). He then outlines the 'ancient doctrine' of reincarnation, that souls perpetually alternate between an embodied state on earth and a disembodied state in Hades, an embodied soul being a living person and a disembodied soul a dead one. The 'ancient doctrine' thus implies that the living come to be from the dead and the dead from the living, and Socrates suggests that it will be sufficient to prove this doctrine if we can show that the living always come to be from the dead (70c5–d5). (He presumably takes it to be obvious that the dead come to be from the living.)

Three observations may be made at this point. Note first that when Socrates speaks of a dead person he does not just mean someone who is not now living, but also one who used to be living. That is why he feels entitled to say that if the living are born from the dead then they are born *again*, which could not happen unless they—or anyway their souls—existed (in Hades) betweenwhiles (70c8–d2). This will prove to be a crucial point. Note second that what Socrates proposes to prove is that one who is living now has come to be living from being dead, and therefore has lived before. It does not follow from this that he will live *again*, though Socrates seems to think that it does. This objection will later be countered. Note finally that the ancient doctrine is first expressed as the doctrine that living *people* come from dead ones, but the argument that follows will make no use of the fact that it is people that we have in mind, for it aims to prove quite generally that *whatever* is living, and has come to be living, has come to be so from being dead, and so has lived before. If it works, then, it will apply to all animals, and indeed to vegetables, and to anything else that can be said to come to be living. So it would not apply to souls, since in Plato's view they are living things but have never come to be living. But it would apparently apply to bodies, and would show that every living *body* has lived before. Yet one cannot suppose that Plato really wanted to prove that.

The argument proper begins by introducing a perfectly general principle about coming to be, which is said to apply to all things that come to be without exception. The Greek verb here somewhat awkwardly rendered 'come to be' (γίγνεσθαι) presents a problem for translators. It may occur with a complement ('come to be so and so'), in which case it is idiomatically rendered by 'become' ('become so and so'). But it may also occur without a complement ('come to be', full stop), in which case it is more idiomatically rendered by 'come into being'.[1] We may assimilate the two uses by always supplying a complement, e.g. 'existing', where it would otherwise be lacking, and I shall presume that we are taking this course. For Plato's very general language indicates that he means to include both uses of the verb. (But I have more to say on this point below, pp. 55–7.) Anyway, the general principle is put thus: if a thing comes to be so and so, and if there is an opposite to being so and so, then the thing comes to be so and so *from* being the opposite to being so and so. That is to say, before it came to be so and so, it used to be the opposite to being so and so (70d7–e6). Before we proceed any further, let us stop and ask: what is meant here by an *opposite*?

A. OPPOSITES (70d7–71a11)

There are three main ways in which the notion of an opposite commonly figures in Greek philosophy, and to distinguish them we must first introduce a little logical terminology, beginning with the distinction between a *property* and a *relation*.[2]

---

[1] This use is rendered 'be born' in the previous paragraph. (In Aristotle's terminology the distinction is that between γίγνεσθαί τι and γίγνεσθαι ἁπλῶς).

[2] This introduction will confine itself to what is needed. For example I only consider what are called 'two-place' relations. (Readers familiar with the etymology of the word 'property' should promptly forget it.)

Many simple statements may be regarded as statements in which some particular object is referred to and something is said about that object. Thus 'Socrates is wise' refers to the man Socrates, and says of him that he is wise. We call such statements 'subject–predicate' statements, and we say that the object referred to is the *subject* of the statement, while the rest of the statement introduces a *property* which is *predicated of* that subject. So in our example Socrates is the subject, and being wise (or wisdom) is the property that is predicated of him. The phrases that introduce properties are called predicates,[3] and in simple cases they may (as here) consist of the copula followed by an adjective ('. . . is wise') or by a common noun ('. . . is a philosopher'), or they may simply be intransitive verbs ('. . . talks', '. . . thinks'). More complex properties may be expressed by more complex adjectival phrases, noun phrases, or intransitive verb phrases. Indeed, any statement whatever which refers to a particular object may always be regarded as attributing some property to that object, no matter how complex. But for our purposes quite simple examples will be adequate. A property, then, is the kind of thing that can be predicated of (or attributed to) a single object in a single statement.

By contrast, a relation is the kind of thing that is said to hold between *two* objects. In any statement that refers to *two* objects, what is said about them can be called a relation holding between them. For example in 'Socrates is shorter than Simmias' the relation of being shorter than is said to hold between Socrates and Simmias (and specifically from Socrates to Simmias rather than from Simmias to Socrates). Once we recognize a relation as the kind of thing that holds between two objects, we can also say that it holds between an object and itself: for example, being as tall as is a relation which often holds between one thing and *another*, but also holds between everything and *itself*. In an extreme case, a relation may hold *only* between a thing and itself, as happens with the relation of being the same thing as, but the point is that a relation always has, as it were, two 'gaps' which both need to be filled by references to objects in order to make a statement.

One complication we can notice at once. The statement that

---

[3] Notice that in the received terminology (which is somewhat awkward) a predicate is an *expression* which introduces property, whereas a subject is not an *expression* which refers to an object but the object referred to.

Socrates is shorter than Simmias can be regarded, as we said, as predicating the relation of being shorter than of the two objects, Socrates and Simmias, to which it refers. But it can *also* be regarded as predicating a complex property of just one of those objects: it predicates of Socrates the property of being shorter than Simmias, and it also predicates of Simmias the property of being such that Socrates is shorter than him. Any of these three ways of looking at the statement is perfectly legitimate, and the complex properties that are introduced by the second and third view are called *relational properties*, since they are made up of a relation together with one of its two subjects. (In a similar way, the complex properties of being shorter than everything, or shorter than something, or shorter than most things, are called relational properties, because they are made up from a relation plus something else. But in this case the something else is not a *subject*. The expressions 'everything', 'something', and 'most things' are not what we call subject-expressions, since they do not make a reference to a *particular* object; rather, they are used to generalize over objects.) The idea of a relational property will be important in what follows, but for the moment let us set it aside and come to our main topic in this section, the notion of an opposite. As I said, there are three main uses of this notion which need to be distinguished.

(i) One *relation* may be said to be opposite to another, and what is meant by this is that the one relation is the *converse* of the other, which is to say that it is the same relation but taken in the opposite direction. Thus if *x* bears any relation to *y*, then *y* will bear the converse of that relation to *x*, and it will not matter whether we say that *x* bears the relation to *y* or that *y* bears the converse relation to *x*, for these are just two ways of saying the same thing. For example if *x* loves *y*, then *y* will be loved by *x*, and being loved by is the converse relation to the relation of loving. Similarly if *x* is above *y* then *y* is below *x*, and the relations of being above and of being below are converses of one another. Again, if *x* is larger than *y* then *y* is smaller than *x*, and the relations of being larger than and of being smaller than are converses of one another. And so on. A logician will say that every relation has a converse; but sometimes the idea of a converse to a relation seems somewhat useless, namely where the relation is the *same* as its converse. For example, if *x* is the same age as *y*, then *y* is also the same age as *x*, so the relation of being the same age as is its own converse. Even where a relation is not the same as its converse, still it may be that one thing can bear both the relation and its converse to something else. For example loving is not the same as being loved by, but of course it is quite possible to love and be loved by the same person. But usually, when the converse of a relation is called its opposite we have in mind relations which are asymmetrical, i.e. relations which cannot hold both from x to y and from y to x. For example, the relation of being larger than is an asymmetrical relation, and its converse is the relation of being smaller than, and these two are quite often called *opposite* relations. The first sense of 'opposite', then, is that one relation is said to be opposite to another when the one is the converse of the other, and this use is especially applied to asymmetrical relations. My remaining two senses apply to properties and not relations, but the first has some *connection* with relations and their converses.

(ii) This is the sense in which we count as opposites such pairs as large and small, hot and cold, dense and rare, loud and soft, high and low, and so on. These pairs introduce a *scale* (of size, of temperature, etc.) and very roughly each member of the pair stands for one end of the scale. For example, to say that something is hot is to say that it is pretty high on the scale of temperature, while to say that it is cold is to say that it is pretty low on that scale. Properties that in this way indicate different ends of the same scale are often said to be opposites of one another, and the connection with opposite relations is easy to see. For example if we take the two adjectives 'hot' and 'cold, and apply the comparative construction to form the expressions 'hotter than' and 'colder than', then these are expressions for relations which are opposite relations in the sense of the last paragraph. A scale will always yield a pair of such opposite relations, which are said to 'order' the points of the scale as higher or lower than one another, according as they represent things which are hotter than or colder than one another. (In technical terms, the ordering will be a 'linear' or 'one-dimensional' order.[4])

The traditionally opposite adjectives marking different ends of

---

[4] For the curious: a relation (such as 'hotter than') will yield a scale in this way whenever (i) for any things x, y, if it holds from x to y it does not also hold from y to x; (ii) for any things x, y, z, if it holds from x to y but not from x to z then it holds from z to y.

the same scale are very often, as with the examples above, somewhat vague adjectives. But this need not be so. We can for example regard '(pure) white' and '(pure) black' as a pair of opposites, with a whole range of shades of grey in between, ordered by the relation 'darker than' (and its converse 'lighter than'). What we cannot do, or at least not without further explanation, is to regard white and black as opposites with all other *colours* falling in between, for there is no obvious ordering relation which arranges all the colours in a (linear) order with white at one end and black at the other. That is, there is no appropriate scale in this case.

Several points may be noted about pairs of opposite properties of this kind. First, they are *contrary* to one another (or *incompatible* with one another), which just means that nothing can have both properties at once. (This is actually just a special case of the more general principle that *any* two points on the scale exclude one another: a man cannot be both tall and short, but he cannot be both tall and of middle height either.) But such opposites are not *contradictories*, which means that it is not also true that everything must have one or other of the two. On the contrary, there will usually be plenty of intermediate cases which have neither of the two opposite properties. Next, observe that not every property has an opposite in this sense, since not every property does mark the end of a scale. (For example, 'grey' or 'of middle height' have no opposites in this sense.) Occasionally, a property will have more than one opposite in this sense, namely when it can be seen as marking the end of two different scales. For example, 'flat' contrasts in one way with 'sloping', and on this scale its opposite would perhaps be 'vertical'. But in another way 'flat' contrasts with 'uneven' (though we have no single word for the opposite on this scale, say 'extreme bumpiness'.) In yet another way 'flat' contrasts with 'curved' (but again there is no maximum curvature). This multiplicity of contrasts with a single adjective is not altogether common.

(iii) My last kind of opposites are simply properties which are *contradictories* of one another, which means that nothing can have both the two properties *and* everything must have one of them. Every property has a contradictory, and only one contradictory,[5]

---

[5] There is a trivial exception to this. Let us call a property self-contradictory if nothing *could* have it, e.g. the property of being both black and not black. Let us

which can always be expressed simply by adding the word 'not'. So in this sense the opposite to 'black' is simply 'not black', the opposite to 'grey' is 'not grey', and so on. Very often we use the notion a little loosely, and call two properties contradictories of one another when it is not strictly true that *everything* must have one or other of them, but only things 'of the right sort'. For example, one might count 'true' and 'false' as contradictories of one another, because the kind of things to which these adjectives apply (statements, beliefs, etc.) must always be either one or the other. Similarly one might count 'odd' and 'even' as contradictories, because again these adjectives apply to (whole) numbers, and every (whole) number must be either odd or even. But of course numbers are neither true nor false, and statements are not (in the relevant sense) either odd or even. So these pairs are not strict contradictories, though we might often accept them as such. But a strict contradictory can always be formed, for any property, just by adding the word 'not'.

This completes my threefold classification of different kinds of opposites, namely as

    (i)   A relation and its converse,
    (ii) Properties at different ends of the same scale,
    (iii) Properties which are contradictories of one another.

We can now put this to work by asking which kinds of opposites are relevant to Plato's general principle about coming to be. The first point to notice is that the opposites that apply here must be opposite *properties*, and not opposite relations, since the complement to the verb 'come to be' is always an expression for a property, when fully expressed. If an argument is needed here, we may offer this consideration. If a thing *x* is said to come to be so and so, then it must be true to say afterwards '*x* is so and so', and in this statement the *property* of being so and so is attributed to *x*. Being so and so must be a property and not a relation, because by hypothesis '*x* is so and so' makes a complete statement: it has not got a further gap, waiting to be filled by another reference to an object. (Of course the property may be a relational property, and it may—as we shall see—be elliptically expressed, but a property it

call a property tautological if everything *must* have it, e.g. the property of being either a man or not a man. Then according to these definitions *every* self-contradictory property is a contradictory of *every* tautological property.

must be if our remark is to make sense.) We can begin, then, by ruling out sense (i) as irrelevant.

When we come to consider senses (ii) and (iii) it appears at first glance that it must be sense (ii) that Plato has in mind. First, the examples that he begins with—beautiful and ugly, just and unjust—seem to illustrate sense (ii), for these are surely not *contradictory* opposites, but leave room for intermediate cases: a girl may be neither beautiful nor ugly but just 'ordinary', and an act may be neither just nor unjust but morally indifferent. Second, it is worth noting that he limits his principle to those properties that do have opposites, and we have seen that this would be a relevant limitation if he has sense (ii) in mind, but pointless if it is sense (iii) he is thinking of: in sense (iii) *every* property has an opposite. On the other hand, if it is indeed sense (ii) that Plato intends, then the principle is very obviously false, just because in sense (ii) the opposites leave room for intermediate cases which are neither one opposite nor the other. Thus if a girl comes to be beautiful, we can certainly infer that earlier she was *not* beautiful, but we cannot infer that she used to be *ugly*. Similarly if a thing comes to be hot there is no need to suppose that it must have been cold beforehand; it is quite good enough if it was, say, lukewarm. Generally, we can say that Plato's principle is *true* only if we are meaning contradictory opposites. It is true in that case because we can say quite properly that if a thing comes to be so and so then it cannot have also been so and so all along, for otherwise there would be no 'coming to be'; hence if a thing comes to be so and so then at an earlier time it was not so and so, which is to say that it had the property which is the contradictory opposite to the property of being so and so. If we take it that opposites in sense (iii) are intended, Plato's principle is thus perfectly correct, while if sense (ii)—or any other sense—is what is meant, the principle is false. So despite the considerations with which I opened this paragraph, it seems better to suppose that contradictory opposites are intended, for otherwise the argument will break down at once.

Unfortunately Plato introduces a considerable complication with his further examples which use comparative constructions (becoming larger, becoming weaker, becoming faster, and so on). The complication arises because on the face of it these are words for relations, and do no signify properties at all. But this must be misleading. Suppose for example that a thing x becomes larger, so that when it has done so it is larger. Clearly we must ask 'larger than what?', for what is larger must be larger than something. There are two possible suggestions worth considering. (*a*) It may be that we are meant to understand a reference to some fixed object *y* throughout, and the idea is that *x* comes to be larger than *y* and after the change *x* is larger than *y*. Does it then follow that before the change *x* was smaller than *y*? Obviously not: it may be that before the change *x* was the same size as *y*, and never had been smaller than *y*. So on this interpretation Plato's comparative examples are mistaken in the same way as his example of 'beautiful' and 'ugly' was mistaken: the properties of being larger than *y* and being smaller than *y* are contraries but not contradictories, for they allow the intermediate property of being the same size as *y*. Let us then try another interpretation, which I imagine probably is what Plato intended. (*b*) When it is said that *x* comes to be larger, perhaps what is meant is that *x* comes to be larger *than it was*; and similarly when it is said that *x* used to be smaller, what is meant is that *x* used to be smaller *than it now is*. At least this makes the examples *true*: if *x* has come to be larger than it was, then it certainly follows that *x* used to be smaller than it now is. Indeed, these are just two ways of saying the same thing. But unfortunately the example does not illustrate the principle it was meant to illustrate. For the relevant *properties* involved are the properties of being larger than *x* used to be, and of being smaller than *x* is now; *x* now has the first of these properties, and used to have the second. But these properties are not in any plausible sense *opposite* properties, because the relations 'larger' and 'smaller' are each filled out in a different way. For example, suppose that *x* used to be five foot tall and is now six foot tall. Then a thing has the property of being larger than *x* used to be if it is more than five foot tall, and it has the property of being smaller than *x* is now if it is less than six foot tall. But these properties are not even contraries: a thing which is five foot six inches tall is *both* more than five foot tall *and* less than six foot tall, so it has both these properties simultaneously.

We must conclude that the comparative examples were a mistake: either the examples are in error (interpretation (*a*)) or they do not illustrate the principle about opposites because the properties concerned are not in any sense opposite properties (interpretation (*b*)). Plato *thinks* he is dealing with opposites, because he simply uses the words 'larger' and 'smaller', which are indeed words for opposite (i.e. converse) *relations.* But to make sense of the example we have to fill in what our thing is being said to be larger or smaller *than*, and (if the example is to avoid error) the filling must be *different* in each case. Once it is put in, we can then see that the two (relational) properties involved are not in any sense opposites to one another. Our object *x* itself had both these properties when it was part way through its change.

All this is, however, of no noticeable importance to the main argument, for the main argument does not use comparatives anyway. It concerns properties which are expressed by simple adjectives, and no such problem arises in their case. Let us come, then, to what Socrates presents as the main argument.

B. THE MAIN ARGUMENT (70d7–72a10)

It appears that all that is needed for the main argument is this. First we require the general principle about coming to be: using the schematic expression 'being *P*' to stand in for having any property, we may set this down as

    (i)   If anything *x* comes to be *P*, and if being *P* has an opposite, then *x* comes to be *P* from being the opposite to being *P*.

We also need the premiss which allows us to apply this general principle to the particular case we are interested in

    (ii)   Being alive has an opposite, namely being dead.

We also need a third premiss

    (iii) Whatever is alive has come to be alive.

From premisses (i) and (ii) we can then infer that whatever comes to be alive comes to be alive from being dead, and from this together with premiss (iii) we can infer that whatever is alive has come to be alive from being dead, or in other words that the living have come from the dead. This is precisely the conclusion that Socrates said he would prove.

Strangely, when you look at the text you find that Socrates seems to think that more is needed. He begins appropriately enough by stating and illustrating his first premiss at 70d7–71a10.

He secures agreement to the second premiss at 71c1–5, and he omits to state the third premiss, but that is hardly surprising because it is after all very generally agreed. (But in fact the third premiss would not be true of souls—or of God—if Plato is right.) He then draws his conclusion at 71d5–15, and at once announces that our souls must therefore exist in Hades. But meanwhile he has introduced some further ideas. After stating premiss (i), and before going on to premiss (ii), he appears to be stating a further premiss at 71a12–b10, which is

> If being *P* has an opposite, then there *is* a process of coming to be *P*, and there *is* a process of coming to be the opposite to *P*

Then after stating premiss (ii) he at once hints at how this is to be applied to the case of life and death (71c6–d3), and goes on to spell it out in detail at 71e4–72a2

> There is a process of coming to be alive (again), just as there is a process of coming to be dead.

So he finally concludes that 'in that way too' (καὶ ταύτῃ) we can reach our conclusion that the living come from the dead. We may note at once that this 'extra' line of reasoning does not supply the premiss (iii) that was missing: even though there may be a process of coming to be alive, it will not follow from this that everything that is alive has been through that process. So that is not the role of the 'extra' reasoning. Let us set aside the question of what its role is meant to be until we have examined the argument as I first set it out.

The most obvious fault with this argument is that its second premiss is false. We have noted that if the first premiss is to be true, then the relevant kind of opposites must be properties that are contradictories of one another, and the properties of being alive and being dead are not contradictories: some things are neither alive nor dead. At least, this is certainly so if part of what is meant by saying that a thing is dead is that it used to be alive. For example a stone is not alive, and is not in this sense dead either, since it never was alive. More importantly to the argument, something that does not yet exist at all—for example my first grandchild—is not now either alive or dead. If the second premiss is to be true, then, we must not take the word 'dead' in this, its usual, sense, but must understand it simply as the contradictory to 'alive'—as meaning just 'not alive', and no more than that. Then indeed Socrates' conclusion follows: those who are alive have come to be alive from being not alive—that is, at some earlier time they were not alive—but clearly nothing can be inferred from this about our souls' existing in Hades. On the contrary it is quite open to us to hold that at any time when a person is not alive, he does not exist at all.

Nor is the 'extra' line of reasoning of any help here. The very general claim that there are always processes in both directions between *any* pair of contradictory opposites is surely too sweeping, but at least it is true for being alive and not being alive. There is a process of passing from being alive to not being alive, namely dying, and there is also a process of passing from not being alive to being alive, namely being born (or better: being conceived). In fact every person undergoes both these processes at some time or other.[6] But this has no tendency to show that any person ever comes to life *again*. If Socrates thinks that it does, this must be because he is not careful to express his two opposite properties as the properties of being alive and being *not alive*, but is using the word 'dead' in place of 'not alive', and then illegitimately relying on the *usual* sense of this word, according to which what is dead has already lived before. But, as we have seen, he is not entitled to do this, because on this understanding 'dead' is not the contradictory of 'alive'. He may also be misled by an accident of Greek vocabulary: he is comparing coming to be alive with waking up, and the Greek verb for to wake *up* (ἀνεγείρεσθαι) begins with the same prefix (ἀνα) as the Greek verb for to come to life *again* (ἀναβιώσκεσθαι). But although 'up' and 'again' may be expressed in Greek by the same word, they obviously do not have the same meaning.

Anyway, it is clear that the argument we have had so far goes nowhere towards establishing the 'ancient doctrine' we began with. It does not show that anything ever lives and dies more than once. But we have more to come. The (illegitimate) claim that there is such a thing as coming to life again is supported when it

---

[6] It may be objected that any change between contradictory opposites must strictly speaking be instantaneous—for at any moment a thing must have one or other of the two contradictory properties—and an instantaneous change should not be called a *process*. Very well then, forget the word 'process' and speak simply of changes instead. The Greek word γένεσις simply means a 'coming to be', and covers any kind of change.

first appears by the rather weak reason that if there were not then 'nature would be lame' (71e9). But Socrates now goes on to add a supplementary argument which is designed to support and strengthen this claim: *all* change, he argues, must 'go round in a circle' (72a11–d3). By this he means not only that there *are* processes of change in both directions between any pair of opposite states, but also that there is a perpetual oscillation between them. So the 'extra' line of reasoning which crept into the main argument is now going to be further developed and strengthened.

C. THE SUPPLEMENTARY ARGUMENT (72a11–d3)

The main claim of the supplementary argument is simply this. For any property *P*:

> If things changed from being not–*P* to being *P*, but never changed back from being *P* to being not–*P*, then in the end everything would be *P*.

Socrates once more illustrates his point with sleeping and waking: if things that were awake went to sleep, and things that were asleep never woke up, then we should end with a state in which everything was asleep. Similarly, he claims, with being alive and being dead. And since things that are alive certainly do change to being dead, there must be such a thing as coming to life again in order to prevent a state in which everything is dead. (In order to make explicit the idea of a *perpetual* cycle we may add this: suppose—as is reasonable—that *every* living thing lives for only a finite time and thereafter dies, and suppose that it can only come back to life again for some finite number of times;[7] then by the same reasoning it will eventually exhaust all its lives, and in this way too everything will end up dead. So to prevent such an ending we must say that if every life is followed by a death, then *every* death must be followed by another life, *ad infinitum*.)

There are two obvious objections to make to this argument. First, Socrates evidently supposes that it is impossible that everything should end up dead, though *we* should see no impossibility here. But second, and more important, it appears that Socrates is just forgetting about the possibility of new things coming into existence. It may well be that once a living thing has

---

[7] More strictly, the argument requires the supposition that there is some maximum number such that no living thing has more than that number of lives.

died it stays dead for evermore. But still, while they are alive living things mate and breed, and so give rise to *new* living things, and in this way the succession of living things may perfectly well go on for ever. Hasn't Socrates just overlooked this point?

Well, I am inclined to suspect that he has, but in fact when one thinks about it more deeply the situation is more complex than it at first appears. We are supposed to be considering a situation in which things do change from being not–P to being P, but never change from being P to being not–P, where being P and being not–P are contradictory properties. Now the proper contradictory to being alive is *not* being dead, but being not alive, and this makes a difference. In the objection which I have just raised, I did indeed suppose that nothing ever changes from being dead to being alive, but I did *not* suppose that nothing ever changes from being not alive to being alive. On the contrary, when a new living thing is brought into existence, then we must say that that thing does change from being not alive to being alive. For while it does not exist it certainly is not alive, and so does have the property of being not alive. So on closer inspection we see that the counter-example I offered is not after all a counter-example to the principle that Socrates himself actually puts forward; my alleged counter-example did permit change from non-living to living, as well as change from living to non-living.

However we can get what we want by suitably redescribing the counter-example. Instead of considering the pairs 'living' and 'not living' let us now turn our attention to the pairs 'dead' and 'not dead'. A thing is dead at any time if it is not living at that time *and* has been living at an earlier time, and it is not dead at any time if it is *either* living at that time *or* still unborn (i.e. it is not living then and has not lived at any earlier time either). The counter-example, then, allows that things change from being not dead to being dead, and does not allow anything to change from being dead to being not dead, and yet it does not have the consequence that in the end everything is dead. It would have this consequence if we allowed Socrates two extra premises, viz. that any any time there are only a *finite* number of things either dead or not dead at that time, and that *everything* which is not dead will eventually become dead. But the first of these extra premises would be quite unreasonable (and again the second would not be true of souls—or of God—if Plato is right). For the 'things' that we are taking into consideration are all the things—or at any rate all the persons—who either did exist, do exist, or will exist. The ones that did exist but do not now exist are the ones that are now dead, and the ones that do exist or will exist are the ones that are now not dead. But it is obviously not fair to assume that there are only a *finite* number of people who *will* exist. If there were, then indeed there would come a time when they were all dead, since each must die at some time. But that is hardly surprising.

If all this sounds a bit peculiar it is because I have deliberately been treating existence as a property like any other, that a thing may have at some times and lack at other times. This need not lead to any problems so long as we remember what we are doing, and do not confusedly suppose that when a thing does not exist it must nevertheless also 'be there' (or 'subsist') in some way, so that its property of not existing has some subject to 'attach' to. Obviously this is just a muddle, and arises because we are apt to take too concretely the idea of a thing *having* a property, as if the thing were keeping a firm hold on the property, or as if the property dwelt within the thing, or were stuck on the outside and could be 'stripped off'. If we take this kind of picture seriously, then certainly there will seem to be some difficulty in the idea of a thing having a property at a time when it does not exist, and it will appear that there could not be such a property as the property of not existing. But there is no need to be taken in by these pictures. A thing has the property of not existing at a certain time if and only if a statement referring to the thing, and predicating of it that it does not exist at that time, is true. There is no mystery about this.

In fact we have to treat existence as a property like any other if we are to accept the leading premiss to this whole cyclical argument, that if a thing comes to have any property then before it did so it had the opposite property. For suppose (like Aristotle) we make a distinction, and say that this principle holds for coming to have an *ordinary* property, when the thing in question exists both before and after it acquires the new property, but we refuse to accept the principle for coming into existence, which we do not count as an ordinary property. (Or perhaps, we do not count existence as a property at all.) In that case we cannot assume without more ado that when a person comes to be alive the principle must apply. For we should *first* have to show that in these cases of coming to be the person does exist beforehand, that coming to be alive is *not* a case of coming into existence. But if we have to do that before we start, it is difficult to see how we could ever get started at all. As I said at the outset, Plato presumably intends his principle to apply to cases of coming into existence just as much as to other cases; he does not indicate any limitations to it, and he could not without begging the question to begin with.

But as a curious postscript it may be worth observing that on Plato's own principles it can be argued that nothing ever does come into existence anyway. For suppose there are indeed changes from not existing to existing. Then to secure a balance in nature there must also be changes from existing to not existing, and these changes must alternate perpetually. As Plato understands this cycle, it implies that the *same subject* must alternate between existing, not existing, existing again, and so on. But he also supposes that if a man is first alive, and then dead, and then comes alive again then he—or anyway his soul—must still exist when he is dead. He does not say why, but presumably his thought is that unless the man's soul existed during the period when he was dead, there would be no reason to say that it was the *same* man that came back to life again, rather than a new one. Although this move could be questioned—and the argument would not be simple—let us just suppose that Plato is right about this. It follows that the distinction between a person and his soul, that we have just been allowing for, must be abandoned. If the continued existence of the same soul is to be enough to ensure the rebirth of the same person then the soul must *be* the person. So we can say more straightforwardly that on Platonic principles the *person* must exist all through, if he can come to life again. But now let us apply this to coming to *exist* again. Apparently we can equally say that if something first exists, then goes through a period of non-existence, and then comes to exist once more, then by the same argument it must after all have existed during the supposed period of non-existence, for otherwise there would be no reason to say that it was the *same* thing that came back to exist once more, rather than a new one. It follows that in fact nothing ever does really go through a period of non-existence: *everything always exists*, not only living things but also everything else. This obviously absurd consequence does seem to flow from the very general principles that Plato endorses, and makes it quite clear that there must be something wrong with those principles somewhere.

We have already seen, in more detail, where the errors lie. What I call the main argument goes wrong when it assumes that 'living' and 'dead' are contradictory opposites. Just as 'sleeping' and 'waking' are not strictly contradictories, but may loosely be called contradictories when we are confining our attention to *living* things, so 'living' and 'dead' are not strictly contradictories, because unborn things are neither. But the argument requires strict contradictories. What I call the supplementary argument simply relies on a mistaken principle. The natural way of putting an objection to it is to say that it seems to overlook the possibility of new things coming into existence. But if we insist that such things are being taken into account, then the objection must be put differently: the argument assumes that the things under consideration—*including* all the (new) things not yet in existence—are only finitely many, and this assumption is unwarranted. Of course it may be that the assumption is true, and that there are only a finite number of (living) things to come, so that eventually there will be no more. But that is not, as Socrates seems to suppose, an impossibility.

I add two further footnotes on this argument, before moving on to the next. The first is an objection *ad hominem*: Plato's own belief is that some souls *do* escape the wheel of rebirth, either by living a suitably philosophic life, or by living a life so bad that they become incurable and are confined to Tartarus for ever (113e). So even on his own account the cycle of life, death, and reincarnation does not always go on for ever, and some souls do end up permanently 'dead'. If, as Plato does, we assume that there is only a finite stock of souls in the first place, and no new souls are ever created, will it not then follow that in the fulness of time *every* soul escapes the wheel of rebirth, and *all* souls are eventually 'dead'?

Second, I should note a little puzzle that arises with the last sentence of the supplementary argument (72d1–3). Explaining what would happen if the living were to die but never come to life again, Socrates says: 'If the living things came to be from the other things, but the living things were to die, what could possibly prevent everything from being completely spent in being dead?' The question is: what are these *other* things which the living things are supposed to be coming from? Since the hypothesis is that the dead do not come to life again, i.e. that the living never do come from the dead, we must presume that these 'other things' are not the dead. But furthermore, our general principle is that the living cannot come from the living, in the sense that what comes to be alive must itself have been not alive beforehand. (Of course its parents were doubtless living, but a thing does not come *from* its parents in the sense of 'from' that this argument requires.) It must follow that these 'other things' from which the living come are neither dead nor living. They are presumably envisaged as souls waiting to be born in Hades, not yet living, but not dead either, because they never have lived. It is these souls, i.e. unborn persons, that the argument presumes to be in finite supply. But notice that if Plato had stopped to reflect on this idea he should surely have seen that 'living' and 'dead' are not contradictory opposites, for neither would apply to persons not yet born. So he should have seen that the main argument simply rests on a mistake. If he had reflected yet further, he might have seen that in *one* sense there do not need to be any 'others' for the living to come from, for coming to be alive may be a matter of coming into existence, the coming to be of a new entity and not a change in an old one.

I suspect that this last possibility was rendered particularly difficult for him by that old and perennially attractive doctrine that nothing can come into existence 'from nothing'. The doctrine need not be taken as implying that no new human bodies could ever come into existence, for in an ordinary and common-or-garden sense of 'from' we may think of a new material object as made *from* already existing matter, which is simply rearranged to form the new object. But for Plato a person is both body and soul, and since souls are immaterial they cannot be brought into existence in this way. So it may have seemed to him that because souls are immaterial there could be no way of creating them, and similarly no way of destroying them either. Each soul must therefore exist for all time. If we add the premises that there are only finitely many souls, and that life on earth will never come to an end, there seems to be no alternative to the doctrine of reincarnation. But clearly *these* are not the reasons that Plato actually gives in the present argument—they have some connection with what he later says in the Affinity Argument—so I shall not now pursue them any further.

IV

THE RECOLLECTION ARGUMENT
(72e–77d)

A. THE STRUCTURE OF THE ARGUMENT (73c1–74a8)

THE Recollection Argument is I think the most interesting argument in the *Phaedo*, and it is also the most difficult. This is not because it is particularly long. In fact the heart of the argument occupies less than two pages, from 74a9 to 75c5. But these two pages present many problems of interpretation. Some of the crucial sentences are ambiguous, and some of the concepts that Plato is using—notably the idea of 'falling short'—are difficult to understand. We shall therefore need to spend some time sorting out these problems before we are in a position to evaluate the argument. But before we plunge into these detailed problems it will be helpful if we begin with an outline of how the argument as a whole is meant to go. This is the more necessary as Plato himself has presented it in a rather misleading way.

The argument aims to show that we existed before birth, and its overall tactic is to show that we know something which we could not have learnt after birth. The knowledge in question is knowledge of a form, and the example chosen is the form of equality, which Plato mostly refers to as 'the equal itself'. No doubt it is intended only as a representative example. We are told in 75c10–d4 that the argument concerns 'not only the equal, the larger and the smaller, but everything of that sort'. For example it concerns the beautiful itself, and the good or just or holy itself, and in fact everything on which we set the seal 'the thing which (so and so) itself is'[1] when we ask our questions and give our answers. (The questions are doubtless those Socratic 'what is X?' questions, which are meant as questions about X itself, and are not to be answered by giving cases or examples of X.) There is room for dispute over just what things there are on which we 'set this seal', i.e. on just what forms Plato thinks there are, and we shall take up

[1] Both the Greek text for this phrase, and its precise translation, are slightly doubtful. But nothing of importance hinges on this.

this question later on. But notice here that Plato seems to imply that the argument would be equally applicable in all such cases. The argument aims to show, then, that we do have some knowledge of forms, and that we could not have acquired this knowledge during our life on earth. Plato seems to take it to be relatively uncontroversial that we do have this knowledge: at any rate, the claim is made and accepted without any supporting argument at the opening of the central section (74a9–b3). The ensuing discussion is therefore aimed to show that we have not acquired the knowledge during this life, and Plato takes it that this will follow if the knowledge cannot be acquired by perception. It is admitted that perception somehow puts us in mind of this knowledge—it reminds us of it, and recalls it to us—but the main claim is that perception cannot itself *provide* the knowledge. But if perception cannot provide the knowledge, then—Plato supposes— nothing in this world can provide it, and we have to admit that we acquired the knowledge in another world, and before we were born into this one.

There is a gap in the argument here which it seems that Plato does not take sufficiently seriously. Why must it be supposed that there ever was a time when we learnt what we now know? Indeed in an earlier version of this argument in the *Meno* Plato had himself drawn the conclusion that we never did learn it, but must have had the knowledge always, i.e. for all the time that there has been (*Meno* 85d). This alternative would evidently be equally suitable for a proof of the pre-existence of the soul. But another possibility is surely this: perhaps we simply came into existence at birth with the knowledge already in us, so we have had it all the time that we have existed, but have not existed for ever, in fact have not existed before this life at all. Plato is not the only philosopher who has claimed that we have some knowledge which our experience in this world cannot account for, but others have usually been content simply to infer that we were born with it. For example Descartes supposed that when God created our souls (at birth) he put the knowledge into them, and Chomsky supposes that the knowledge is inherited in our genes. (I do not mean to imply that Plato, Descartes, and Chomsky were all agreed on just *what* knowledge we are born with.) At one point our text appears to notice this possibility (76c14–d6), but it is dismissed by an argument which wholly begs the question. We shall later have to consider whether Plato could have given a more convincing reply at this point.

That, then, is the overall structure of this central section of the argument. It opens at 74a9 with the claim that we do have knowledge of 'the equal itself', and then proceeds to argue that this knowledge is not to be explained as given to us by perception. From this Plato infers that the knowledge was not acquired during this life, and so concludes that it was acquired earlier. He apparently overlooks the possibility that it was acquired *at* birth, and jumps straight to the claim that it must have been acquired *before* birth, thus reaching his desired conclusion at 75c4. That completes the argument.

Now you will notice that in this summary of the argument the notion of recollection (ἀνάμνησις) plays no part; the main argument simply does not need it. It has a minor role to play in the explanation of why our knowledge of the equal itself cannot be said to be given to us by perception, for it is admitted that the knowledge is in some way due to our perceiving examples of equal sticks[2] and stones, but contended that this must be a matter of being *reminded* by these examples of something we already knew before. Since it is implausible to suppose that a new-born child is already bursting with information about the forms—or anything else—those who believe in innate knowledge have always held that the knowledge is somehow *latent* at birth, and comes into consciousness as we grow up. In Plato's version, it is our experience of equal sticks and so on that prompts us to recollect what we were once fully conscious of (though the recollection is—for most of us—only somewhat partial, as we shall see). But the only claim that is really crucial to the argument is the negative claim that perception cannot by itself yield a full explanation of our knowledge; it is admitted that it does have some role, but that role can only be an ancillary one. The idea that we can thus be reminded of something we knew before is in this way a relevant part of the total picture, but it is not one of the important premisses to the argument as a whole. Unfortunately Plato's own presentation of the argument rather obscures this point, for he chooses to begin by assembling some points about being reminded,

---

[2] I depart from Gallop's translation here. The Greek ξύλα can mean 'sticks' just as well as 'logs', and sticks seem the more natural candidates for things that are equal (sc. in length).

as if it were these that the whole argument would depend on. This was something of a mistake on his part.

Our topic is introduced by Cebes, who in 72e–73a briefly outlines the argument of the *Meno*, which is presented as an argument to show that all learning is really recollection (*Meno* 80d–86c). I shall come back to a comparison between the *Meno* and the *Phaedo* when we have worked through the *Phaedo*'s argument, but for the present let us set it aside. As Socrates indicates at 73b3–4, the version now to be presented is not meant to be the same as the *Meno*'s version.

In this version he begins by observing that if I am reminded of something then I must previously have known it (73c1–2). He at once goes on to say that one kind of way in which reminding occurs is when I perceive and recognize one thing and thereupon think of something else 'of which the knowledge is not the same but different' (οὐ μὴ ἡ αὐτὴ ἐπιστημή ἀλλ᾽ ἄλλη). The first point states a *necessary* condition of being reminded: if I am reminded of something, then I knew it before. The second point is apparently meant to state a *sufficient* condition: if on perceiving one thing I think of another, then I am reminded of that other. (This is one way, but presumably not the only way, of being reminded.) If we put the two points together we can evidently infer: if on perceiving one thing I think of another, then I knew that other before. But it is at once clear that this is not true. If I am James Watt, and I perceive (and recognize) a kettle boiling, I may be led to think of a steam-engine (a machine in which the power of steam is harnessed to do useful work.) It obviously does not follow that I knew a steam-engine before: this may be the *invention* of a steam-engine.

Let us add a few more points with this example in mind. Although Plato does not quite say so, he evidently means that my perceiving (and recognizing) one thing should be what *leads* me to think of the other—it would not be good enough if the perception of the one thing just happened to be followed by the thought of the other, without any connection—but that constraint is evidently satisfied in this example. Plato does imply that my thought of the second thing should be a case of knowledge coming to be present (73c4–5), but why should we not say that that too is satisfied here? James Watt, we may suppose, proceeded to think about the possibility of a steam-engine in such detail that by the end he did indeed know what a steam-engine would be like. And finally, whatever exactly Plato meant by his obscure condition that the knowledge of the reminding thing, and of the thing it reminds us of, should not be 'the same knowledge', why should we not say that the example satisfies that condition as well? After all, men knew what boiling kettles were for centuries before they ever thought of steam-engines, and conversely it would be quite possible for a man to know about steam-engines who had never met (or thought of) a boiling kettle (e.g. if he had no use for hot water). All Plato's conditions are apparently satisfied, but James Watt did not already know of steam-engines beforehand.

The truth is, then, that Plato's allegedly sufficient condition for being reminded of something is not actually sufficient, because in fact it does *not* imply that I knew the thing beforehand. At a first glance, it looks as though this is a crucial objection to the argument, because it looks as though Plato meant to argue as follows. When I look at equal sticks and stones and so forth, then (i) I am led to think of something else, namely 'the equal itself', and (ii) my knowledge of equal sticks and my knowledge of the equal itself are 'not the same knowledge'. Hence, by the allegedly sufficient condition, I am being *reminded* of the equal itself, and then, by the necessary condition, I must have known the equal itself beforehand. As a matter of fact this *does* appear to be Plato's argument at 74c13–d2, where he infers that we must be dealing with a case of being reminded, and at 74d9–e4, where he goes on to claim that we must have known the equal itself beforehand. (On the first of these occasions the extra premiss is that equal sticks are not the same as the equal itself, and on the second that they 'fall short of' the equal itself. On this way of looking at the argument these points are each supposed to justify the claim that knowledge of equal sticks is not the same knowledge as knowledge of the equal itself.) But on this approach the objection I have just raised is surely damaging: why should we not say that we *invent* the idea of the equal itself, and never did know it beforehand?

However the argument which I originally outlined did not rely on any such false premiss about reminding, since in fact that notion played no crucial role in the argument at all. It was supposed to be an independent premiss that we do know the equal itself, and then to be argued just that perception cannot explain this knowledge. It is true that the objection just raised makes it clear that it will not be easy to argue that perception is not an adequate explanation. For we now see that what has to be shown is that the knowledge cannot be explained by perception *and human invention* working together. But this is not such a hopeless task as one might have thought, for we shall see that 'inventing' the equal itself would not be at all the same kind of thing as inventing the steam-engine. That must wait, however, until we have seen just what 'the equal itself' is supposed to be. Meanwhile, let us just observe that Plato's own presentation of the argument apparently does invoke a premiss about reminding, but since the premiss is not true we shall do better to avoid using it if we can.

As we read on, we find what seems to be yet another premiss being introduced about reminding. Plato illustrates the premiss we have just had by speaking of how a lyre may remind me of its owner, of how Simmias or his portrait may remind me of Cebes, and finally of how Simmias' portrait may remind me of Simmias himself. This last is a case where I am reminded by something *like* what it reminds me of (and, presumably, I am reminded by it *because* it is like), and here Plato makes another general claim: when I am reminded of one thing by another that is like it, then there is something else that must always happen to me as well: I must notice whether the thing that reminds me is a perfect likeness of what it reminds me of, or whether it falls short in some way (74a5–7). This premiss is very puzzling, not only because on the face of it it is fairly obviously false, but also because one cannot see how Plato meant to use it in the argument. In the argument itself he certainly does not claim first that equal sticks are *like* the equal itself and then use this premiss to infer that we must notice whether they fall short of it. On the contrary he first says that it does not matter to the argument whether the equal sticks are like the equal itself or not (74c11–13), and then goes on to assert independently that we always do see that in fact they fall short of the equal itself (74d4 ff.). I wonder whether perhaps he had really meant to state this premiss the other way round. Perhaps he had intended to argue that because equal sticks remind us of the equal itself, but also—as we see—fall short of it, we can infer on that ground that they must be like it. But in fact the text seems careful not to commit itself either way on whether equal sticks are like the equal itself or not, and certainly it does not use the premiss here introduced in either direction.

It seems simplest, then, just to put this premiss on one side, like the previous one, and not to fuss overmuch about the puzzling notions they introduce. It is clear that Plato does think that knowledge of the equal itself is 'not the same knowledge' as knowledge of equal sticks, and his ground for this is quite clear: equal sticks are grasped by perception, but the equal itself is not. It is also clear that he believes that equal sticks do 'fall short of' the equal itself, and we shall later have to enquire what exactly he means by this. (We shall also enquire whether he thinks equal sticks *resemble* the equal itself, though falling short of it.) We shall, then, pay some attention to these notions as they are applied to the relation between forms and particulars, which is the application Plato chiefly has in mind. But I do not think it is worth asking how, or whether, they apply to reminding in general. For we have seen that what Plato tells us about reminding in general is actually no help with the main argument at all.

To recapitulate briefly, the main argument begins with the premiss that we do know what the equal is, and this is the first point that must be elucidated. It then tries to show that this knowledge is not given to us by perception, and here we can distinguish two steps which I take in order: first that the equal itself is not the same as the equal sticks and so on that we can perceive, and second that they fall short of it. In the course of elucidating these points we shall be led to an account of how Plato conceived his forms, and what exactly their function is. This will also enable us to explain why he seems to overlook the possibility that we were simply born with knowledge of them, but never acquired the knowledge before birth. Finally, when the whole line of reasoning is made clear, we can then turn to an evaluation and ask how much it does succeed in establishing.

B. 'WE KNOW WHAT THE EQUAL IS' (74a9–b3)

The argument opens with the claim that there is such a thing as 'the equal itself'. 'We say that there is something which is equal—I don't mean a stick ‹equal› to a stick, or a stone to a stone, or anything else of that sort, but some further thing beyond all those, the equal itself (αὐτὸ τὸ ἴσον)' (74a9–12). To this Simmias answers with some enthusiasm 'We most certainly should say so, unquestionably'. Socrates goes on without pause 'And do we know what it is? (ἐπιστάμεθα αὐτὸ ὅ ἐστιν)', and to this again he receives a very positive answer 'Certainly'. The main question we have to ask here is just *what* it is that we are agreeing to the existence of, and are agreeing that we know. But as a preliminary it is worth raising the question: who are the 'we' who have this knowledge?

There are two possible answers worth considering. One is that *everyone* will agree that there is such a thing as the equal itself, and that he knows what it is, and the other is that it is only rather special people—including evidently both Socrates and Simmias— whom we may label *the philosophers*. At a first glance, one might naturally suppose that it is just the philosophers, for it is clearly a form we are talking about, and earlier in Socrates' Defence it was the special mark of philosophers that they concern themselves with forms. Most ordinary people, one imagines, pay no particular attention to forms. Indeed Plato says elsewhere (notably in *Republic* v. 475d–476d) that ordinary people do not recognize that there are such things as forms, so they certainly would not agree that there is such a thing as 'the equal itself', and obviously would not say that they know what it is. If this is right, then the leading premiss to our argument is one that most people would reject, and Plato does nothing to convince us of its truth.

This is in itself rather unsatisfying, and it also leads to a further problem. The argument is supposed to prove the pre-existence of the soul, but it only applies to the souls of those who do know what the equal is, which means (on the present proposal) that it only applies to the soul of a philosopher. In that case, it will only be philosophers who are proved to have had an existence before this life. But Plato did not believe that only philosophers have had a previous existence; he clearly believed that all men have, and he himself speaks of this argument as proving the pre-existence of the soul quite generally, with no limitation to philosophers' souls. That is surely a difficulty for this proposal.

Another difficulty may be drawn from the apparent contradiction between the way the argument opens, with Simmias claiming that 'we' do know what the equal is, and the way in which it closes, with Simmias admitting that no one (except possibly Socrates) does know this (76b10–c3). In this latter passage Socrates has offered Simmias a choice: supposing that we did acquire this knowledge of forms before birth, should we say that we have retained the knowledge ever since, or should we say rather that at birth it was forgotten? (75c7–76b2). Simmias does not know how to choose, but Socrates helps him to make up his mind by suggesting that a man who knows something must be able to 'give an account' of what he knows. That convinces Simmias that we do not know the forms, for indeed no one (save perhaps Socrates) can give an appropriate account of them. So he eventually concludes that the knowledge must indeed be forgotten at birth, and during life we are subsequently reminded of what we once knew (76b3–c5). On any account, this passage is somewhat odd, but one can make no sense of it at all without supposing that two different levels of knowledge are in play. What we may call proper philosophic knowledge of a form involves the ability to give an account of it. This is something that philosophers aspire to, but even they do not generally attain it. At any rate, Simmias has not attained it, and he thinks that no one else has either (except possibly Socrates). But there must also be a more homely and humdrum knowledge of forms, not involving the ability to give an account, for this is what people have when they have been 'reminded'. And the implication of the text is that *everyone* has been thus reminded. (At 76c1–5 we are told that it is not true that all men know, but they—i.e. all men—are reminded.) It is natural to suppose that the knowledge that Simmias says that 'we' have at the beginning of the argument is again this more humdrum knowledge that comes through being reminded. For if we do not suppose this, then there must actually be *three* levels of knowledge in play: there is the proper philosophic knowledge which practically no one has, and anyway Simmias does not have; there is the humdrum knowledge which comes through being reminded, which everyone has; and on this account there is yet a third intermediate kind of knowledge which at the beginning of the argument 'we philosophers' have, including Simmias. But *three* levels of knowledge seems altogether too extravagant, when two will do perfectly well. So I conclude that when Simmias says at the beginning that 'we' know what the equal is, he has in mind the ordinary humdrum knowledge which *everyone* has, simply as a result of being reminded: there is no special limitation to philosophers in this claim.

(In parenthesis, I add a note on the oddity of the closing passage, which we have not dispelled. Socrates evidently supposes that before this life we once had proper philosophic knowledge.

But if his reason for supposing this is to explain how we now have a
humdrum knowledge, the explanation seems needlessly extravagant. Why not just suppose that what we acquired before birth
was itself merely humdrum knowledge? Plato's answer to this will
emerge when we have probed more deeply into what knowledge of
a form really is, according to him.)

Having now settled that it is everyone who is supposed to know
what 'the equal itself' is, and therefore to recognize that there is
such a thing, we may now pass to the question of *what* it is that we
are all supposed to know. The Greek phrase 'the equal' (τὸ ἴσον,
a definite article and an adjective in the neuter) has three main
uses. It can be used to continue a reference to some equal thing
already introduced, meaning roughly 'the equal thing in question'.
It can also be used in a generalizing way, to mean 'whatever is
equal'. (Compare the English idiom '*the* whale is a mammal'.) But
finally, it can be used as a variant on the explicit abstract noun
'equality' (ἡ ἰσότης), and is simply interchangeable with it. This
last must presumably be the use we have here, for neither of the
first two seems to make much sense in the present context, and it is
quite natural to take the role of the word 'itself' as an attempt to
focus on just this use. We can fairly safely say, then, that the
phrase 'the equal itself' is supposed to mean the same as the noun
'equality' which occurs a few lines later (74c1).

But still, what does that mean? What does Plato have in mind
when he says that we shall all agree that there is such a thing as
equality, and that (in an ordinary, humdrum sense) we all know
what it is? Instead of exploring various possibilities I shall simply
make a *suggestion* about this, and we shall then see as we go on
how this suggestion works out. The suggestion is that what Plato is
talking about is the *meaning* of the word 'equal'.[3] So when he
claims, and expects us all to agree, that there is such a thing as
equality, what he is relying on is just that the word 'equal' does
have a meaning. Similarly when he claims that we all know what
equality is, what he is relying on is that we all know what it means.
After all, the word 'equal' is not an especially difficult and

[3] To prevent confusion: Plato is not of course talking of the English word 'equal'
in particular, nor yet of the Greek word ἴσον in particular. His topic is the meaning
of any word in any language which means the same as ἴσον in Greek (and
therefore the same as 'equal' in English).

recherché word: we all do master that word perfectly easily, and use it in our talk without encountering any problems. So in an ordinary and common or garden sense we do indeed know what 'equal' means, and it is perfectly natural to say that what the word means is equality, and hence we do all know what equality is. So the first point to be observed in favour of this suggestion is that it makes very good sense of the leading premiss to our argument, and indeed renders that premiss very obviously true.

The next point to observe is that the suggestion also makes very good sense of the two levels of knowledge that we have already seen to be involved in this argument. In an ordinary sense, you know perfectly well what the word 'equal' means, and would be quite indignant if I suggested that you did not. But now suppose that, like Simmias in 76b5-7, you are led to agree that for your understanding to count as *knowledge* in the strict and proper philosophical sense you must be able to 'give an account' of what you know. What this means in the present context is that you must be able to *define*[4] equality, to give an adequate answer to the Socratic question 'what *is* equality?', which picks out the *one* thing common to all cases and examples of equality, in virtue of which we call them all 'equal'. Can you do this? Well, I challenge you, and I'm confident that after a few attempts you will agree that it doesn't seem to be an easy task at all. We are in much the same position with all the words that Socrates used to ask his awkward question about—words such as 'beautiful', 'good', 'just', 'holy', and so on. In an ordinary sense, we understand them well enough, and we use them in our ordinary conversation without any difficulty. But we do not know how to define them, so in the strict sense of 'philosophic' knowledge we do not really know what beauty, or goodness, or justice is. The suggestion, then, that what Plato is talking about is our knowledge of what these words mean makes very good sense of the two levels of knowledge that we must recognize to be involved in this argument.

So far the suggestion is standing up well enough, though we have one slight difficulty which should be mentioned. If, at the beginning of this argument, the point that Socrates wants to make is just the simple and obvious point that the word 'equal' does have a meaning, and we know what it means, why should Simmias be so

---

[4] The word λόγος, which is here translated as 'account', has many meanings, but one standard meaning is 'definition'. See p. 159.

specially enthusiastic in his agreement? It is hardly convincing to say that he is specially enthusiastic just *because* the point made is obviously true; it must have some interesting significance for him. Indeed it is obvious what the significance is. Socrates is clearly talking about a form, and Simmias has already shown (in 65d) that he is familiar with the notion of forms and regards them as supremely important. But can these mysterious and marvellous forms be really nothing but the ordinary meanings of words? Well, that is a point that we shall learn more about as we proceed. But before we do I here pause to note one passage *outside* the *Phaedo*, where Plato associates forms, the understanding of language, and recollection.

The theory of recollection occurs first in the *Meno*, but there it is not connected with understanding language or with forms. (In my view, the *Meno* was written before Plato had reached his theory of forms; I shall have something to say on the *Meno*'s use of recollection later.) Recollection is not mentioned in the *Symposium* or the *Republic*, though there is no reason to suppose that Plato has repudiated the doctrine. It does reappear (for the last time) in the *Phaedrus*, where the so-called 'myth' that forms Socrates' second speech (244a–256e) treats several of the themes from the middle dialogues in a somewhat 'poetical' manner. The passage that concerns us is in 249b–c, where we are told that souls which have fallen from the blissful state in which they behold the forms are incarnated in various forms of animal life, but 'only the soul which has beheld truth [i.e. the forms] may enter into this our human form—seeing that a man must needs understand the language of forms, passing from a plurality of perceptions to a unity gathered together by reasoning—and such understanding is a recollection of those things which our souls beheld aforetime' (tr. Hackforth). Now the phrase here translated as 'to understand the language of forms'—more literally, 'to understand something said in accordance with form' (συνιέναι κατ' εἶδος λεγόμενον)—is not perhaps entirely pellucid. But since it refers to something which *every* human must be capable of doing, it is not likely to mean anything specially exhalted, and I think it most probable that what Plato means is just that every human must understand language. This understanding involves 'passing from a plurality of perceptions to a unity gathered together by reasoning' insofar as it involves seeing how many different sticks, stones, and so on, can all be called by the one word 'equal', and this word is something 'said in accordance with form' insofar as it applies to the various sticks and stones in virtue of one form which they all share. If this is right, then Plato says in the *Phaedrus* that men understand language only because they once beheld the forms and can (dimly) recollect them, just as (on my suggestion) he says in the *Phaedo*. Other still later passages could be cited where Plato seems to say that all language involves forms—for example *Sophist* 259e: 'A statement (λόγος) comes into existence only through the weaving together of forms'[5]—but we do not have anywhere else a connection between understanding language, and forms, *and* recollection.

It must be admitted that the *Phaedrus* is rather later in composition than the *Phaedo* (and the *Sophist* is very much later), so it is rather weak evidence for what Plato believed at the time when he was writing the *Phaedo*, though not altogether negligible. But it is more to the point to see how well the suggestion works out as we continue with the *Phaedo*'s argument, which I now return to. We have so far just considered the premiss that we do know what 'the equal itself' is; we must now turn to the reasoning which is supposed to show that this knowledge cannot be explained simply on the basis of perception.

C. 'THE EQUAL ITSELF IS NOT THE SAME AS EQUAL STICKS, ETC.' (74b7–c6)

Plato begins with the apparently very straightforward claim that the equal itself (i.e. equality, or what the word 'equal' means) is not the same as equal sticks and so on. Our knowledge of it does in some way come from seeing sticks or stones or other things that are equal, but it is not the same as they are. No doubt he also means to imply, though he does not quite say so at this point, that whereas sticks and stones obviously are perceptible things, the equal itself is not. This claim appears to be very straightforward. Plato might simply have said that equality is *one* thing that is common to *all* the various perceptible objects that are equal, and therefore cannot be the same as any of them. With a little more subtlety he might have added that the meaning of the word 'equal'

---

[5] Compare also *Parmenides* 135b–c (if διαλέγεσθαι there just means discourse in general).

remains the same no matter what new things come to be equal, or what old things cease to be equal, so it cannot be identified with (the class of) all the equal things taken together. Indeed the word would still have a meaning, and the same meaning, even if it came about that there were no longer any equal things at all (for we should still be able to *say* 'there is now nothing that is equal'). But the argument that he does offer is none of these, and unfortunately it is full of problems. It is clear that the general strategy of the argument is to claim that equal sticks and stones have a certain property which the equal itself does not have, namely that they 'sometimes seem equal to one but not to another', and for that reason they cannot be the same as it. But the language he uses here is extremely ambiguous, and we must first try to sort out this ambiguity, because it is important to see just what property he thinks the forms do *not* possess. Then in the next line we are faced with another problem: we expect him to say that the equal itself does not have this property, but instead he says that *the equals themselves* never seem unequal. What does he mean by this plural expression? And finally he says that equality never seems to be *inequality*, which again seems to be the wrong thing to say. I tackle these problems in turn.

(i) *'Seem equal to one but not to another'*

The Greek verb here translated by 'seem' (φαίνεται), has two distinct uses. In one it is followed by a participle (φαίνεται ὄντα), and the meaning is 'seem to be and are' or 'are observed to be'. In the other it is followed by an infinitive (φαίνεται ἑῖναι), and the meaning is simply 'seem to be' or 'appear to be', with room for the addition 'but are not'.[6] Our present text is elliptical, and the relevant participle or infinitive is omitted, so we lack this guide to the meaning. That is one ambiguity. Another is that it is not clear how we are to construe the datives here translated as 'to one . . . to another' (τῷ μέν . . . τῷ δέ). They may be dependent on the verb 'to seem', in which case they must presumably mean 'seem to one *man* . . . but not to another'. In this case we should no doubt understand an infinitive, for our sticks will seem to one man to be equal, and will seem to another man to be unequal, but presumably they will not actually *be* both equal and unequal: one of the men will be mistaken. On the other hand the datives may

---

[6] As the tag has it: 'φαίνομαι ὤν quod sum; quod non sum φαίνομαι ἑῖναι.'

not be dependent on the verb at all, but on the adjective 'equal', and in that case the meaning is likely to be 'equal to one *thing* . . . but not to another'. It will then seem probable that we are to understand a participle with the verb, for a stick may perfectly well seem, and be, equal to one stick but not to another. Let us set down these two possible interpretations without more ado: the meaning could be either of

(*a*) Equal sticks sometimes appear to one man to be equal, and to another man to be not equal.

(*b*) Equal sticks are sometimes observed to be equal to one stick but not to another stick.

Within the second main line of interpretation, according to which we understand a participle with the verb and the meaning is 'are observed to be' there are some further variations. The datives τῷ μέν . . . τῷ δέ may not after all mean 'to one thing . . . to another thing'. They *could* mean 'in one respect . . . in another respect,' and the thought will be that a pair of sticks may for example be equal in length but not in thickness. This is rather an attractive interpretation, but it must be confessed that it is not a very natural reading of the Greek. (One would certainly expect τῇ μέν . . . τῇ δέ.) Another point worth noting is that there is a respectable manuscript tradition in favour of a different reading τότε μέν . . . τότε δέ, meaning 'at one time . . . at another time'. On this reading, the point will be that equal sticks, while remaining the same sticks, are at one time equal and at another not, because they have changed. This contrasts with the form equality, because it never changes, as is later emphasized (78d–e). But although this suggestion does have some corroboration from elsewhere in the dialogue, still I think it implausible, for if Plato had meant to make the point that perceptible things change whereas forms do not, he surely would not have chosen sticks and stones as his examples. No doubt stones do actually change over time, but very very slowly, and they certainly do not strike one as a *natural* example to illustrate the point that particular things may change in size. I am inclined to think, then, that these further variations are less plausible than our first two interpretations, and I henceforth restrict attention to those.

One may first remark that the presence of the word 'sometimes' is a little awkward for interpretation (*b*), for presumably a stick which is equal to one stick will *always* be unequal to some other.

The point is not a very serious objection, but it does perhaps create some presumption in favour of (*a*). But the more serious difficulty is this. On interpretation (*a*) we are considering a *pair* of sticks, which together form an instance of the form equality, and we are saying that men may make mistakes over whether any pair of sticks are indeed equal, though one never makes such a mistake about the form itself. By contrast, on interpretation (*b*) we are considering a *single* stick, and remarking that it may be equal to one thing but not to another, which is possible because equality is essentially a *relation* between two things. But (i) Plato says, as we have seen (75c9–d1), that his argument applies not only to such terms as 'equal' and 'larger' and 'smaller', but also to 'beautiful', 'good', 'just', 'holy', and so on; yet these do *not* appear to be terms for relations. Besides (ii) the implied contrast with the form equality must now be that it is equal but not equal *to* anything, and surely this is a *very* peculiar idea. Since equality is a relation, we must surely say that nothing can be equal without being equal *to* something. It thus seems that interpretation (*b*) leads only to nonsense. But for all that, I believe that interpretation (*b*) *is* probably the right one, and Plato's doctrine *is* indeed very peculiar. For the moment, I support this belief simply by appealing to a very similar passage at the end of book v of the *Republic*.

At this point in the *Republic* Plato is contrasting the genuine philosopher who loves genuine truth with others whom he calls 'lovers of sights and sounds'. It soon becomes clear that the main point of the contrast is that philosophers concentrate their attention on forms, for genuine truth only pertains to forms, whereas other men think only of perceptible things, and about them Plato maintains that there is no genuine truth or knowledge, but only opinion. The passage I wish to concentrate on is at 479a–c, where Plato is trying to convince us of this last point. He begins by asking

Is there one of these many beautiful things which will not seem ugly, or one of the many just things which will not seem unjust, or one of the many holy things which will not seem unholy?

And to this he receives the reply

No. These things necessarily seem both beautiful in a way and ugly, and similarly with the others you ask about.

At once he goes on

> And what of the many double things? Do they seem any less half than double? And the large things and the small, the light and the heavy, should they be any more called what we do call them than the opposite?

And again the reply comes

> No. Each of them will always partake of both.

Let us pause here, and take stock.

In the *Phaedo* the argument claims that equal things seem unequal, and adds that the same applies to beauty, goodness, justice, and so on. In the *Republic* we begin with the claim that beautiful things will seem ugly, just things unjust, and so on, and then at once go on to make the same claim about things that are double, or large, or heavy. In both dialogues Plato evidently means to be applying the same line of thought to both kinds of case. But what is this line of thought? The same verb 'seem' (φαίνεται) is used in both passage, and still without an explicit infinitive (εἶναι) or participle (ὄντα) to resolve its ambiguity. At first one might naturally suppose that it is the infinitive to be supplied (interpretation (*a*) of the *Phaedo*): it is a common enough thought that what appears beautiful to one man may appear ugly to another, but we need not infer from this that it *is* both beautiful and ugly. But when we go on at once to things that are double, this interpretation seems most unlikely. It is surely not at all common for a thing to appear to one man to be double something else, and to appear to another man to be half of *that same thing*. Here interpretation (*b*) of the *Phaedo* is far more natural. The obvious point is that being double is a relation, so a thing can be double *one thing*, and half *another*. Similarly with the next examples: a thing can seem, and be, large compared with one thing and small compared with another.

In the last reply quoted above, the interpretation (*b*) begins to be quite strongly confirmed, for that states that our things actually do partake of both the opposite characteristics, and not merely that they appear to. As we read on, this interpretation seems unavoidable. Plato asks

> So should we say that each of the many *is* rather than *is not* whatever one says that it is?

The reply adverts to the riddle about how a man who was not a man (a eunuch) threw a stone that was not a stone (a pumice stone) at a bird that was not a bird (a bat), and then adds

> In these cases too there is an equivocation, and one cannot firmly believe that any of them either is or is not either both or neither.

So Plato finally concludes

> Do you know what to do with them then? Can you put them in any better place than between being and not being?

What is abundantly clear from this is that in Plato's view particular things do not merely *appear* to have both of two opposite characteristics: they *actually* have both. The verb we have been neutrally translating as 'seem to be' must actually be being used in the sense 'are observed to be' (φαίνεται ὄντα), because Plato is prepared to infer from the premiss that things 'seem' to be thus and so to the conclusion that they *are* thus and so.

I conclude that the *Republic* passage demands interpretation (*b*), and will not tolerate interpretation (*a*). Since the *Republic* is reasonably close in date to the *Phaedo* this affords a strong presumption that interpretation (*b*) is also right for the *Phaedo*, and we therefore have to face up to the problems that it involves. Some of them are perhaps not really so difficult. When Plato says, for example, that whatever is beautiful is also ugly he may perhaps mean that it will be beautiful compared with one thing but ugly compared with another, or beautiful in one setting but ugly in another, or something else of this sort. (I shall elaborate on these suggestions later, p. 97.) The idea will be to treat the property of being beautiful as if it were, despite appearances, a kind of relational property which a thing has only in relation to something. But at the same time we shall have to say that the form is beautiful all by itself, and not in relation to anything. As one might also put it, the form is beautiful without any qualification, while particular examples can only be said to be beautiful in some qualified way. Perhaps, in the case of beauty, this is not quite so unintelligible a doctrine after all. (Compare *Symposium* 210e–211b, quoted below, p. 93.) But I confess that in the case of equality it still does seem very weird indeed. No doubt we can say that equal things can only be equal in a qualified way, namely by being equal *to* something. But can we attach any sense to the idea that the form is equal all by itself, and without any such qualification? It certainly seems very difficult.

Though I do have more to say on this topic, I shall postpone it until we have worked our way through more of the problems that this argument involves. At the moment, we have merely discussed the ambiguous claim that equal sticks 'seem equal to one but not to another', and of various possible interpretations I have argued for interpretation (*b*). But since it undeniably has its difficulties, I shall also keep interpretation (*a*) in mind in what follows. We expect Plato to say next that whereas equal sticks do 'seem equal to one but not to another', this never happens with 'the equal itself'. But in fact that is not quite what he does say.

(ii) *'The equals themselves'*

Where we expect to find Plato referring to 'the equal itself', we instead find the quite unexpected expression 'the equals themselves' (αὐτὰ τὰ ἴσα). What does this mean? There are two main alternative suggestions: either it is really another way of referring to 'the equal itself', and the plural is not supposed to make any difference, or the phrase introduces some new entities. Let us take the second alternative first. What new entities might these be?

All that we have to go on 'is that these 'equals"have never seemed to you unequal', which is presumably meant to contrast with the equal sticks that do 'seem equal to one but not to another'. According to interpretation (*a*), then, the point is that they are equal and never *appear* to be unequal to anyone: nobody makes this mistake about them. According to interpretation (*b*) the point must be that they are not unequal to anything, but are simply and unqualifiedly equal, all by themselves. It is difficult to see how anything *at all* could satisfy interpretation (*b*), including even the form of equality itself, so there is surely no prospect of finding a whole set of equals that fulfil this condition. But with interpretation (*a*) there are at least two suggestions one might make.

One takes its start from the fact that, according to Aristotle's report (*Metaphysics* A, 987^{b}14–18), Plato believed that as well as forms and sensible particulars there were also things of a third kind, namely the things studied in mathematics. These differ from sensible particulars in that (like forms) they are imperceptible and eternal, and they differ from forms in that (like particulars) there are many of each sort, whereas each form is unique. The doctrine was presumably meant to apply to the objects of geometry, those (perfect) squares, circles, triangles, and so on that the geometer considers as congruent to one another, but I deliberately take a more unexpected example, the numbers. There is reason to suppose (e.g. from *Republic* vii. 525d–526a) that Plato understood the equation '2 = 1+ 1' to state that the number two was made up of a pair of ones, and that these 'ones' were absolutely equal to one another in every way. Would not these 'ones' qualify for the title 'equals themselves'? It could quite plausibly be said that no one has ever thought that one mathematical 'one' was unequal to another. (Of course, there is something very wrong with this way of viewing the number two, but I leave that aside as not very relevant to the present issue.)

A quite different suggestion is that Plato is here anticipating the doctrine of 102d–103b, according to which if Simmias is equal to someone in height he will participate in the form equality and that means that there is such a thing as 'the equality in Simmias'. Whereas Simmias himself may grow or shrink, and so cease to be equal (to whoever it was) while still remaining Simmias, Plato claims that the equality in him *must* be equal, and cannot cease to be equal without ceasing to exist. Perhaps, then, the equality in Simmias might be one of 'the equals themselves', and the equalities in other people will be other 'equals themselves'. Since such an entity apparently has to be referred to *as* 'the equality in so and so', anyone who could speak of it at all would have to know (on Plato's doctrine) that it was equal and could not be unequal.[7] (Again, I here set aside the merits of this doctrine, which surely is very muddled indeed.)

But the reply to both these suggestions, and to others that one might make, is that they are too far-fetched. Plato cannot have supposed that any reader would be able to see what he had in mind, if it was either of these suggestions that he did have in mind. (Obviously, his readers would not have had the benefit of having read Aristotle's report in *Metaphysics* A, which in fact reports a doctrine that is not clearly to be found in *any* of Plato's dialogues.

---

[7] Since the equality in Simmias apparently cannot be unequal, it might also seem to be an example of something equal 'without qualification'. But apparently it would still be equal *to* something, viz. to the equality in the other person to whom Simmias was equal.

Nor would the reader be reading the *Phaedo* backwards, so that he knew the doctrine of 102b–103d before he came to 74c.) We can generalize this point. So far in the *Phaedo* Plato has spoken of sensible things, such as equal sticks and stones, and of forms, such as the form of equality. But we have been given no suggestion that there is also some third kind of entity intermediate between the two. If Plato had meant to introduce a third kind of entity, he could not have imagined that the bare phrase 'the equals themselves' would reveal what he had in mind. Therefore, he did not mean to introduce a third kind of entity. The phrase must be intended to refer to something we have had before, and in that case it can only be a alternative expression for the form.

The unexpected plural can in fact be parallelled from a later dialogue, the *Parmenides.* At 129b1 in that dialogue there is a clear occurrence of the analogous phrase 'the similars themselves' (or 'the like things themselves'; αὐτὰ τὰ ὅμοια), where the context makes it quite clear that it is the form of similarity (or likeness) that is meant. (Indeed a little later the bare phrase 'the many things' (τὰ πολλά) is used to mean the *form* of plurality, without even the help of a 'themselves' (129b7, where the reading may be suspected, and 129d5, where there is no reason for suspicion).) But although the use can be paralleled, this does little to explain it. How could Plato use a plural expression to refer to a single form?

One line of explanation is that Plato occasionally (but by no means usually) uses a plural expression for forms whose instances would be plural. This, it is suggested, is because the form is supposed to *resemble* its instances, and so must be composed of a plurality itself. Thus if we take interpretation (*a*) the instances of the form of equality will be *pairs* of sticks, stones, or whatever, and if the form is to resemble its instances then it seems that it too must be composed of some pair of ideally equal things. That is why 'the equals themselves' will do as a title for it. However this explanation does rather conflict with Plato's insistence that forms are *not* composite things, at 78c–d, and are for that reason indissoluble. I note also that the explanation produces something of a problem for the forms of 'larger' and 'smaller', which Plato classes along with the form of 'equal' at 75c9. By parity of reasoning one would suppose that the form of 'larger' must be composed of two things, one 'ideally' larger than the other, and the form of 'smaller' will similarly be composed of two things, one 'ideally' smaller than the other. But then what is the difference between these forms? On this description, they seem to be entirely indistinguishable, but it is impossible to believe that Plato thought that these two forms were really the same form. (It is much more probable that he identified them with the forms of 'large' and 'small' respectively. In any case, he would clearly consider them as 'opposite' forms.) This line of explanation, then, is not without its difficulties, and besides it is only available to us if it is interpretation (*a*) that we are adopting. Upon interpretation (*b*) an instance of the form of equality will be a *single* stick that is equal (to some other), and there is therefore no call for a plural form to 'resemble' it. Can we, then, suggest any other explanation?

There is an alternative explanation, and it goes back to my earlier suggestion that what Plato is trying to talk about is the meaning of the word 'equal'. This word is an adjective, and in Greek (but not in English) adjectives agree in number with their nouns. So where we have a singular noun the adjective will also occur in the singular (ἴσον), and where we have a plural noun the adjective will occur in the plural (ἴσα). But the adjective means the same whether it occurs in the singular or the plural, so if we are trying to talk about its meaning it does not matter which form we cite it in. To make the point clear in English, where adjectives do not agree with their nouns anyway, let us suppose that we are interested in the meaning of a verb. You might say (in all ignorance, let us imagine) 'what is the meaning of the verb "to berate"?' Or perhaps you might prefer to put your question this way 'what is meant by "berating"?' Or perhaps you simply ask 'what does "berates" mean?' Although these three ways of asking the question use three different forms of the verb, 'to berate', 'berating', and 'berates', still it is quite clear that in an important sense it is exactly the same question being asked. Similarly, the meaning of the adjective 'equal' in the singular is exactly the same as the meaning of the adjective 'equal' in the plural.

The reason why the adjective is cited first in the singular and then in the plural is easily enough seen from the context; it is first picked out of a sentence in which it occurs in the singular, and then picked out of a sentence in which it occurs in the plural. To make clear the kind of thinking that I am here attributing to Plato, I shall deliberately make use of explicit quotation marks, which is a device that Greek lacks. In 74a10–12 he says first that a stick (singular) may be equal (singular) to a stick, or a stone to a stone, and goes on to ask whether this 'equal' itself also exists. The 'equal' itself is, he suggests, something quite different from an equal stick or an equal stone. So far, the adjective has only occurred in the singular, and so it is cited in the singular. But then it is suggested that the 'equal' itself is not something different, so in 74b7–c1 we argue that it is, in this way: stones (plural) which are equal (plural), and sticks (plural) too, sometimes seem equal (plural) to one but not to another, but what about this 'equal' itself. Has the 'equal' itself ever seemed unequal? Here the adjective is naturally cited in the plural, since it has just occurred in the plural. But what we are trying to talk about, when we cite the word, is its meaning; and that has not changed.

However there is a complication. What I have just said is not yet an accurate rendering of our Greek text, because my whole phrase 'the "equal" itself' is still a singular phrase, even though the word cited within it is plural. But the proper Greek for what I have just said (which would be τί δέ; αὐτὸ τὸ ἴσα ἔστιν ὅτε ἄνισόν σοι ἐφάνη;) would surely *sound* ungrammatical to a Greek ear, because its final adjective 'unequal' would be in the singular, though what it characterizes would be introduced by a word 'equal' in the plural. Besides, the antithesis between 'equal' and 'unequal' would be spoilt, because one word is plural and the other singular. To restore this, the two adjectives would inevitably be made to agree with one another, and so the final adjective would become plural too (yielding τί δέ; αὐτὸ τὸ ἴσα ἔστιν ὅτε ἄνισα σοι ἐφάνη;) I think it is quite a possible conjecture that this is in fact what Plato wrote, at least as his first draft. But now we have a sentence which, although it *sounds* all right (at any rate, to me), really is ungrammatical by the proper rules of grammar. The *thought* which the sentence is trying to convey requires the two adjectives to agree with one another, which they now do, both being plural. But the rules of grammar demand that the plural adjective 'unequal' should have a plural subject, and strictly speaking our subject-phrase is still singular, since it is the whole phrase 'the "equal(s)" *itself*' (αὐτὸ τὸ ἴσα). So either Plato himself, or some copyist after him more zealous for grammar, allowed everything to get attracted into the plural. This restores the grammar all right, but at the cost of introducing the puzzling phrase 'the "equal(s)" *them*selves' which has led us such a dance. I am sorry if this explanation sounds rather involved to one not familiar with the Greek language, but I think it is a perfectly satisfying explanation, and it allows us to maintain that the plural phrase 'the equals themselves' results only from the peculiarities of Greek grammar. It still means just the same as the singular phrase 'the equal itself', for both of them are phrases used to pick out that entity which the adjective 'equal' signifies. This, Plato thinks, is something that does not suffer from the defect that it seems equal to one but unequal to another, for it never seems unequal. Another word for the same entity is the noun 'equality', so we could equally say that equality never seems unequal. Unfortunately, what Plato does go on to say is not quite this: he asks rather whether equality ever seems to be inequality.

(iii) *'Equality never seems to be inequality'*

It should first be mentioned that our Greek text *could* be so translated as to avoid the difficulty. Since Greek lacks an indefinite article, we might feel that we were free to insert one, and translate 'equality never seems to be *an* inequality'. Being *an* inequality could then be understood as a matter of being a case or example of inequality, which just means being unequal. In that case, Plato has said the right thing after all. But I agree with most commentators in thinking that this translation is really very unlikely,[8] and the difficulty should not be thus swept out of sight.

The problem is not, of course, that it is wrong to say that equality never seems to be inequality, but that it is irrelevant to the present argument. What the argument is trying to do is to distinguish equality itself from such things as equal sticks, on the ground that equal sticks have a property which equality does not have. But that property is *not* the property of seeming to be inequality. No doubt it is true that equality never seems to be inequality, but then it is *also* true that equal sticks never seem to be inequality, so this property marks no distinction between them. What does mark the distinction (according to Plato) is that equal sticks sometimes seem unequal, while equality never seems unequal, but being unequal is not the same property as being inequality.

---

[8] One would certainly expect the Greek to be ἥ ἡ ἰσότης ἀνισότης τις, if this is its meaning.

It is possible that Plato is thinking of the argument in a slightly different way, like this: equal sticks are also capable of being their opposite, unequal sticks, but the form equality is not capable of being *its* opposite, inequality. The idea would then be that the opposite to an equal stick is again a stick—an unequal one—whereas the opposite to a form is another form.[9] But in each case we are talking about a thing and its own opposite. If this is Plato's idea then it is still a mistake, but for a rather different reason. The kinds of things that can be opposites, in the sense which concerns us (pp. 45–8), are basically properties (or relations). Since forms either are or are closely related to properties (or relations), it is quite in order to say that one form is opposite to another, and that the form equality is opposite to the form inequality. But an object such as a stick cannot *be* an opposite except in a quite different sense. For example, several sticks may be arranged in a pattern so that we can say that one stick is opposite to another. But here we are talking of being *spatially* opposite, and forms (or properties) do not stand in such spatial arrangements. Rather, they are *logically* opposite to one another, and sticks do not stand in such logical relations. The properties of being equal and unequal are logical opposites, but not the objects that have them, and in the only sense in which such objects as sticks can be opposites an equal stick is not opposite to an unequal stick. (And it is not possible for a stick to *be* the stick that it is opposite to.)

If we try to put this mistake about opposites right, then we come back to the same error as before. What is true of an object such as a stick is that it can *have* opposite properties (can 'admit opposites', as Plato later says), so again the proper contrast with the form would be that the form cannot *have* opposite properties. And to say that the form equality cannot *have* the property inequality is, once more, to say that it cannot *be unequal*, not to say that it cannot *be inequality*.

I think there is nothing one can do about this except to say that it is a mistake on Plato's part. A more difficult question is whether we should set it down as a mere slip, and something of no importance, or whether we should regard it as a symptom of a deeper and more fundamental error. This is relevant to the

---

[9] Something like this idea is generalized to all relationships at *Parmenides* 133–4, where Parmenides suggests that sensible things can be related only to sensible things, and forms only to forms.

question of how we are to understand the fact that Plato apparently maintains that equality *does have* the property of being equal, i.e. that it is an equal thing. (I discuss this claim further below, pp. 89–94.) For one might suggest that if Plato can here make the mistake of confusing being unequal with being inequality, then perhaps he constantly makes this kind of mistake. Perhaps he similarly confuses being equal with being equality—in his language, being equal and being *the* equal—and perhaps *that* is why he thinks that the equal itself is equal. What he really has in mind is that the equal is the equal—which is a trivial tautology—but because he fails to make the distinction he constantly talks as though the equal were equal. After all it certainly looks like a *mistake* to say that equality, or the equal, is equal, and this would give us a very simple explanation.

Now I fear there may be *something* in this line of thought, but I am quite sure that it is not the whole story. Plato has other, and more important, reasons for holding that the form of the equal is itself equal, and it is by no means obvious that this must be regarded as a mere 'mistake' on his part. But I shall come to those in due course, and meanwhile let us just bear this suggestion in mind. We have not finished yet with the argument as Plato sets it out. Indeed it may seem that we have hardly got started. So far we have been considering merely the initial claim that the equal itself is not the same as equal sticks and so on, though it is our perception of such equal things that somehow 'puts us in mind of' the equal itself. But that does not yet seem a good enough ground for saying that perception cannot explain our knowledge of the equal itself. To make out a case for this, we must apparently pay some attention to the further claim that the particular things we can perceive always 'fall short of' the equal itself, for this is where the main thrust of the argument seems to lie.

D. 'EQUAL STICKS ETC. FALL SHORT OF THE EQUAL ITSELF' (74d4–75b9)

The claim that all perceptible equal things 'fall short of' the equal itself is introduced at 74d4–7, apparently as a new point. It is then re-expressed in various ways. To begin with it is just said that equal things do not seem to us to be equal in the same way as the form (οὕτως ἴσα εἶναι ὥσπερ αὐτὸ τὸ ὃ ἔστιν); they fall short of it in being such as it is (74d6–7). Next we are told that they *seek* to be like it, but cannot succeed and are inferior (74d9–e2), they *strive* to be like it but fall short (75a2–3, b1–2), they *desire* to be such as it is, but are inferior to it (75b7–8). Obviously, these expressions are somewhat metaphorical, but when the metaphor is stripped away what actually do they mean? What is this apparently new point that the argument here introduces?

A suggestion that has regularly appealed to one commentator after another is that what Plato is trying to say is that no two perceptible things are ever *exactly* equal; for example, no two sticks will ever have exactly the same length, but one will always be just a fraction longer or shorter than the other. There are perhaps two main reasons why this suggestion should have proved so attractive. One is that the commentators themselves think that no perceptible things ever are exactly equal, and they think that Plato would have agreed with them, because of some things he says *elsewhere* about the lack of perfection in physical things. For example they cite *Republic vii.* 529c–530b, which really says only that you ought not to expect the motion of the planets to be entirely regular; or *Timaeus* 29c–d, which simply cautions us that in many questions of physics one cannot be sure that one has the right answer. These are not very compelling parallels. The other reason is that they think (with rather more reason) that Plato holds that you will not find 'perfect beauty', 'perfect justice', and so on, on this earth. We then have only to add that 'perfect beauty' is what matches up to some ideal standard of beauty, in just the way that 'perfect equality' might be what matches up to our quite ordinary standard of exact equality, and we seem to have an appropriate kind of similarity between all Plato's examples. (But they usually omit to explain what it would be like to match up to some standard of being perfectly or exactly larger or smaller, and why perceptible things cannot ever meet this standard.)

Although this suggestion has always proved attractive, I think the objections to it are overwhelming. The first and most obvious objection is that our text simply never mentions the notion of perfect or exact equality at all; there is no expression in the text which could properly be thus translated.[10] Second, I see no reason

[10] I am afraid that readers who are dependent on a translation, and are not using Gallop's translation, may be surprised at this statement. But it is perfectly correct.

to suppose that Plato would have believed that no two sticks could have exactly the same length. Indeed in the *Timaeus* (admittedly a much later dialogue) he puts forward an atomic theory of matter in which there are four different kinds of atoms and each atom of a given kind is exactly the same size as any other of that kind. Two sticks, then, may match one another perfectly if they are each made of the same number of atoms in the same arrangement. But, quite apart from this, what evidence could Plato possibly have had for such a sweeping claim about *all* physical things? If he had believed it, he would surely have been extremely rash. Third, let us consider the context. What the argument is concerned with is the question of what can be gathered from perception, and the present suggestion is that the concept of exact equality (e.g. in length) could not be got in this way, because there are no perceptible examples of it. But now we see that what the argument requires (on this suggestion) is not just the claim that no two sticks ever *are* exactly equal, but more strongly that no two sticks even *look* exactly equal. ('Do they [the sticks] *seem to us* to be equal in the same way as the form?') So long as the sticks *look* exactly equal, we shall be able to gather the idea of exact equality from them, even if they are not quite equal in fact. But now the claim is surely absurd. You may possibly have some high-flown theory of the physical world which tells you that no two sticks ever are quite equal, but it is mere folly to say that no sticks ever *appear* to be exactly equal. Anyone with a box of matches will prove you wrong. Finally, let us think again about the extreme generality of this claim. Notice that while we have been concentrating on the notion of length in particular, that was our doing, and Plato's text just speaks quite generally about being equal, presumably in *any* respect. But one respect in which (collections of) things may be equal is that they may be equal *in number*. *Could* Plato *possibly* have believed that I can never have *exactly* the same number of coins in my left pocket as in my right pocket? The idea is ridiculous.

I conclude that this suggestion will not do; it cannot be what Plato actually means. One can of course make various other suggestions as to what new point this talk of 'falling short' is getting at. For example, it seems a plausible idea that while two sticks may be equal in *some* respects (e.g. in length) there are bound to be other respects in which they are not equal (e.g. in their distances from all other objects). (A possible objection to this is that any object will be equal to *itself* in all respects whatever.) But to any such suggestion we can always be sure that we have at least this objection: it is not in the text. Our text supplies no further argument to show that perceptible things always do fall short of forms, and it supplies no further elucidation of what this claim might mean. One looks in vain for any further hint of what the supposedly new point might be. The obvious moral to draw from this is that the point is not actually meant as a *new* point at all: it must be just a repetition of something we have had already, but now re-expressed in a more picturesque way.

There are still two alternative proposals as to what the point might be. On one interpretation, it is a repetition of the *premiss* of our opening argument, that perceptible equal things 'seem equal to one but not to another', whereas the equal itself does not. On the other, it is merely a repetition of the *conclusion* of that argument, that perceptible equal things are not the same as the equal itself. I begin with the second proposal.

This proposal is determinedly unexciting. According to it, to say that perceptible equal things 'fall short of' the form means only that they *are not* the form: falling short of something is simply a matter of not being the same thing as it, and consequently everything whatever falls short of everything else in this way. Two advantages might be claimed for this proposal. The first looks back to the premisses about reminding which open our argument, and in particular to the premiss at 74a5–7, where we first meet this notion of falling short. We are told there that when we are reminded of one thing by seeing another which is like it, then it must also happen that we think whether the thing that reminds us is or is not lacking in its similarity to what it reminds us of. I remarked earlier that, when taken in an ordinary way, this premiss seems fairly obviously to be false. I may surely glimpse a portrait of Simmias, and thereby be reminded of some point about Simmias, without at all pausing to reflect on how good a likeness the portrait is. But on the present proposal this objection does not arise, for I shall inevitably notice that the portrait 'falls short of' Simmias (or 'lacks something in its similarity') just by noticing that it is a portrait, and therefore *is not* Simmias. Alternatively, suppose (improbably) that I do not realize that it is a portrait I am looking at, and I think that it is Simmias himself. Then again I am led to think of one thing (Simmias) by perceiving another (his portrait), and again I 'experience something further', for in this case I think that what I see is *not* lacking in its similarity to Simmias, because I think that it *is* Simmias. Either way, I surely shall have an opinion on whether what I see is or is not the thing it leads me to think of. On the present proposal, that is all Plato means when he says that I shall think whether or not what I see 'falls short of' what I think of, so the proposal has the advantage that, if it is correct, then this remark about reminding is after all *true*. (But one might also observe that, on this proposal, there was no reason for Plato to limit this remark about reminding to cases in which I am reminded by something *like* what it reminds me of. It would be equally true in cases where I am reminded by something *unlike* what it reminds me of. So the claimed 'advantage' is perhaps rather double-edged.)

The second advantage that might be claimed is that Plato is now exonerated from the charge that he conceives the form of equality to be an equal thing. It is true that he is quite prepared to say that the form 'is equal'. This is implied by the way he first introduces it in 74a9–10 ('We say that there is something equal . . . the equal itself'), but still more by his talk of falling short. For example he says that equal things 'are not equal in the same way' as the form, implying that both *are* equal, though in different ways. But the main thrust of the present proposal is that these statements can be interpreted in an entirely innocuous way. The form 'is equal' *only* in the sense that it is *the* equal, it is identical with the equal. So Plato's vocabulary is perhaps misleading, but his thought is entirely straightforward. By contrast, particular things 'are equal' in the ordinary sense: they 'participate in' the form (as Plato will later say, e.g. 100c5), but they also 'fall short' of it, which simply means that they are not identical with it. On this proposal, it is a mistake to say that particular things are not 'as equal as' the form, as if we could make some kind of comparison of the degree of equality attained by each. For the two are 'equal' only in quite different senses: one is, i.e. is the same as, the equal; the others are not the equal, i.e. they fall short of it, though they do participate in it. (But notice that they participate perfectly well. There is nothing wrong with their participation, except that participation is not identity.) In effect, then, this proposal makes use of the point that Plato's terminology does not properly distinguish between being equal and being equality, as we noted earlier that he failed to distinguish between being unequal and being inequality (pp. 84–5), but it insists that although his terminology may be odd his thought is quite straightforward. The necessary distinction is marked by the claim that particulars fall short of the form, for this means that they are equal but are not equality, while it is equality (and is not equal).

One's first reaction to this proposal might be that it construes what seems to be an interesting and exciting metaphor in a flat and uninteresting way. For example, not being the same as is a symmetrical relation, and if this is all that falling short means then it should be equally true to say that the form falls short of the particulars. But would Plato say this? Would he be happy to say that the form *wants* to be like the particulars, it *strives* to be like them, but cannot succeed and is inferior? This seems very improbable. But perhaps we can answer this objection, and explain the metaphor, in this way. The reason why the particulars *want* to be the form is that they are trying to tell us what the form is. The best way they could do that would be by *being* the form. But unfortunately they cannot succeed in that endeavour, for they simply are not the form, but can only participate in it. Or rather, to get the desire located in the right place, it is *we* who want to know what the form is, and *we* who should therefore like the particular things we can perceive to tell us. But that they can not do, simply because, as we have said, they *are not* the form. All they can do is to participate in the form, which is not enough to tell us what we want to know.

I am inclined to think, then, that even in this very flat and anaemic account of what 'falling short' really comes to, we can still give a tolerable explanation of the picturesque metaphors that Plato employs, and I do not think that there is serious ground for objection on this score. The main ground for objection lies deeper, and comes to grips with the heart of the question. Did Plato think, or did he not think, that particular equal things *resemble* the form? The present proposal is that there is no resemblance at all. It is true that the same *word* 'equal' applies to both, but it applies in quite different senses, and so no more indicates a resemblance than does the fact that the same word 'bar' applies both to bars that serve alcohol and to bars of soap. We need something more than that if we are to claim that Plato thought the form was in any genuine sense *like* the things that participate in it.

Curiously, the text of the *Phaedo* is quite unforthcoming on this question. All commentators have noted that the opening remarks on how reminding takes place seem designed to lead up to the case of being reminded by things that are like, as a portrait of Simmias may remind us of Simmias himself. One naturally supposes that this will be the kind of reminding that is to play a part in the sequel: particular equal things will remind us of the form by being *like* it. But when it comes to the point, our text remains studiously non-committal on this issue. It twice observes that it does not matter to the argument whether particulars remind us of forms by being like them, or despite being unlike them (74e11–13, 76a3–4), and we are told nothing further. It is true that one might be pushed to explain how particulars do remind us of forms if it is not by being like them, for it is not as if we had *previously* set up some mental association between the two, which might explain how the sight of the one leads to the thought of the other. But this is a speculation which goes beyond anything that the text explicitly says, and so far as that text is concerned, we can only say that it contains several suggestive points but nothing definite.

The situation changes if we may bring in the evidence of *other* dialogues. Some further evidence can indeed be extracted from later on in the *Phaedo* (101a–b, concerning forms as causes), but I leave that until we come to it. The *Republic*, however, is conclusively in favour of the idea that particulars resemble forms: it explicitly uses the relation between a picture and what it is a picture of as an analogy to the relation between particulars and forms, and it constantly speaks of that relation as a relation of resembling, or being a copy of, or being a reflection of. (See especially *Republic* vi. 509d–511e, and x. 595a–605b.) The same terminology is found in other post-*Phaedo* dialogues.[11] In view of this, it seems fair to conclude that when, in the *Phaedo*, Plato says that the form of the equal is itself something equal he means to be taken in a more straightforward way than the present proposal will allow. He does mean this to imply that the particulars and the form are *alike* in both being equal, and he does think that that is how the particulars remind us of the form. But of course the particulars are in another way *unlike* the form, for they are equal only in the

[11] E.g. *Phaedrus* 250a–b; *Timaeus* 29b–c, 39e, 48c, 50c–51a.

defective way that they 'seem equal to one but not to another', while the form 'never seems unequal'. That is no doubt the explanation of why he never does affirm straightforwardly that the particulars are like the form rather than unlike it.

The evidence of the *Republic* would still leave it as a possibility that Plato changed his opinion between writing the *Phaedo* and writing the *Republic*. Perhaps in the *Phaedo* he was not yet prepared to commit himself to the view that particulars were resemblances of forms, while by the time of the *Republic* he had made up his mind that they were. One difficulty with this suggestion is to see why Plato might have changed his mind, for at least as I reconstruct his thinking—which I shall do in a moment—his major reason for supposing that there were forms always included the idea that forms have in an unqualified way those same characteristics that particulars also have, but defectively. Another difficulty is the evidence of the *Symposium*, which seems to me entirely in harmony with this 'resemblance' view, and which is admitted on all sides to be very close in date to the *Phaedo*. But before I come to develop this point, I should just pause to point out the direction that my argument is taking.

I said earlier that we now had two interpretations of 'falling short' to consider. According to one, to say that particulars fall short of forms is merely to say that particulars are not the same as forms, which was the *conclusion* of the argument we began with. I have recently been putting some objections to this interpretation, the main objection being that it leaves out—indeed, it aims to deny—a point that seems to me important, namely that the form and the particulars that are 'called after it' both share a *common* characteristic, in our case the characteristic of being equal. But to argue for this objection must at the same time be to argue for the alternative interpretation that I mentioned, according to which to say that particulars fall short of forms is to repeat the *premiss* of that opening argument: particular equal things will 'seem equal to one but not to another', whereas the form 'never seems unequal' (but always seems equal). It is in this way that particulars fall short: what they are trying to do is to be always equal and never unequal, but since they are particulars they cannot succeed in this; only the form can succeed. (The elucidation of the metaphor remains as before, p. 90).

We have already discussed (pp. 73–8) various possible ways of taking this 'defect' of particulars, and I have argued in favour of interpretation (*b*). On this approach, the main point is that particular things can be equal (or beautiful, or just) only with a qualification, which therefore allows them to be at the same time unequal (or ugly, or unjust) with a different qualification. By contrast the form is equal (or beautiful, or just) without any such qualification, and so cannot also be unequal (or ugly, or unjust). As my final piece of evidence in favour of this interpretation, I now quote a passage from the *Symposium*.

In the central speech of the *Symposium* Socrates is reporting Diotima's teaching on the subject of love and beauty, and towards the end she describes the quest for beauty as a kind of ascent. The lover begins by loving the beauty of a particular body, and then progresses first to an appreciation of bodily beauty in general, then to the beauties of the soul, then to the beauties of laws and institutions, and then to the beauties of every kind of knowledge (210a–d). Finally he will see one knowledge which is knowledge of a thing beautiful in this way:

He will see something marvellously beautiful in its nature, the very thing all his previous labour was undertaken for. First it is always [*sc.* beautiful?] and neither comes to be nor perishes, neither increases nor decreases. Next it is not beautiful in one respect but ugly in another, nor beautiful at one time but not at another, nor beautiful in relation to one thing but ugly in relation to another, nor beautiful here but ugly there, as being beautiful to some but ugly to others. This beauty will not appear to him as a beautiful face, or hands, or anything bodily, nor as a piece of reasoning (λόγος) or knowledge, nor will it be *in* something else, as for example in a living creature, or in the earth, or in the heavens, or in anything else at all. It exists alone, itself by itself with itself, and always of a single form; and the other beautiful things participate in it in such a way that while they come to be and cease to be, it neither grows nor diminishes nor suffers any change at all. (210e4–211b5.)

This is the *Symposium*'s description of the form of beauty. One thing that is quite clear about it is that the form of beauty is itself a (supremely) beautiful thing. Another thing that is quite clear is that it is beautiful without any qualification at all. It may be noted that one of the qualifications here ruled out is in fact the qualification that interpretation (*a*) finds equal things to suffer from: they seem equal to one man but not to another. Another of the qualifications is the one that interpretation (*b*) begins from:

equal things are equal in relation to one thing but not in relation to another. But clearly the intention of the *Symposium* is to exclude *all* such qualifications from the form. That is why it is beautiful in a way that nothing else can be, but it still *is* beautiful. The deflationary proposal we were discussing, according to which a form does not *have* the characteristic it represents but simply *is* that characteristic, surely cannot survive this evidence. I conclude that the falling short of particulars consists in the very point that was mentioned at the start of the argument: they can only exhibit *with qualification* the characteristics that forms exhibit without qualification, and consequently they will exhibit both the two opposite characteristics at once, which a form will never do.

If we now pause for a moment to take stock, the extravagance of Plato's thought will seem absolutely breathtaking. He begins (as I interpret him) from the safe and quite uncontroversial premiss that we do, in a perfectly ordinary sense, attach some meaning to words such as 'equal' or 'beautiful'. He ends with the conclusion that there must therefore be entities to which these words apply without any qualification—entities which are not accessible to the senses, which are not in fact in this world at all, but which we must at some time have seen. How on earth does such a surprising conclusion come from such an innocuous premiss? I devote the next section to a (somewhat conjectural) reconstruction of just how Plato was led from his premiss to his conclusion, so that we have the doctrine fully articulated before we turn to evaluate it.

E. FORMS AS MISSING PARADIGMS

I mentioned in my introduction (pp. 6–7) that one of the background influences which surely played some part in the formation of Plato's theory of forms was Socrates' propensity to ask 'what is *X*?' questions, especially about concepts of ethics (or aesthetics), and to be dissatisfied with the answers. Let us begin with this, for it is a frequently recurring theme in Plato's dialogues. Thus the *Laches* is wholly devoted to the question 'what is courage?', the *Charmides* to 'what is temperance (σωφροσύνη)?', the *Euthyphro* to 'what is piety?', and the *Hippias Major* to 'what is beauty?' We may add that half of the *Meno* is an attack on the question 'what is virtue?', the *Lysis* could be said to be asking 'what is friendship?', and

Republic i is built around the question 'what is justice?' In each case the question remains unanswered at the end of the dialogue. Even where a dialogue is officially concerned with some other question Socrates is apt to conclude by saying that the reason why they have made no headway is that they should have concentrated first on the relevant 'what is X?' question (e.g. *Protagoras* 361 c; compare *Meno* 100b, *Republic* i 354b). Nearly always he speaks as though this were the first and most important question to answer in any philosophical enquiry, and his failure to reach any answers does not deter him.

Several presuppositions can be discerned in the way that Socrates handles his question. First, if we suppose that the question can be answered without hedging, we are evidently assuming that the term 'X' is univocal, and this is quite an interesting assumption for the terms Socrates is concerned with. For example, you might say that one of the major faults in the argument of *Republic* ii–iv is the assumption that 'justice' applies in the same sense to men and to states. (When we speak of just men, just acts, just laws, and just states, the senses of the word 'just' are surely connected but *not* identical.) On one occasion (*Meno* 73a) a disputant does raise the question whether 'X' means the same in all its various applications, but Socrates brushes the question aside somewhat carelessly. He takes it to be pretty obvious that there is some *one* thing common to *all* the men, women and children who are virtuous, despite their different pursuits, for why else, he might say, do we use the same word in each case?[12]

Another assumption is that being X is in some sense analysable, though it is not easy to see just what sort of analysis Socrates is looking for. He very commonly insists that he does not want a list of the *many* things that are X, but rather the *one* thing that is common to all the many instances, and this one thing is described sometimes as what *makes* the various X things X, and sometimes as a 'paradigm' by which to *judge* whether a thing is X or not. It may well be doubted whether these two requirements can be jointly satisfied, for one apparently concerns an underlying cause of the characteristic in question, while the other asks for a mark by

---

[12] It is one of Aristotle's well-known objections to the Platonic theory that this assumption is false, at any rate for the word 'good' (*Nicomachean Ethics* A6, 1096a23 ff.).

which we recognize its presence, and one would not expect these
to be the same. Besides, it is often natural to suppose that what
Socrates is really looking for is a definition in roughly our sense,
and is therefore also requiring that an answer must provide an
expression with the same *meaning* as '*X*'. In fact it is not easy to
find direct textual support for this suggestion,[13] but it would go
some way towards explaining why Socrates so emphasizes the
priority of his 'what is *X*?' question. One could understand the view
that before we do anything else we must be clear about what we
mean, whereas it is not so very easy to see why underlying causes,
or even marks of recognition, have to be settled before any other
question can sensibly be raised.

There is more to be said on the question of what Socrates would
count as an adequate answer to 'what is *X*?', but I leave that topic
on one side as not very relevant to my present concern. I also leave
on one side the issue of whether Socrates is right to lay so much
emphasis on the priority of his 'What is *X*?' question. But what we
can fairly say is that Plato took over from Socrates the assumption
that this question is a sensible question, and one that is of crucial
importance. He assumed, that is, that indeed there *is* some one
thing which is common to all that is just, or all that is beautiful, or
all that is good, and that it is sensible and in fact vital to ask what
this thing is. But we now have to ask where this assumption led
him.

I conjecture that Plato became more and more impressed
by the fact that it seemed so excessively difficult to find answers to
these questions. In some cases it is apparently quite simple. For
example the question 'what is quickness?' may be answered by
saying that quickness is doing a lot in a short time (*Laches*
192a–b), and the question 'what is shape?' may be answered by
saying that shape is the limit of a solid (*Meno* 76a). But with the
interesting and important cases that Socrates was so concerned
with, no such simple answers seemed available. Worse, every
effort to explore more complex answers seemed always to reveal
some difficulty. So at this point a further question arises: what is it
that makes it so difficult to discern the *one* thing common to the
many instances in these cases? I should like to suggest that
reflection on this problem led Plato in the end to think that the
trouble lay—at least partly—in the instances themselves. One

[13] The best evidence would seem to be *Euthyphro* 10a–11b.

cannot even cite an unambiguous *instance* of courage, or beauty, or justice, and if that is so it would surely explain why it seems so difficult to find the one thing common to all these alleged instances.

Let us illustrate this with some of Plato's examples. To take a familiar case from the *Republic*, one might have thought that paying one's debts was at least *one* case of justice, though no doubt there are others too. But on reflection we can see that paying one's debts is *not* always the just thing to do; there are circumstances in which one definitely ought not to return what one has borrowed, e.g. if one has borrowed a gun from a madman (*Republic* i. 331c). Or again, one might have been inclined to say that for a soldier to stay in his place in the ranks was at least *one* way in which he could be courageous; but again on reflection we can see that there are circumstances in which this would not be the courageous thing to do (*Laches* 190e–191c). In a slightly different vein, one might have supposed that at least *one* sort of beautiful thing was a beautiful girl, and yet this looks an essentially unsatisfactory example, since a mere girl would appear plain beside a goddess; or one might have supposed that gold was a beautiful material, but again it has to be said that this holds only for *some* objects, and only in *some* settings, and so on (*Hippias Major* 289a–b, 289e–291b). Further ·examples of this sort can easily be culled from the early dialogues. Generally, we may say that Plato inherits from Socrates a preoccupation with the question 'what is X?' where the values for 'X' are concepts of ethics (or aesthetics). From Socrates also be inherits the assumption that this question is to be understood as asking for the *one* thing common to the *many* cases of X. But what he notices, I suggest, is that there seems to be a serious difficulty even over the various *cases* of X: one cannot specify any such case which is not also in some ways or in some circumstances a case of non-X.

Now if, when we consider the concept of X-ness, it seems hard even to collect any unambiguous *cases* of things that are X, one is liable to wonder how it is what we ever came to acquire this concept in the first place. For surely the *usual* way of acquiring a concept is with the help of 'paradigm cases'. We learn what the word 'red' means by being shown examples of red things, and the same account no doubt goes for 'stick' and 'stone' (*Phaedo* 74b) and for 'finger' (*Republic* 523b–e). But if everything that was red was also not red, it is clear that pointing to examples of red things could not distinguish the meaning of 'red' from that of 'not red', and so would not help in the slightest. And we have just said that, for *interesting* values of '*X*', it is indeed true that everything that is *X* is also non-*X*, so there are no suitable paradigm cases that we can use. In that case, how do we ever come to understand '*X*' at all? That, it seems to me, was Plato's new problem, and was what led him to the theory of forms.

Whether or not the Socratic questions we began from should be understood as questions about meaning, the new problem they have led to very clearly is a problem about meaning. It is the problem of how we can come to understand a word when there are no appropriate paradigm examples to illustrate what it means. When put in this form, Plato's answer to it is that we cannot. He *retains* the natural idea that a word can be understood only with the help of a suitable paradigm, and so posits forms to be the needed paradigms when ordinary sensible paradigms are missing. The role of the form is to be a clear and unambiguous example of *X*, an example that is not *also* an example of non-*X*, and forms are needed wherever all ordinary sensible examples are ambiguous in this way. We may note a small extra assumption at this point. Plato supposes that if all ordinary sensible examples are thus ambiguous, then an unambiguous example would have to be non-sensible. It must be grasped, as we metaphorically say, with the eye of the mind rather than the eye of the body. What seems a much larger assumption is that we cannot perform this feat during our life on earth, and so must have done it in some previous time when not encumbered by a body. Why not suppose that we *now* have this 'mental vision' of non-sensible paradigms? Plato's answer to this goes back to the Socratic problem he began with. If we really did have available to us, in this life, suitable (non-sensible) examples of beauty, goodness, justice, and so on, then surely we should now be able to answer the Socratic questions that we do not seem able to answer. Besides, it must be admitted that in fact we cannot form any clear picture of what an unambiguous example would be like. Nevertheless we must have had *some* acquaintance with the examples, because we do succeed in attaching some meaning to these words, even though we cannot say how we do it. The idea that we now have a dim and hazy memory of an experience that took place before birth thus seems to answer all problems.

Even so, the theory still seems over-bold. Would we not expect Plato to show more hesitation about it than he does? In the introduction I suggested, rather speculatively, that Plato's belief may have been reinforced by thinking further about numbers and mathematics, which would be a likely consequence of increased contact with the Pythagoreans (pp. 12–14). Let us carry these speculations a little further. First, numbers appear to be a further case of something we understand, but without the help of unambiguous paradigms. A finger, for instance, will be an example of something that is one (finger) but also three (joints) and in general many (parts) (*Republic* 524d–525a). The same will hold of any sensible example of a number; it will also illustrate some other number as well. Second, the numbers themselves may well appear to be suitably unqualified examples of the properties they represent since the number two, for example, is just two; it is not two *of* anything and therefore not some other number *of* something else. But we may also (inconsistently) be tempted to think that the number two is in a way a paradigm pair, as being two ones, and so something that sensible pairs may imitate. If we allow ourselves to think of the numbers now in one of these ways and now in the other, they may seem to fulfil all the conditions we have set for forms. Moreover, numbers are not sensible things, but they clearly do exist, and we know quite a lot about them. In fact the study of numbers, i.e. arithmetic, is a star example of a science that is quite independent of perception: it does not rely on observation or experiment, but we appear simply to be able to draw the knowledge out of ourselves.

This last point was, apparently, what first put Plato on to the idea of recollection, in the *Meno*. Though nothing is said about forms in that dialogue, still its problem has something in common with the *Phaedo*'s problem, and mathematics was there taken as supplying the key to it. The problem arises in this way. Socrates and Meno have been attacking the question 'what is virtue?' and failing to answer it. This prompts Meno to ask why they should suppose that success is even possible. Perhaps his most interesting question here is: even if you were to stumble across the right account of what virtue is, how would you know that it *was* the right account? (*Meno*, 80d). In reply, Socrates somewhat tentatively suggests that we all knew the right answers once, and the problem is to recollect them. (Presumably he supposes that if I did know the right answer once then I shall recognize it as the right one if I meet it again). In order to convince Meno of this he then tries to demonstrate, using an ignorant slave, that we are capable of recognizing the right answer to a mathematical problem, even if we have never (in this life) heard it before (*Meno* 81a–86b). So the general moral of the *Meno* is that mathematical knowledge certainly is possible, and this gives us some reason to hope that proper philosophic knowledge (of, say, virtue) is also possible. For mathematical knowledge comes from within, it has (when one properly understands it) an unshakeable certainty, and—though the *Meno* itself does not stress this point—it is independent of perception. These characteristics are explained if it is indeed nothing but recollection of something once known with perfect clarity.

Well, I simply leave it as a speculation that Plato's confidence in his theory was considerably bolstered by the fact that it did seem to make good sense of mathematics. Since the speculation receives no notable support from the *Phaedo*, which hardly mentions mathematics, I shall ignore this aspect of the theory when we come to evaluate it. Before I do that, I should just like to add two brief remarks on the *Phaedo*'s theory, as I have expounded it.

First, I have made no attempt to explain how anything could be equal without being equal *to* something (and therefore unequal to other things). I have tried to make clear why Plato believed there *must be* such a thing, but I do not imaginë that even he had any conception of how it would appear to the eye of the mind. (You will notice that even the description of the form of beauty described it largely in terms of what it was *not*.) Plato would not claim to have himself attained the proper philosophic knowledge of forms that he speaks of.

Second, notice that Plato will quite naturally take an expression such as 'the equal itself' as a name of that non-sensible paradigm example of equality that he believes to exist. This can lead to confusion, since he *also* uses the word interchangeably with the abstract noun 'equality' (as is quite normal Greek idiom), and equality—the property of being equal—cannot be identified with any paradigm example of equality. The paradigm example *has* the property, and has it paradigmatically, but it *is not* the property. I shall have more to say about this in my last chapter, when I take up the theory of forms once more, but so far as the main arguments of the *Phaedo* are concerned, I think we can be charitable. Sometimes when Plato speaks of a form what he says applies to the paradigm example, and sometimes it applies to the property which that paradigm example is an example of. But usually we can see well enough what he is really thinking of. The connection between the two is of course very close, for he thinks that we know what the word 'equal' means, i.e. we know what equality is, only because we are (dimly) acquainted with its perfect paradigm.

From these considerations about Plato's view of forms in general, let us now return specifically to the argument of the *Phaedo*.

F. EVALUATION OF THE RECOLLECTION ARGUMENT

We may begin by briefly recapitulating the main points of the argument. The heart of it runs from 74a9 to 75c5, beginning with the claim that we all know, in a perfectly ordinary sense, what the word 'equal' means. We may put this, if we like, as the claim that we all know what equality is, and the challenge posed is to say how we know this. The first point made is that equality is not the same as any of the equal things that we can perceive, and it is not itself a perceptible thing at all. According to what we may call the 'simple' interpretation of the argument, that is the only point made, for when Plato goes on to claim that perceptible equal things all 'fall short of' equality itself, he is simply re-expressing this same point in other words. On this construction, the argument would presumably apply to all general terms without exception. But as I construe the argument it is more complicated, and only applies to rather special words. For on my version the next claim is that perceptible things cannot even provide any clear examples of equality: perceptible things are indeed equal in a way, but they are also, and at the same time, unequal. From this we are meant to infer that our knowledge of what equality is cannot be explained as given to us by perception. Yet we must also admit that it is our perception of equal things that somehow 'puts us in mind of' the notion of equality, for the knowledge is manifested just as soon as we learn to classify sticks and so on as equal (cf. 74e9–75a3). This is not actually as soon as we are born, as the argument may seem to suggest (75a11–b12), but the point is that there has been no opportunity between birth and our first classification of things as equal to acquire the relevant knowledge. For once we are born perception is the only source of knowledge, and we have agreed that perception cannot explain this knowledge. We must infer, then, that we have the knowledge when we are born, though it somehow remains latent until the perception of equal things triggers it.

Notice that up to this point in the argument we have made no use of any controversial thesis about forms. We have said that any example of something equal is also an example of something unequal, and we have also claimed that in this life perception is the only source of knowledge. But we have not yet needed to make any positive claims about what our knowledge of equality is, or how it is acquired. However we do need to say something more about this if we are to overcome the objection that the argument so far does not show that we existed before birth. For all that we have had so far, it is open to an objector to maintain that we were just born with this knowledge of equality, but did not have to learn it at any previous time. When Plato himself belatedly notices this objection, at 76c14–15, he gives a reply which can only be regarded as missing the point. He takes it to be already established that the relevant knowledge must be both acquired and forgotten, and that it is forgotten at birth, and objects that it can hardly be acquired and forgotten at the same time. But if the hypothesis is that before birth we did not possess this knowledge, then of course there is no reason to say that we ever did forget it at any time (76d1–4). Plato may perhaps believe that the rather dim state of our present knowledge—in a sense, we know what the word means, but we cannot *say* what it means—can only be explained if we once had a much fuller and more explicit knowledge which we now only partly recollect. But that is a claim that would need a lot more argument.[14] So it seems simplest at this point to bring in more of his doctrine about how meanings are learnt, and in particular that they can be learnt only by acquaintance with paradigm examples. (This is, in a way, implicit in the claim that perception is the only source of knowledge in this world.) It will then follow that we were at some time acquainted with an example of equality that was not

---

[14] The argument might have to introduce the (doubtful) premisses that fuller, and properly philosophic, knowledge is possible, and that when it is reached it will 'click into place' as a memory does. (And support for these premisses might draw upon an analogy with mathematical knowledge.) See the next section, on the *Meno*

also an example of inequality, and such an example must therefore exist somewhere. Granted this, it will then seem very plausible—though still not, strictly, necessary—to say that we met the example before birth rather than at birth. On any view, the argument does falter at this point, but when we take into account more and more of Plato's total picture it becomes progressively easier to see why this did not strike him as a serious objection. (Plato is himself notably careless about just how the theory of forms enters into the argument. He concludes at 76d7–e7 by saying that the claim that there are forms and the claim that our souls existed before birth must stand or fall together, but this is obviously a gross exaggeration. Either claim *could* be true while the other was false.)

However, I shall pay no more attention to the question of pre-natal existence. The argument I set out in the first paragraph of this section, which aims to show just that we were born with a knowledge of what equality is, is itself quite sufficiently contro-versial, and I restrict attention to that from now on.

Suppose we begin with the 'simple' version of the argument, which would apply to all general terms, even to such a simple term as 'red' or 'round'. In this version, the argument simply points out that the meaning of a word is not itself a perceptible thing, and then challenges us to say how, in that case, the meaning can be learnt. But the reply seems to be very simple. According to a very traditional approach to the notion of meaning,[15] we learn the meaning of general terms not by perception alone but by perception *plus* abstraction. That is, we observe a number of examples of things to which the word applies—for example red things—and we then 'abstract' the property that they have in common. In other words, we notice that our red things all resemble one another in a certain way, and we thereby form a conception of this resemblance that they all share, and concentrate our attention selectively on it. We see that there may be yet other things that resemble our original examples in the same way, so we are ready to apply the word 'red' not only to these examples but to other things as well that have the appropriate resemblance to them, and when we have done this we have formed the general idea of redness. In brief, then, we perceive the examples *and* we notice

[15] The approach is perhaps especially associated with Locke (*Essay*, book III).

their resemblance, thus 'abstracting' their common feature. Because all human minds do have this ability to 'abstract', you may say, if you like, that they are born with it. But this is not at all the same as to say that they were born with an understanding of redness in particular. We were born simply with a general ability to notice resemblances, and thereby abstract any number of general concepts from different sets of examples.

Now I certainly admit that there are difficulties in this traditional idea of 'abstraction'. Perhaps one of the more interesting difficulties is that any actual set of examples will in fact resemble one another in indefinitely many different ways, and it needs to be explained how we manage to pick out the 'right' resemblance. For example, the things presented to me may all be red, but they may all be painted too, and yet 'red' does not mean the same as 'painted', nor even the same as 'painted red'. In this case, you can clearly correct my error by presenting me with further examples of things that are painted but not red, or red but not painted, and pointing out that the word 'red' does or does not apply to them as appropriate. But, at least in theory, there are always infinitely many ways in which I might generalize wrongly from any finite set of examples, however large, so you could not guard against them all. Besides, you could not in this way prevent this mistake: all the red things I have ever seen have been both red and seen by me, but 'red' does not mean 'red and seen by me', yet if I thought it did you could not put me right by showing me an example of something that was red but *not* seen by me. On reflection, then, we see that there must be something more to it than the traditional doctrine allows for, and in fact the problem has led some philosophers to say that we must be programmed from birth (by our genes) to generalize only in certain ways and not others. But all this takes us a long way from Plato, and what he says gives us no reason to suspect the traditional notion of abstraction.

Let us move on, then, to the more interesting version of the argument, in which it is only meant to apply to words for which we cannot point to perceptible examples. As a preliminary, let us first start with a very simple case where perceptible examples are indeed missing, the word 'mermaid'. You did not learn what this word means by seeing clear and unambiguous examples of mermaids, for there are none. (Of course there are pictures of mermaids, but pictures of mermaids are not mermaids, and 'mermaid' does not mean 'picture of a mermaid'.) The traditional account here is that you know what this word means because its meaning can be explained in terms of *other* words, which are words for things you have perceived. In this case, the relevant other words are obviously 'woman' and 'fish', and perhaps we should add 'top half of' and 'joined to' and 'bottom half of' (roughly). So the traditional account allows *three* operations as relevant to learning the meaning of words—perception of examples, abstraction from those examples, and explanation of some words in terms of others already known. With this in mind, let us turn to consider the words Plato himself is interested in.

Unfortunately, what he has to say about the particular example that his argument uses, the word 'equal', can only be dismissed as a mistake. The word 'equal' is a word for a *relation*, and a paradigm example for a relation must consist of *two* objects and not one. No doubt any single object will be equal to one thing but unequal to another, but since no single object will illustrate the meaning of a relation anyway that is simply not to the point. The same reply applies to the examples 'larger' and 'smaller' that are mentioned later; again we need an example of *two* objects to illustrate these relations, but Plato seems to be supposing that we ought to be able to do it with just one. We have seen an instance earlier in this dialogue of Plato mistakenly treating relations as if they were really properties of a single thing (pp. 49–51), and we shall see another instance later (pp. 181–3). The present passage seems yet another.

Since this result seems so disappointing, let us just canvass a few other interpretations of the argument. Suppose first that, as interpretation (*a*) had it, the point is meant to be that *two* sticks which seem equal to one man may seem unequal to another. Then the obvious reply seems to be that we have procedures of measurement which will *settle* the dispute. As Plato has himself remarked in an earlier dialogue, men do quite seriously disagree with one another on questions of right and wrong, good and bad, justice and injustice, but they do *not* seriously disagree on whether one thing is equal to another, or larger than it, or smaller than it. We have perfectly good methods of settling any disagreement of this kind (*Euthyphro* 7b–e). Let us take another suggestion then. Perhaps the point is that two sticks which are equal in one respect (e.g. length) will also be unequal in another. To resolve this, one has only to observe that the 'abstraction' in this case will in fact proceed in two stages. First we shall use some appropriate pairs of objects as examples from which to abstract the notion of equality in length, some other pairs to abstract the notion of equality in weight, yet other pairs to abstract the notion of equality in volume, and so on. That is, we first abstract the different notions of equality in this or that special respect, and for this we have perfectly good examples. Then as a second stage we may review all these various notions of equality in particular respects, and 'abstract' from them in turn the feature that they have in common, viz. that they are all kinds of equality. The doctrine of abstractions seems quite capable of handling this case, provided we add a little complication.

It is also quite capable of handling the matter if we suppose that the point is that there are no examples of *exact* equality (say in length). Let me illustrate with a simpler example first. Suppose that we understand what 'perfectly beautiful' means, but that there are no examples of things that are perfectly beautiful. Nevertheless there will be examples of pairs of things such that one is more beautiful than the other, and we can use these examples to introduce the *relation* 'more beautiful than'. In terms of this relation we can then explain what it means to say that a thing is perfectly beautiful: it means that nothing else could be more beautiful than it. To apply the same technique with the notion of exact equality is a little more complex, for we must now begin with a relation which holds between one *pair* of sticks and *another pair*, namely when the first pair is 'more nearly equal' than the second. There will at any rate be perfectly good examples of this, even if no two sticks ever are exactly equal. But we can then explain what it means to say that two sticks are exactly equal: it means that no pair of objects could be more nearly equal than they are. Perhaps—though I very much doubt it—Plato would hold that it is never *true* to say this, but even so there would still be no problem about its meaning.

As a final illustration of this approach, let us turn from the comparative expressions 'larger' and 'smaller' to the positives 'large' and 'small'. These are not on the surface relation-words, but they do seem to suit Plato's case: for example, a large mouse will at the same time be a small animal. But since the relation 'larger than' is already understood, we can explain being a large mouse as a relational property, the property of being a mouse larger than most *mice* (and similarly a small animal is an animal smaller than most *animals*). When a thing is said to be large, there will always be a 'comparison class' of this kind, explicit or implicit, which the speaker has in mind, and if there is not we may fairly say that what he says has no meaning after all.

I conclude that those of Plato's examples that involve relations (covertly or overtly) are in fact quite easily handled by the traditional doctrine in terms of perceiving examples, abstracting a common property, and explaining one idea in terms of others already understood. This seems to hold *however* we construe the argument he puts. If Plato does not see this, it is apparently because he has never really grasped that relations are not properties, and relations need two terms to exemplify them and not one. I am afraid this may seem a rather elementary mistake, but I see no way of interpreting Plato that would avoid it.

So I come, finally, to the cases that Plato himself evidently thought the most crucial and important, namely beauty, goodness, justice, and so on. There is nowhere in Plato any decent argument to show that all perceptible examples of these will also be examples of their opposites, and the few hints that he does give are usually quite easy to answer. To illustrate, I briefly deal with two of the list of examples given earlier (p. 97). The *Republic* suggests that returning what one has borrowed both is and is not just, since although it is often just to give back what one owes, it is not always. For instance, one should not return a lethal weapon to a homicidal maniac, even if it is his. Here the point is that there is a general *type* of act of which some examples are just and others not. So you might perhaps wish to say of the general *type* that in a way it both was and was not just. But the *particular* examples which are acts of that type will be either just or not just, as the case may be, and need not in any way be both. So there is really no problem here at all. To take a different kind of example, the *Hippias Major* suggests at one point that a beautiful girl no doubt is beautiful in a way, but is also not beautiful, since she would appear plain beside a goddess. Accepting this suggestion for the sake of argument, we can still easily explain what is going on in terms of the comparative relation 'more beautiful than'. Plato is construing the phrase 'a beautiful girl' (like the phrase 'a large mouse') as if it means 'beautiful *for* a girl', i.e. (more beautiful than the majority of girls). This is of course quite compatible with being less beautiful than a goddess. I leave it to you to disentangle his other examples. Anyway, a mere handful of examples would not of course establish the perfectly general thesis he is aiming for. What is needed is a general reason for supposing that there is *always* something wrong with *any* examples that one might use to introduce these words.

Although, as I say, no such reason is to be found explicitly in Plato's writings, still I think we can supply one for him. It goes back to what I called interpretation (*a*) of our opening argument about equality: things will seem equal to one man but not to another, which is to say that men disagree on the topic. Now I argued at the time that this is not likely to be what Plato does mean to say about equality, and I have argued recently that anyway the point has no force when applied to equality, for such disagreements can easily be *settled*. But in the case of beauty, goodness, and justice we have *no* any procedure for settling these disagreements, and this is a point of some importance. For if a word is to be introduced in terms of examples, it seems necessary that the examples should be in a sense undeniable. The word 'red', for example, surely is introduced via paradigm examples, in much the way as the traditional approach suggests. Now suppose that a man, in full view of a paradigmatically red object, denies that it is red—suppose, indeed, that he does this for a fair range of paradigmatically red objects. Of course, he may be teasing us, or he may be a victim of some trick of the light, or there may be some disorder in his visual apparatus, and so on. But if we cannot account for his denials by such means as this, then we can only conclude that he does not after all understand what the word 'red' *means*. For its meaning is given by just such examples as these, so one who does not believe that they are examples must have misunderstood its meaning (unless some other special explanation is available). By contrast, examples of beauty, goodness, or justice are *never* undeniable. No matter what we choose as our paradigm of something good, another man may always say that he does not think it is good, and this will never force us to conclude that he has not understood what the word means. Essentially this is because words like 'good' are used not only—and sometimes not at all—to *describe* the things they are applied to, but also to *set a value* on them. Another man may agree completely about how the thing is to be described, but he may evaluate it differently from us, and if he values things differently he will of course apply the word 'good' to different things, but this is *not* because he attaches a different meaning to the word. On the contrary, we are each of us using the word with the same meaning, for our disagreement is a genuine disagreement about values, and not simply a verbal misunderstanding.

The distinction between *description* and *evaluation* that I have just been relying on is somewhat controversial, and this is not the place to give it a proper examination. But it is difficult not to agree that it is a feature of such terms as 'good' or 'just' or 'beautiful' that they can quite sensibly be denied of *any* suggested example whatever, and that they therefore cannot be terms whose meaning is given directly by paradigm examples. To this extent, it seems to me that Plato was entirely right. We have, admittedly, a further question to consider: can the meaning of such terms be explained by means of other words which *are* understood via paradigm examples? On this I shall say nothing, but simply challenge you to produce the required explanation. (There are *many* theories concerning how these words are to be explained. I do not myself think that any of them are wholly successful, but that again is too large a question to be discussed here.) I simply conclude by giving it as my opinion that in fact the traditional account, as so far developed, *cannot* explain how we understand the meaning of these words. Are we then forced to agree with Plato that we must have been born with an understanding of the relevant concepts?

One point worth observing is that even if we do agree with Plato on this point, we have still not really met the problem. For even if we are born with a (latent) knowledge of these concepts, still it is altogether too much to suppose that we are also born knowing which *words* express them. So we still have to discover this, and this seems still to present just the same problems as before. But it is more to the point to bear in mind that all I have said so far is that the *traditional* account cannot explain how we understand these words, and this may well be because the traditional account is too narrow anyway. Indeed a little reflection shows that the traditional account certainly is too narrow. One kind of word which it obviously cannot explain are the 'little' words that we are so apt to overlook until a study of logic brings them to our attention. I mean words such as 'if' and 'or' and 'not'. It is absurd to suppose that we

can *perceive* ifs and nots, and it would be hopeless to try to explain
the meaning of these words in terms of other words which do stand
for things we can perceive. (And the hypothesis that we *once* met
an if and a not in a pre-mundane existence is not likely to tempt
anyone.) Another famous 'little' word, which first vexed Hume
and has since vexed everyone, is the word 'because' ('by cause of',
'cause'). Also of interest to philosophers are the words 'must' and
'might' ('necessity' and 'possibility', and we might here add
'probability'), and similarly 'should' and 'ought', or again 'in order
to' and 'on purpose'. Nor is it only these 'little' words that create
problems for the traditional account. Consider for example
'freedom' or 'the mind' or in a different direction 'atom',
'electron', 'energy', and so on. Clearly the list could be prolonged
indefinitely. It *cannot* be true that the meaning of each single word
we understand is given, one by one, by examples of things that the
word applies to.

You may ask: if the traditional account is wrong, what should
we put in its place? I am afraid I shall make no attempt to answer
that question. I shall even have to leave it open whether Plato (and
the Empiricists after him) were right to claim that in this world our
sole source of knowledge—including knowledge of meanings—is
perception. There are now some theories of meaning which claim
to conform to that principle, and there are objectors who argue
that no attempt to conform to it can succeed. The matter is still
thoroughly controversial, and far too complicated for me to
summarize in a few words. So I simply leave the issue like this. If
Plato, and what I have called the traditional account, are right in
saying that the only way we can learn the meaning of a word in this
life is by association with perceptible paradigm examples, then
there are indeed very many words which we know the meaning of
but have not learnt in this life, and the words 'good', 'just', and
'beautiful' are among them. But it seems much more likely that
Plato, and the traditional account, are wrong about the only way
of learning the meaning of a word.

G. APPENDIX: THE *MENO* ON RECOLLECTION

Although I cannot discuss all the problems that arise from the
Meno's first introduction of recollection, it may be useful if I
expand a little the brief comments I made earlier (pp. 99–100). The

doctrine is offered as a reply to Meno's question of how one could hope to succeed in discovering what virtue is: how, he asks, should one set about the search, and how indeed should one recognize the answer when one has found it (80d)? As a matter of fact Meno poses his question in rather general terms, and Socrates apparently takes him to be asking how it is ever possible to discover anything at all (80e). Equally Socrates replies in very general terms, suggesting that all learning whatever is really a matter of recollecting what we knew before (81d). But it does not seem at all likely that he really means it so generally. Some knowledge of a perfectly ordinary kind, for example my knowledge of how to get from Athens to Larissa, can surely be explained well enough as based on perception (97a). Taken in context, Meno's question is about how to attain knowledge of the special philosophic sort, and Socrates' reply is presumably meant to be limited to this also. At any rate, all that it directly argues for is that *mathematical* knowledge is due to recollection.

Considered as an argument, the passage is not notably successful, and seems to omit some crucial points. Socrates takes an ignorant slave-boy to practise on, and asks him how to find a square which is double the area of a given square. The boy first makes a few guesses, and by pointed questioning Socrates easily convinces him that these guesses are wrong, thus leading him to admit that he does not know (82b–84d). Socrates then himself draws a crucial figure, and by leading questions takes the boy through a proof that the central square, constructed from the diagonals of the four smaller squares, is twice the area of each smaller square. So this is the answer to our problem (84d–85b).

Commenting on what he has done, Socrates claims that on each occasion the boy was merely questioned, and gave as answer an opinion (δόξα) that was already in him. He emphasizes that the boy already had true opinions in him, but seems to pay no attention to the fact—which the first half of the passage made clear—that he also had false opinions in him too. Finally he remarks that at present the (true) opinions are but newly aroused, and do not amount to knowledge, but 'if the same questions are put to him many times and in many ways, you can see that he will end by knowing as accurately as anyone. He will know not because someone has taught him but because someone has questioned him, and he will recover the knowledge from himself' (85c–d).

Perhaps the most obvious drawback to this little demonstration is that it makes it seem that no one can thus 'recover knowledge from himself' unless someone else, who already knows the right answer, can put the appropriate leading questions to him. But clearly the important feature of mathematical knowledge is that people can work it out all by themselves, without help from outside; in Socrates' terms, they can ask *themselves* the right questions. Another rather surprising feature is that Socrates claims that the boy does not yet *know* what he has been led to see, but will know it if the process is repeated often enough. What difference will mere repetition make? One might rather say that a crucial characteristic of mathematics is that mathematical proof is *conclusive*, so once a result is proved it is thereby known, and we do not need to seek any further confirmation. Admittedly, Plato's hesitation is quite intelligible, for you must properly understand a proof before you can be said to know its conclusion, and there is always a danger that people will think they understand when they do not. But the hesitation nevertheless does some harm to Plato's argument, for here is our slave who has been led to the right answer but apparently it does not at once strike him that this *must* be the right answer, in the way that a memory may 'click' into place as something already familiar. Finally, it is worth noticing that although Socrates is anxious to rule out the suggestion that it is his own knowledge of the answer which has led the boy to the truth, he does not ask whether there may be something else that is the source of his conviction, perhaps his *perception* of the diagram Socrates has drawn. He could certainly raise objections to this suggestion: he could say that if the boy understands the proof he will see that it holds for *any* square, and not just the one drawn in front of him; he will also see that in fact the proof holds only of *perfect* squares, whereas the figure in the sand is probably not a perfect square anyway. Later, Plato shows himself perfectly aware of this point (*Republic* 510d), but in the *Meno* the distinction between knowledge that is based on perception and knowledge that is not has not yet become a prominent theme.

I feel, then, that if Plato had been writing the *Meno* a little later in his philosophical career, he would have presented the argument in a rather more convincing way than he actually did. But for all that, one can still see that he is on to a good point. Mathematics has always struck philosophers as the star example of a branch of purely a priori knowledge (which just means knowledge *not* based on perception). It satisfies any condition one might reasonably impose on what is to count as 'knowledge' in a strict sense. For Plato, this is a matter of being able to 'give an account', and in mathematics one can indeed given an 'account', i.e. a proof, of one's assertions. It is true that Plato later came to think that mathematical proofs, as presently pursued, did not quite match the standard he intended, since these proofs themselves had premisses that the mathematicians gave no account of (*Republic* 511a, 533c); but he also thought that this defect was remediable (*Republic* 511d, 533d). That, however, is a more sophisticated reflection, and it was doubtless his position in the *Meno*—and, I imagine, in the *Phaedo* too—that mathematics was an example of knowledge in the strict and philosophical sense. That is why it affords us a hope that strict and philosophic knowledge will also be attainable in the more important field of ethics, for this is the moral which Plato is most concerned to draw in the *Meno*, and he is therefore less certain that recollection is an essential part of the total picture (*Meno* 86b).

It will be noticed that whereas the *Meno* invokes recollection to explain how philosophic knowledge may be possible, the *Phaedo*— as I interpret it—uses recollection to explain the ordinary and everyday understanding of words such as 'virtue' or 'equal', which falls far short of philosophic knowledge. This is no doubt why the *Meno* treats this theory as rather tentative, while the *Phaedo* shows no such hesitation: after all, there is no doubt that we do have an ordinary and everyday understanding of these words, though there is genuine room for doubt as to whether a philosophic knowledge of what they signify is indeed possible. Of course the two approaches are quite compatible, and it is only to be expected that there should be a connection between our means of knowing what, e.g., virtue is in the everyday sense and in the philosophic sense. For if we can recognize a philosophic account as correct that must be because we can see that it 'fits' with the everyday knowledge we began with. Yet although the two dialogues do dovetail quite nicely with one another in this way, commentators have sometimes doubted whether Plato would assign to recollection these two very different roles. They would rather think that recollection is always to be regarded as the source of philosophic knowledge, and so try to interpret the *Phaedo* too as concerned only with philosophic knowledge from start to finish.

I have already argued against this interpretation on pp. 67–8, where I claimed that the premiss 'we know what the equal is' must be meant as asserting that we all have an ordinary and everyday understanding of the word 'equal'. On the rival interpretation this premiss should rather be 'we (philosophers) believe that (philosophic) knowledge of what equality is must be possible (though we also admit that we do not at the moment have it)'. This is a far cry from what the text actually does say. Moreover we (philosophers) surely do not think that this *philosophic* knowledge, if we attain it, will come to us from our perception of equal sticks and stones, though Plato tells us that the knowledge he is thinking of does arise in that way. So although this interpretation would certainly be in line with the *Meno*, our text in the *Phaedo* is very strongly against it. One may feel some sympathy for those commentators who believe that Plato would not have invoked those sacred entities the forms in order to explain the ordinary humdrum everyday understanding of language that we all possess. But the *Phaedo* shows that they are wrong, and I would rather applaud his recognition that if philosophic knowledge is possible it must stem from the same source as our ordinary and everyday grasp of meanings.

As for Plato's suggestion that the source in question is an experience in some other world, though we are not likely to agree with this, we should recognize that Plato did have good reasons for it. One is his discovery of a priori knowledge, i.e. his discovery that we can come to know some truths independently of experience, apparently drawing the knowledge out of ourselves, and recognizing at once that it is knowledge of an unshakeable sort. This phenomenon certainly needs explanation, and it was not altogether a foolish idea to suggest that it could be explained if it is really a recollection of something once known but since forgotten. That is the *Meno*'s contribution, but it is much strengthened by the further points added in the *Phaedo*. For Plato is perfectly right to see that there is a problem over how we come to understand such concepts as beauty, justice, and goodness, and that an explanation is called for. (He is quite wrong to suppose that the same problem applies to relations, but let us ignore that.) Moreover the explanation in terms of recollection has two clear points in its favour: it allows one to retain the simple and natural idea that the meaning of a word is given by examples to which it applies, and at the same time it justifies the hope that proper philosophic knowledge of these concepts should be attainable. And here it ties in very nicely with the *Meno*'s suggestion about a priori knowledge, for Plato is surely right to suppose that philosophic knowledge of what goodness is, if it is attainable at all, must be attained a priori. It could not be reached by investigating the good things of this world, since we begin with too much uncertainty on which things are good.

V

THE AFFINITY ARGUMENT
(77e–80b)

A. THE PROBLEM

SO far, we have had two arguments for immortality. The Cyclical Argument was an attempt to show that no soul ever begins or ends its existence, but it told us nothing at all of the nature of the soul. This is obvious when we reflect that if the argument were a good one it would actually show that nothing at all ever begins or ends its existence. By contrast, the Recollection argument is specially about souls, because it is concerned with explaining our knowledge, and knowledge is something which souls have but other things do not. On the other hand this argument only bears directly on the *pre*-existence of the soul, and by itself it gives us no particular reason to suppose that the soul will go on existing after its present life. When Simmias and Cebes make exactly this point (77b1–c5), Socrates replies that future existence will be secured as well if we put the two arguments together (77c6–9), but this is rather an odd thing for him to say. For the Cyclical Argument professed to prove both past and future existence at once, and if it is a good argument it therefore establishes by itself that the soul will go on existing after death. On the other hand if it is not a good argument it is not clear how it will help to add the Recollection Argument to it.

As a matter of fact, what Socrates actually says is that we must combine the Recollection Argument with our previous admission that the living come from the dead. Perhaps, then, he does not mean to cite the *whole* of the Cyclical Argument: he is concentrating on what I called the *main* part of the Cyclical Argument (70d–72a), and excluding what I called the *supplementary* argument (72b–d) as being more doubtful. At first sight, this does seem to be exactly his idea, for it is just the proposition that the living come from the dead that he repeats with emphasis in his next sentence: 'if the soul does have a previous existence [from the Recollection Argument?], and if when it enters upon living and being born it must come from no other source than death and being dead [from the Cyclical Argument], surely it must also exist after it has died?' (77c9–d4). But if this was his idea, it will not work. For *both* the propositions cited are concerned with the *past* existence of the soul, and cannot show that it will survive its *next* death. That is doubtless why Socrates does not end his sentence where I have just ended it, but adds 'given that it has to be born again'. But we need the *whole* of the Cyclical Argument to provide a reason for that extra clause. In fact the best we can say seems to be that the Recollection Argument provides an independent confirmation of one half of the Cyclical Argument, and this may be thought to shore up the other half as well. But clearly it does not help very much.

As commentators have often pointed out, the two arguments can be seen as complementing one another in a different way. The Cyclical Argument shows that the soul always exists, but says nothing of its nature, whereas the Recollection Argument shows that the disembodied soul still retains some 'power and wisdom' (70b3–4, 76c12–13). However it is hardly possible to see the present text as making this point, and besides the point is somewhat dubious in the light of Plato's full theory. For the Recollection Argument shows that at some point before this life the soul had 'wisdom' insofar as it acquired knowledge of the forms, but Plato does *not* suppose that disembodied souls always enjoy unfettered knowledge of the forms. So far as most of us are concerned, bound to the wheel of rebirth, we shall know no more of the forms after death than we knew in life. It is difficult, then, to make very much sense of the suggestion that we 'combine' the two arguments we have so far had.

What in fact happens from now on is that the Cyclical Argument is pretty well abandoned. Quite rightly, Plato evidently feels that it will not carry conviction. The much deeper argument from recollection is retained, and is several times referred to as an argument to be trusted (77a–b, 87a, 91e–92a, 92d. *Cf.* 95c and perhaps 107b: 'the initial hypotheses', plural). But the trouble with the argument from recollection, as we said, is that though it may prove that the soul existed *before* this life it does not prove that it will continue to exist *after* it. But that, as everyone agrees, is the really crucial point. To make headway with this, Plato now sets himself to argue that the soul is not the *kind* of thing that would be expected to dissolve at death. Though the Greek word 'soul' (ψυχή) is etymologically connected with the word for to breathe or blow (ψύχειν), and though breath is just the kind of thing that can be blown apart by the wind, he thinks that the soul is not really like this at all. In the present argument he tries to show this by drawing analogies between the soul and other, admittedly imperishable, things. These analogies are pretty well destroyed by the objections that follow them, but in the final argument he reverts once more to what kind of a thing the soul must be supposed to be.

B. THE ANALOGIES

It is important to notice that two quite different analogies are drawn in this argument, one between souls and forms (78b–79c), and one between souls and gods (80a). We begin with the forms.

Socrates first points out that a thing that can be dispersed must be composite, and goes on to suggest that things that do not change are most likely to be simple, uniform, and incomposite, while things that do change are likely to be composite. Now forms are not liable to change, and are in fact uniform (μονοειδές, 'having just one form': by this Plato probably means that whereas particular things will participate in many, and indeed opposite, characteristics, a form will have only one character, viz. the one it is a perfect example of). Moreover, forms are invisible and of course eternal. By contrast, the particular things that 'bear the same name' as the forms are always changing—notice how Plato exaggerates this—and they are visible and of course they are not eternal. So we have these two kinds of thing: the one invisible, unchanging, and eternal; the other visible, changing, and perishable. Presumably Plato does not believe that *all* things must be of one of these two kinds, for he does not believe that souls, or indeed gods, are in *all* ways like forms. That is why he next asks, not which of the two kinds the soul belongs to, but which it more resembles.

Now the body actually is something that is visible, changing, and perishable. The soul can at least be said to be invisible, though there is an interesting hesitation in the argument here (79b7–15). Perhaps the reason for it is that forms are not just invisible, they are totally immaterial. But although Plato evidently *believes* that the soul is equally immaterial, he would not be entitled to expect general agreement on that point. (For example, Democritus held that the soul was material all right, but made of such very small, fine, mobile atoms that it could not be seen.) We have to content ourselves, then, with the claim that at least the soul is invisible to ordinary human eyes.

Though we can say that the soul is invisible (even if we cannot add that it is immaterial), we evidently cannot say that the soul never changes. What Plato offers us instead is the idea that the soul is subject to change when it perceives the physical world—in fact it 'wanders' like the things it perceives, and 'is confused and dizzy, as if drunk'—but it finds peace and rest when it isolates itself from the body and contemplates the unchanging forms. On the face of it, this assigns the soul a chameleon-like character—it simply takes on the nature of whatever it is thinking of—and is not much of a ground for saying that it is more like what is unchanging than what is changeable. Indeed one wonders why Plato dared to make this comparison at all, for it is obvious that the soul *is* a changing thing, and in this respect is like the body and *not* like the forms.

As if to put matters right, Plato at once switches to a different comparison. The gods are immortal, and their nature is to rule the mortal, and it is also the nature of the soul to rule the body, when it is in a body. The comparison is not very exact, for presumably gods succeed in ruling mortal things without being *in* them. Moreover, although it may perhaps be the 'nature' of the soul to rule, and the 'nature' of the body to be ruled, still it seems that the soul does not always succeed in its attempt to rule the body. At any rate it can give in to the desires and emotions which the body prompts in it. But presumably gods do not fail to rule in a similar way.

On the basis of these somewhat shaky comparisons, Plato concludes that the soul is 'very similar' to what is divine, immortal, intelligible, uniform, indissoluble, and never changing, and hence that it is 'completely indissoluble, or something close to this'. In fact all that has been argued is that the soul is invisible, that it is at rest when contemplating forms (but not at other times), and that it is its 'nature' to rule (even if it does not always succeed in doing so). It is obvious that it does not *follow* from this that it is indissoluble, or in any way close to being indissoluble. (You will notice that we have said nothing on the apparently crucial question of whether it is composite or incomposite; I observed earlier that this question caused Plato some problems (pp. 40–1).) Fairly

obviously, Plato does not himself think that the conclusion strictly
follows from his premisses, but knows well enough that analogies
can never count as conclusive proofs;[1] from the fact that the soul is
like the forms (or like the gods) in one way, it will never follow
that it is like them in other ways too. For all that, analogies can
quite often be *persuasive*, especially if they are full and detailed.
But the present analogies really are not: on the contrary, there
appear to be equally good analogies pointing in the opposite
direction, as Plato himself goes on to point out.

Simmias suggests (85e *ff.*) that the soul may just as well be
compared to the attunement of a lyre. Of this you may say that it is
'something unseen and incorporeal and very lovely and divine',
but for all that it lasts no longer than the lyre itself. At the very
least this makes the simple point that not everything invisible is
eternal, for an attunement is invisible but not eternal. In the next
chapter we shall take up the question of how much more there is to
this counter-analogy, but we can say now that Plato does regard it
as a serious objection to his present argument, for he spends some
time refuting it.

More whimsically Cebes suggests (87a–88b) that the soul may be
compared to a weaver, who weaves himself many cloaks and lives
longer than any of them. But for all that he dies in the end, and his
last cloak outlasts him. (This is directed in particular at what
Socrates says in 80c–d.) Cebes' analogy starts from the claim that
during a single life the body is constantly being worn out, and is
renewed by the soul from new materials. Then he suggests that the
soul may perhaps eventually discard one body as no longer
repairable, and begin upon a new one, as the weaver may do with
his cloaks. But this continual task of keeping its bodies in trim, one
after another, may so weaken the soul that in the end it too will
perish, longer-lived than any of its bodies, but still outlasted by the
last of them. And who can ever say that the body he now has will
not prove to be his last? This analogy can be seen as directed at
Socrates' other comparison, for it admits not only that the soul
may last longer than the body, but also that it rules and controls
the body, yet still it need not be immortal. The whole of the final
argument of the dialogue is ostensibly devoted to rebutting it.

All I wish to conclude at the moment is that Plato certainly knew

---

[1] *Cf.* 92d1–5. The phrase διὰ τῶν εἰκότων, which Gallop renders as 'based upon
likelihoods', *could* perfectly well be translated 'based upon analogies'.

that analogies are not proofs, and that this applies just as much to the analogies that Socrates puts forward as to those of Simmias and Cebes. Without more ado, let us press on to consider more closely Simmias' thesis that the soul is a kind of attunement, and the objections that Socrates brings to it.

VI

THE SOUL AS A HARMONY
(85e–86d, 91c–95a)

A. THE THESIS (85e–86d)

IN this instance I have retained in my title the traditional translation—or rather transliteration—of the Greek word ἁρμονία as harmony, mainly because of its associations with other areas of Greek philosophy. But I am perfectly happy to accept Gallop's 'attunement' as a much better approximation to the meaning that the word has in our context. Note first that it is taken as obvious and agreed by all parties that a 'harmony' or 'attunement' is not eternal: it is thought of as belonging to a particular lyre as some kind of state *of that lyre*, and therefore incapable of surviving the lyre itself. So it cannot be something like a melody, or a chord, or key, for these things do not belong to any particular lyre, and when one lyre is broken they may perfectly well persist in another. But also, a 'harmony' is construed as a relatively long-lasting state of a lyre: it is not something that lasts a few seconds while a particular note is struck, or a chord, nor even a few minutes while a melody is being played. If this were the meaning, the idea that the 'harmony' of a lyre is its 'soul' would be very strange indeed. We may conclude that it is indeed the lyre's state of attunement that is meant—its state of being tuned in such a way that the sounds given forth by its various strings are in such and such relations to one another. If the lyre is well-tuned, these relation-ships will be 'harmonious' in roughly our sense.

The attunement of a lyre is due to the tensions (and lengths, and weights) of its various strings. This is what enables it to play a number of different chords and melodies, and this state of being in tune will also stay with it while it is playing nothing. (Compare: a man's soul is what enables him to do many different things, and is still with him when he is doing nothing, but is, say, asleep.) The state of attunement may naturally be called invisible, and one might also say that it is 'very lovely and divine' because of the very lovely and divine things that it enables the lyre to do. We might be less happy to call it 'incorporeal', because it is a state of some very clearly corporeal things, namely the strings. But this is the main point of the comparison, for the idea is that the soul too is just a state of corporeal things, the elements of the body: 'our body is kept in tension, as it were, and held together by hot and cold, dry and wet, and the like, and our soul is a blending and attunement of these same things, when they're blended with each other in due proportion' (86b7–c2). It was a well-known Greek view that all physical bodies are made up of four elements, sometimes called earth, air, fire, and water and sometimes (as here) the hot, the cold, the wet and the dry.[1] Simmias' rather vague addition 'and the like' shows, I think, that he is not intending to commit himself to any particular account of just what the elements of physical bodies are, and we do no harm to his theory if we adopt a rather more modern perspective, speaking instead of the blending and attunement of hydrogen, oxygen, carbon, and such elements. For it surely is the *physical* elements of bodies he is thinking of, and comparing to the physical parts of the lyre and their mutual tensions. The soul, he suggests, may be no more than this 'tuned' state of the physical elements of the body.

In fact, he goes further. Something of this sort, he says, is what *we actually take* the soul to be (86b6–7); but he leaves us to speculate on whom he here means by 'we'. It is tempting to suppose that he means 'we Pythagoreans', for (i) we have already observed that Simmias, Cebes, and Echecrates all have Pythagorean connections (p. 11), and Echecrates too admits that he once held this view of the soul and still finds it attractive (88d3–6); moreover (ii) we know independently that the Pythagoreans laid special emphasis on the notion of 'harmony' (p. 12). If the theory is indeed Pythagorean in origin, then one might plausibly suggest Philolaus as its author. But it is a strong objection to this view that we also know that the Pythagoreans believed in the immortality of the soul, and yet Simmias introduces the theory precisely because it is incompatible with that belief. Should we perhaps infer that only *some* Pythagoreans believed in immortality? But I shall not discuss that speculation further: the theory itself is more interesting than the question of where it comes from. However, one thing is

[1] Aristotle ingeniously brought the two views together by saying that earth is cold and dry, water cold and wet, fire hot and dry, and air hot and wet. (One wonders about hot bricks, warm water, and the cold dry wind from the North).

worth adding, and that is that the theory is surely not the popular
and ordinary view of the soul. If you had asked an ordinary
Athenian what he understood by the 'harmony' (attunement) of
hot and cold, wet and dry, within the human body, he would have
known at once what you were referring to: it was a well-known
medical theory that *health* was just such a 'harmony'. But we do
not usually think that a man's state of health is the same thing as
his soul. However that *is* pretty much what the present theory
comes to.

We can think of the theory as beginning from the idea that the soul
is what is responsible for life, which is to say that it is a man's soul
that enables him to do all those various things that manifest that he
is alive. If we first think mainly of those bodily activities that men
share with other animals—eating, breathing, sleeping, walking
about, and so on—it is very plausible to say that what enables a
man to do these things is just the proper organization and
functioning of the various parts of his body. But the proper
functioning of muscle, bone, and sinew, or again of lungs, heart
and stomach, is simply due to the way in which they in turn are
made up of their physical elements, and the way those elements
interact with one another. For example, the intake of oxygen
during breathing is merely a consequence of the structure of the
lungs, the chemical composition of the blood, and so on. So in the
end it all comes down to the purely physical composition of the
body; that is what explains the body's 'life', and so that is what the
soul (as cause of life) turns out to be. And note that it is just the
same thing that also determines the body's state of health.
      When Simmias expounds the theory, he omits to pay any special
attention to a man's conscious activities—desires, emotions,
thoughts, and so on—which we think of as more closely connected
with the soul. But presumably he must intend the theory to cover
these too, and we are in a position to fill in more detail here than
he could have done. Conscious activities, we shall say, are due
mainly to the proper organization and functioning of a man's
brain, for that (as we now know) is where consciousness resides.
But the brain is just as much a physical entity as the rest of the
body is, and its functioning is likewise determined by the physical
elements of which it is made, and their ordinary physical
interactions (electro-chemical interactions, we might add, in a

superior way). So long as the physical elements of the brain remain in due order, receiving stimulations from the other organs of the body and appropriate supplies of oxygen from the blood, normal brain-activity will continue, and that will result in a normal 'mental life'. According to this theory, conscious activities are due to physical happenings in the brain just as other activities of living are due to physical happenings in other parts of the body. So in the end it all comes down to the proper arrangement of the physical elements of the body—to their being, as Simmias puts it, blended with each other in due proportion, in a fitting 'attunement' one with another.

Seen in this way, the theory would nowadays be called a *materialist* theory, for its main point is to deny that there are any such immaterial entities as souls are supposed to be. The soul was supposed to be the cause of life—and perhaps of 'mental' life in particular—but on the present theory that cause is nothing other than the proper arrangement of the body's physical elements. That is itself quite enough to explain life—including 'mental' life—and we do not have to posit any special 'animating agent', a mysterious 'prisoner' in the 'tomb' of the body, to account for life. In other words, the soul is not a special and peculiar kind of extra ingredient in a person, over and above the ordinary physical ingredients of his body, for there are no such non-physical ingredients. There are of course living people, but what enables them to live—to feel and think, just as much as to digest and breathe—is simply the way their ordinary material elements are arranged and organized. It obviously does not matter whether we present the theory as claiming that there are no souls (as popularly conceived), or as allowing that there are souls, but they are just organizations (or 'attunements') of bodily elements. Either way, it clearly follows that there are no disembodied souls and the theory must therefore be one that Socrates has to reject. Let us pass straight on to the arguments that he uses against it.

B. THE REFUTATIONS (91c6–95a3)

Socrates begins by pointing out that the theory is incompatible with the consequence drawn from the Recollection Argument, that our souls acquire some knowledge before they enter their present bodies. Since everyone present agrees that the Recollection

Argument is worthy of acceptance, it appears that this rival theory can be rejected without more ado (91c–92e). As a matter of fact the theory is not incompatible with the simple claim that we are born with some knowledge already latent in us, for the materialist could perfectly well explain how that might happen: the structure of our DNA molecules is fixed at conception, and this determines the physical conformation of the brain, which in turn determines how the brain will react to stimuli from perception. So it may perhaps be that we are thus 'programmed' from birth in such a way that the brain will eventually reach that state which is the knowledge Socrates is speaking of. But as we saw the Recollection Argument in fact claims more than this: it claims that the knowledge is knowledge of a form, only to be got by acquaintance with that form, which in turn can only take place when we are disembodied. (Notice how Simmias stresses the importance of forms to the Recollection Argument at 92d.) If we grant all this, then certainly we cannot also hold that there are no disembodied souls, as the Attunement theory requires.

However Socrates does not rest his case on this point, but goes on to offer some independent arguments against the theory. Confusingly, he presents these as if they formed one continuous train of argument, but in fact there are two quite different arguments woven together. As all commentators have observed, he begins at 92e4–93a10 by extracting some premises for an argument that he does not actually present until 94b4–95a3. Let us call this Argument A. In between, he has broken off to press a different argument, which runs consecutively from 93a11 to 94b3. Let us call this one Argument B. From the way in which he runs the two together, it seems natural to infer that he regarded them as closely connected with one another. But in fact there does not seem to be any very close connection, and we can perfectly well treat them separately. (*Perhaps* the connection of thought is this: Socrates begins with the idea behind Argument A, that the soul rules the body, but is then struck by the thought that some souls do it better than others. Reflecting on this, it then occurs to him that the attunement theory cannot even explain how some souls could be better than others, so he breaks off to argue for this in Argument B, before returning to finish his interrupted Argument A. But if this is the connection he sees, it remains unimportant for the arguments as he actually presents them. Argument B makes no use of the idea that a better soul is one that is better at ruling the body.)

I take Argument B first.

(i) *Argument B*

This argument begins with the rather obscure claim that an attunement is an attunement in the same way as it has been tuned (93a11–12), which is explained as meaning that it is more an attunement if it has been more tuned, and less an attunement if it has been less tuned (93a14–62). Unfortunately the explanation is actually a little more complex than this, for two reasons.

(i) What Socrates says is that an attunement is an attunement 'more and to a greater extent' if it has been tuned 'more and to a greater extent' (μᾶλλον καὶ ἐπὶ πλέον). The two phrases 'more' and 'to a greater extent' may simply be intended as synonyms, as is perhaps indicated by the fact that they recur together in 93b4–6 in application to souls, but only the first is used when this is recalled in 93d1–2. Again, both are applied to attunements in 93d3–4, but only the first is repeated a line later in 93d6–7. This would be quite natural if the phrases are synonyms anyway. But it is also possible that they are not synonyms but represent genuine alternatives. The phrase 'to a greater extent' (ἐπὶ πλέον) could naturally mean 'extending over more elements', and the idea might be that, say, the attunement of a harp was an attunement 'to a greater extent' than the attunement of a lyre, because a harp has more strings than a lyre. On this interpretation, it would still be natural for the alternative to be dropped in the course of the argument, since it would not be a relevant alternative in the case of souls: each soul would be an attunement of the same number of elements, namely all the physical elements to be found in the body. Since it appears that if the phrase does mark an alternative it is not in the end a relevant alternative, it may seem that the point is of no importance. But it does in fact affect the next problem.

(ii) Socrates says that an· attunement which has been tuned more and to a greater extent, 'if it is possible for that to happen', will be more and to a greater extent an attunement. Supposing that he means 'more' and 'to a greater extent' to indicate *different* suggestions, it may then be only the second suggestion which he indicates is not always a possibility. Indeed, we have just observed that it would not be a possibility in the case of the soul. But if this is what he has in mind, it is slightly surprising that he never says it. Besides, even if we do take the phrases 'more' and 'to a greater extent' as marking different alternatives, still it is quite natural to read the qualifying phrase 'if that is possible' as covering both of them. Does Socrates wish to suggest that no attunement ever can be 'more tuned' than any other? Indeed, does he not affirm this outright in 93d3–4?

I do not believe that he does wish to suggest this, and certainly we cannot say that he himself affirms it. What he affirms in 93d3–4 is that this would *follow* from the hypothesis that souls are attunements, together with our admission that no soul is more a soul than any other. Obviously he does not himself believe the hypothesis. Moreover it evidently does not follow from these premises that no attunement whatever could be 'more tuned' than any other, but at best that no attunement *which is a soul* could be more tuned than any other. Although this is not quite what Socrates actually says, we should surely take it that this is all he means, since it is all that his argument requires.

As I see it, Socrates begins the argument with the idea that being an attunement *is* usually a matter of degree—one attunement can indeed be more of an attunement than another—whereas being a soul is *not* a matter of degree. From this he wishes to argue that being a soul cannot be the same as being an attunement. But a possible objection is that there may be *some* kinds at attunement where degrees do not come into it, and that is what leads him to put in his hedging remark in 93b1 'if that is possible'. What he has in mind here is that some kinds of attunements may be exempted from this general rule, namely if all attunements of that kind are 'equally tuned'. So he now has to show that the soul is not an attunement of this special kind. This he tries to do by pointing out that some souls are better than others (93b8–c1), and suggesting that the good soul is one that is more tuned, or more harmonious, than the bad soul (94c3–8; cf. *Republic* 443d–e). Souls do, then, partake in greater or lesser degrees of attunement, so they cannot be said to be all equally tuned (93d6–e9). It follows that they are not exceptions to the general rule about attunements. In Socrates' view, the soul *has* a greater or lesser degree of attunement, namely its goodness or badness, and therefore cannot itself *be* an attunement but must be something else.

The major fallacy in this argument comes in its first step, which we may represent as:

Suppose (i):	Every soul is an attunement.
Nevertheless (ii):	No soul is more a soul than any other.
Hence (iii):	No soul is more an attunement than any other.
That is (iv):	No soul is more in tune than any other.

To see that there must be something wrong with this reasoning, compare an analogous objection to the very traditional idea that man may be defined as a rational animal. It would go like this:

Suppose (i):	Every man is a rational animal.
Nevertheless (ii):	No man is more a man than any other.
Hence (iii):	No man is more a rational animal than any other.
That is (iv):	No man is more rational than any other.

The conclusion is evidently absurd, but we need not on that account reject the definition we began from.

For the sake of argument we may accept the premises that no man is more a man than any other, and that it is a defining characteristic of men that they are all rational animals. (Of course one *could* perfectly well stickle over either or both of them.) But it obviously does not follow from this that all men are equally rational. When it is claimed that all men are rational, what is intended is that there is some *minimum* standard of rationality which all men meet. Some men will no doubt be well above that standard, and they will be more rational than some others, but this does not mean that they are 'more men' than those others, for they do not 'more' meet the criterion of reaching the minimum standard. In other words, rationality is no doubt a matter of degree, but reaching or not reaching a given standard of rationality is not a matter of degree. Similarly with the thesis that the soul is an attunement. There are no doubt degrees of being in tune—or, to cash the metaphor a little, of having one's parts arranged in due balance and proportion—but we may easily suppose that some minimum degree of tuning is what is necessary for soulhood—i.e. for being alive. Higher degrees of tuning may be possible, and are no doubt what makes one living body more healthy than another. But just as the healthy body is not 'more alive' than the unhealthy one, so equally its attunement is not 'more a soul': to be a soul it merely has to reach the minimum degree which produces life.

The point may be illustrated perfectly well from the example of the lyre that we began with. A lyre whose strings are broken, or so slack that they will not sound a note, has its parts in *some* organization, but it is so far from the desired organization that we shall not count it as reaching the minimum standard. So the lyre is 'dead' until all its strings are capable of sounding a note, but once they are it can 'sing' and is 'alive' and has a 'soul'. But there is still plenty of room for improvement in its tuning, for we desire the notes sounded by its different strings to be in harmony with one another, and the lyre is not perfectly in tune until the desired harmony is reached. So one lyre may be more in tune than another, though both are 'alive' since both have reached the minimum degree of tuning. This illustration also shows that we could have put our criticism differently, by distinguishing two different senses of 'being in tune'. In one sense a lyre counts as 'in tune' if it reaches our minimum degree, and in this sense a lyre either is or is not in tune, and there are no degrees of being in tune in this sense.[2] But in a different sense one lyre may be 'more in tune' than another, though both are 'in tune' in the first sense, namely if its tuning is closer to the desired harmonious tuning. Then we could say that a lyre's soul is its attunement in the first sense, and this attunement may 'have within itself, being an attunement, a further attunement' (93c6–7), namely the attunement in the different sense of a more or less harmonious attunement. But it may seem rather artificial to introduce two different senses, and the first way of putting the point is probably simpler.

In view of all this, Socrates' objection in Argument B clearly collapses, and we need not discuss his suggestion that virtue and vice are themselves the result of good or bad tuning.

(ii) *Argument A*

The main outline of Argument A is clearly this: the soul is capable of ruling and opposing the body, whereas an attunement cannot

---

[2] We have this complication: what should we say if *some* of the lyre's strings can sound a note while others cannot? The same problem affects the soul, i.e. life: a man may be dead in some ways (e.g. mentally) while still alive in others. Yet we do commonly suppose that being dead or alive is not a matter of degree, and so begin to dispute over the 'correct' definition of death.

oppose its elements. Socrates begins with the latter point in 92e4–93a10. Construing an attunement as a compound thing (σύνθεσις), compounded from the tuned elements, he claims that if the attunement can be said to be in any state, or to do anything, that must be because its elements are in that state, or doing that thing. This is overstating his case, for although we can agree that any state or action of the attunement must be due to some states or actions of its elements, they do not have to be the *same* states and actions. (For example, the lyre may be tuned in a minor key, and this is a feature of its attunement as a whole. But none of its strings taken individually can be said to be 'in a minor key': this description only applies to attunements as wholes, and not to the tuning of individual strings). But perhaps what we can agree is good enough for Socrates' purpose: if any state or action of the attunement must be due to some states or actions of its elements—whether the same or not—then it is surely fair to conclude that the attunement does not *direct* its elements, and cannot be *opposed* to them. (Even here there is room for doubt, for we can and do speak of an association of men as directing or opposing one of its members, when all the other members together direct or oppose this one. But since it turns out that this point is not crucial to the argument, I shall not dwell on it.)

In 94b4, after completing Argument B, Socrates turns to his other premiss, that the soul does rule the body. More exactly, he claims that (at least in a wise man) it opposes the bodily feelings such as hunger and thirst (94b8–10), or appetites and angers and fears (94d5). It is seen as countermanding these 'feelings of the body' (παθήματα τοῦ σώματος), rebuking them, and generally keeping them in their place. To take just the simplest illustration, I may be thirsty and in the presence of drink, but my soul will say 'Don't drink that: it isn't yours', or 'it will make you ill', or something of the sort. And if I am wise I will not drink it. What Socrates is thinking of, then, is the way in which *reason* may control *desire and emotion*. But why should he regard this as a case of the soul opposing the body?

The first thing to note is that it seems not to be Plato's own view that desires and emotions are literally felt by the body, as if when I long for drink it were actually my dry throat that is doing the longing, or as if when I fear the dentist's drill it were actually my tooth that is afraid. The idea is intrinsically somewhat absurd, and anyway not consistent with his view that practically all desires and emotions are in some way 'bodily' and yet can continue into the soul's disembodied state (pp. 27–9). Rather, his usual view seems to be that these desires and fears and so on are felt in the soul, but at the prompting of the body. Indeed in the *Republic* (437–441) the very same conflicts as he here seems to call conflicts between soul and body are characterized rather as conflicts within the soul, one part of it against another. That is one ground for doubting the argument here. Another is that Simmias' theory anyway never claimed that the soul was an attunement of such things as desires and emotions. These were not the 'elements' he spoke of, but rather the hot and the cold, the wet and the dry, which are surely to be seen as representing the *physical* elements of which the body is composed. At first sight, then, Socrates' objection seems to be guilty of *ignoratio elenchi:* it is an objection to a quite different theory, and not the one supposed to be under discussion.

One might, however, try to defend Socrates in this way. According to the theory we are meant to be discussing, *everything* that I do is the result of the physical interactions between physical parts of my body, and this applies to desires and emotions no less than anything else. No doubt, when I am afraid we shall not locate the fear simply in the tooth, but will say that it is mainly due to the happenings in the brain (with perhaps some assistance from the adrenalin, and other such physical features). We need not pick on any one part of the body which can be said to 'fear', but may insist that it is only a whole person that can be said to 'fear', even though his fearing is due to activities in some parts of his body rather than others. (Compare: when I sit down or jump up, that is because various muscles of mine are expanding or contracting in various ways. But no individual muscle can be said to 'sit down' or 'jump up'.) Still, the point remains that according to the materialist theory desires and emotions are indeed bodily activities at bottom. Does this allow us to conclude that Socrates' objection is not so misguided after all?

No, it does not. For according to the materialist theory reasoning too is merely another such bodily activity. According to that theory the 'conflict' Socrates has in mind is a conflict between one bodily activity and another, and is thus a conflict within the body. If we suppose that reasoning can be located in one part of the brain, and desire for drink in another, we may speak of a conflict between two different bodily parts. We might go on to suggest that this often happens in a disordered body: to take a trivial example, an ingrowing toenail will 'conflict' with the flesh it grows into. Perhaps a conflict between reason and desire—especially when the desire is stubborn, and will not give way—should equally be regarded as a sign of disorder? But all this is needlessly fanciful, and in fact it does not seem very plausible to locate reason and desire in different parts of the brain. The important point is just this: the materialist does not identify the soul with reason in particular. For him, reasoning is just one of the many activities of living, and the soul is what enables a man to perform all those activities. This, he claims, is simply the way his physical elements are arranged. It is no objection to this theory if some of the 'activities of living' can be seen as sometimes 'opposed' to others; occasional opposition is quite compatible with general co-operation, and in fact (he may add) neither reason nor desire could achieve anything without some co-operation from the other.

Curiously, then, the conflict which Plato is here interested in is on his own mature theory a conflict within the soul, and on his rival's theory a conflict within the body. It can only seem to be an objection to either theory if we mistakenly incorporate elements from the one theory while discussing the other.

I conclude, then, that Socrates' arguments do not provide us with any good objections to the materialist theory, and I add by way of aside that good arguments either for or against this theory are not easy to come by. The matter is still hotly disputed. One little observation is perhaps worth adding. Plato is the first of a long line of philosophers who have held that reasoning is the most 'unbodily' of our activities, and cannot be explained merely as the working of the material elements of a man. Yet now we have succeeded in inventing purely material objects, computers, which do seem to be able to perform something very like this traditional function of the soul, while we still have no idea how to produce something that could plausibly be said to have desires and emotions. The invention of computers has indeed led to a renewed interest in the materialist theory of the mind, precisely because computers seem to offer us some clue as to how a purely material thing could think. But of course the opponents of materialism are not much cowed by this. For the sake of argument we might agree that computers can manipulate symbols in roughly the same kind of way that humans do when they think, but still there seems to be this crucial difference: humans *understand* their symbols—they attach some *meaning* to them—while computers do not. But I cannot pursue this issue any further without quite losing sight of our proper topic, Plato's *Phaedo*.

To come back to the *Phaedo*, then, we have now discussed a fundamental objection to Socrates' own theory, an objection which maintains that there simply are no immaterial souls at all, either out of the body or in it. Socrates cannot be said to have disposed adequately of this objection, though he certainly cannot be accused of ignoring it. We now turn to Cebes' objection, which allows that there are immaterial souls, and that these can be regarded as 'ruling' the body, and that they may indeed last very much longer than a body. But it still does not follow that they are immortal. To meet this objection Socrates now launches on his long final argument, in which he tries to show that the soul's nature is such that it simply cannot suffer destruction. His overall tactic is to start from the same premiss as Simmias started from, that the soul is the cause of life. But he reaches a quite different result from Simmias, partly because he has very decided views on what kind of a thing a cause must be. Accordingly, his argument begins with a long preliminary section on the nature of causes, which leads on to some interesting remarks on the proper method of tackling such a question, namely by 'hypotheses'. I shall discuss these two topics first, so it will be some time before we come back to the nature of the soul.

VII

CAUSES, REASONS, AND EXPLANATIONS
(95e7–102a2)

AFTER recapitulating Cebes' objection (95a4–e6), Socrates begins his reply by saying that we must start with a perfectly general discussion of the *reason* for coming to be and ceasing to be (95e7–9). The Greek word αἰτία here translated as 'reason' is not especially precise: one could equally say that Socrates is concerned with the *cause* of coming to be and ceasing to be, or with what is *responsible* for it, or with the *explanation* of it. These English expressions too shade into one another, and I shall use them indifferently when commenting on what Socrates says. One preliminary remark that may be made is that a reason (or cause, or explanation, etc.) is always something that answers a question 'why?' or 'on account of what?' (διὰ τί), but this is not yet much of a restriction: there are, as we shall see, all sorts of different senses in which a 'why' question can be asked and answered. Another preliminary remark worth making here is that although Socrates says he is interested specifically in reasons for *coming to be*, his discussion is not in fact limited to changes which are to and from existence:[1] he is equally concerned with acquiring or losing any property, or indeed with just *having* a property. The question he is ultimately going to apply his discussion to is 'why is a thing alive?' rather than 'why does a thing come to be living?', and for most of the time he ignores any difference between being and becoming. Our topic, then, is really the *very* general topic of why things either are or come to be anything at all. It is hardly surprising that Socrates does not actually promise to give us a thorough treatment of this topic, but merely to 'relate his own experiences on these matters' (96a1–4), hoping that they will prove helpful. What in fact happens is that he first discusses and rejects the kinds of causes that physicists enquire into, then he discusses and despairs of the idea that mind is the cause of

---

[1] We noted earlier (p. 43) that the Greek for 'coming to be' covers both coming into being and coming to have any property. But the word here used for ceasing to be (φθορά) does usually mean 'ceasing to exist'.

everything, and finally he introduces his own idea of forms as causes.

A. PHYSICAL CAUSES (96a6–97b8; cf. 100e8–101c9)

Once upon a time, he tells us, he had a great interest in natural science (ἡ περὶ φύσεως ἱστορία).[2] For example, does life begin from rottenness (as Archelaus suggested)? Do we think with our blood (Empedocles), or with our breath (Anaximenes), or with our vital heat (Heraclitus), or with our brain (Alcmaeon)? (Notice that the soul is not one of the alternatives.) He also looked into how life and thought ceases, how the stars behave, how we get thunderstorms, earthquakes, and so on. These are typical questions investigated (or anyway answered, somewhat rashly) by his predecessors in this field. But eventually Socrates decided that he was no good at this kind of enquiry: it simply muddled him.

As a first example of something that muddled him, he sketches an account of growth which I think is meant as the kind of thing *anyone* would say about growth. In fact it contains hints of a theory of Anaxagoras which really is muddling—Anaxagoras inferred that there must be small bits of flesh and bone in the bread we eat, and generalized this to the puzzling claim that there is a little bit of everything in everything—but I do not imagine that that is what Socrates is adverting to. He presents it as if, on its own level, and as far as it goes, it is a perfectly sensible kind of thing to say about growth. Nevertheless he evidently thinks that it is quite unsatisfactory as an account of the *reason* for growth, though he does not explain why. We begin to get some hint when he sums it up as an account of how human beings get *larger*, and goes on to consider other cases of being larger. For example, one man may be said to be larger than another 'by a head', or we may say that ten is larger than eight 'because it has an extra two', and so on. These are on the face of it quite different accounts of why or how a thing is or becomes larger ('by eating', 'by a head', 'by the extra two'), and this seems to be the point he is getting at.

At any rate, this is one of the points that he clearly does make about his next example, coming to be two. If there is already one piece of chalk on the table, then I may bring it about that there are two by adding another piece, or I may instead break the one that is there into halves. But Socrates thinks that I cannot give it as the *reason* for there coming to be two bits of chalk on the table that this came about either 'by addition' or 'by division'. His ground is, it appears, that addition and division (construed as putting together and taking apart) are opposites to one another, and it cannot be right to say that each of two opposite causes may equally be the reason for the same effect. We may add here a similar point that emerges from his later remarks on one man being larger than another 'by a head' (100e8–101b3): if you say that someone is larger, and (someone else?)[3] smaller, by a head, then the larger will be larger and the smaller smaller by the same thing. That is, if 'by a head' were to be a *reason*, then the same reason could be cited for two opposite effects, and this too Socrates seems to regard as inadmissible. So we may set down two conditions which Socrates thinks that any acceptable reasons or causes must satisfy:

(i)   Two opposite causes cannot have the same effect.
(ii) The same cause cannot have opposite effects.

A third condition also emerges from the latter passage: 'it's surely monstrous that anyone should be large by something small' (101b1–2), or more generally

(iii) A cause cannot be the opposite to the effect it has.

But for the moment I ignore this third condition and stay with the first two.

Now suppose, as is the case with most of Socrates' examples, we are considering the cause of some single thing having or coming to have a particular property, say the property of being P. (This is not the case with the desired cause of coming to be two, as Socrates' own remarks at 96e6–97a5 reveal.) The cause will then be something else about that same thing; say, that it is Q. So Socrates' first two conditions then amount to the following: if the cause of anything's being or becoming P is that it is or has become Q, then

(i)   Nothing which is (or has become) the opposite to being Q can thereby by made to be (or become) P.

---

[3] The text at 101a 6–7 seems to envisage *one* person being both larger (than someone) and smaller (than someone else), as at 74b7–9 on my interpretation, and at 102b10–11. But in the next line (7–8) it seems rather to be different people, larger or smaller than each other, as at 100e8–9. The point is of no importance.

    (ii) Nothing which is (or has become) *Q* can thereby be made to be (or become) the opposite to being *P*.

For simplicity, we may omit the distinction between being and becoming, and we may leave out the notion of causing, and say that Socrates' conditions certainly entail

    (i)   Nothing which is the opposite to being *Q* can be *P*.
    (ii) Nothing which is *Q* can be the opposite to being *P*.

Finally, let us suppose that when Socrates speaks of opposites he simply means contradictory opposites (pp. 47–8), so that a thing is the opposite to being *Q* simply if it is not *Q*. Then our conditions simplify further to

    (i)   Nothing which is not *Q* can be *P*.
    (ii) Nothing which is *Q* can be not *P*.

The first of these says that everything which is *P* must be *Q*, and this is what we mean when we say that being *Q* is a *necessary* condition for being *P*: nothing can be *P* without being *Q*. The second says that everything which is *Q* must be *P*, and this is what we mean when we say that being *Q* is a *sufficient* condition for being *P*: no more is needed, for being *Q* is enough. Under this interpretation, then, Socrates is requiring that causes should always be both necessary and sufficient conditions for their effects.

    If this is on the right lines, we can easily explain what he finds wrong with the ordinary and simple view that the reason why human beings grow is that they eat. Eating is not *sufficient* for growth, because many people eat but do not grow. Nor is it *necessary* for growth, since non-human things grow but do not eat. It is not natural to think of vegetables as 'eating', though they do perhaps do something similar. But metals expand (or 'grow', i.e. become larger) upon being heated, water expands upon being cooled below 4 °C, and mountains grow by quite another method (namely by the movement of the earth's crust). If, as Socrates seems to suppose, the proper explanation for becoming larger must also apply to being larger, then it is clear that eating is a hopeless candidate: one table is not larger than another because it has eaten more.

    It must be admitted that the interpretation suggested goes rather beyond anything Socrates says, principally by assuming that when he speaks of 'opposites' he just means contradictory opposites, which does not really seem very likely. But if we stick more closely to the conditions he formulates himself, and take the notion of an 'opposite' in a fairly natural way, it will not be so clear what is wrong with the explanation that one grows by eating. No doubt eating does not always cause growth, but can we say that it sometimes causes the 'opposite' to growth, presumably shrinking? Or again, growth is not always caused by eating, but is it ever caused by the 'opposite' to eating, perhaps excreting? I think, then, that the more general conditions I have formulated very probably do represent something he had in mind, though they are not what he says. But there is a difficulty here, in that somewhat later, when Socrates progresses to what he calls a 'subtler' kind of cause in 103c10–105c8, he himself cites examples of causes which are perhaps *sufficient* conditions for their effects but are certainly not *necessary*. For example, we may perhaps grant that putting something in the snow *always* makes it cold, but obviously it is not the *only* way of making things cold (103c10–d9). Again we may grant that one who has a fever is always ill, but it obviously is not true that one who is ill always has a fever (105c3–4). This seems to show that Socrates does not insist that causes should always be necessary conditions for their effects: he may be holding to the principle that the same cause always produces the same effect (sufficient condition), but not wishing to endorse the converse principle that the same effect is always due to the same cause (necessary condition). Since, as I remarked, eating is not sufficient for growth (for becoming larger), we still have an explanation of what he finds wrong with the ordinary view. But at the same time it does not seem to be the explanation his own exposition suggests. For what he himself does is to pass on to other cases of being larger which cannot be explained by eating, and this could be regarded as a way of pointing out that eating is not necessary for largeness, but does not impugn its sufficiency in the slightest. I am inclined to conclude, rather tentatively, that at this point in the dialogue Socrates does have in mind both our very general requirements— causes should be both necessary and sufficient for their effects— though he later relaxes one of them. (On the 'subtler' causes, see further pp. 184–9.)

In any case, on this interpretation the main drift of his complaint is that the explanations popularly offered are not sufficiently *general*: they do not apply to a sufficiently wide range of similar cases. Is this a reasonable complaint? At first sight, it may seem very right and proper. Our own ideal of a good scientific explanation is that particular facts should be explained by *general* causal laws, and the more general the laws are the better we like it. The laws should state conditions which genuinely are sufficient for the effect in question, so the mere fact that a man eats is not yet an adequate explanation of why he grows: more conditions are needed. Like Socrates later on, we do not insist that the laws state necessary conditions too, for very often there just are many different ways of bringing about the same effect, but if we can find conditions that are both necessary and sufficient we welcome it. Yet at the same time one must add that where it is a *particular* fact to be explained, *part* of the explanation will not be general at all, but will cite *particular* circumstances relevant to that fact, and in some cases these will seem a more important part of the explanation than the general law. For example if we have to explain why there are now two bits of chalk on this table, we shall usually be quite content to say simply that there was one there already (left over from yesterday, let us suppose) and I brought another and added it. This seems a perfectly good explanation by itself, and apparently it does not mention any general law at all. But in fact the explanation does involve a law,[4] only it is so obvious it has gone without saying. It is: when there is one thing of any kind in any place, and without change to it another thing of the same kind is put in the same place, then there are two things of that kind in that place. Of course, anyone who asked for an explanation would know that law already, which is why we should not bother to state it. What he presumably did not know was that that was the law which covered the present situation, and that is what we show him by citing the particular facts that we do cite. This sort of thing often happens with our ordinary everyday explanations, and provided that we do really know the general laws that we imply without stating there is nothing wrong with them. (But it must be admitted that in practice we often cannot supply the general laws. 'Why is he so fat? He eats a lot.' In practice we might be perfectly content with this. But there are people who eat a lot and do not get fat, so the explanation is not

---

[4] I do not mean to imply that this law is what we ordinarily call a 'causal' law.

fully adequate. The precise connection between eating and getting fat is actually a very difficult question.)

I have here introduced a contrast between the kind of explanations that we give one another all the time, and those that we look to science to provide. Which is Socrates actually talking of? The answer seems to be that his examples are a very mixed lot. He begins with the question of why men grow, which seems a perfectly good question for the scientist, even if the answer he sketches looks more like the kind of answer any ordinary man might give (96c7–d6). He ends apparently with the question of why there are two bits of chalk on the table, or something similar, which is surely not a suitable question for the scientist at all, just because no scientific theorizing is likely to be relevant to the answer. An ordinary everyday explanation seems all that one would wish for here (97a5–b3). But in between what has happened? He has pointed out that if one man (or horse) is taller than another 'by a head', that does not give the reason, but presumably no one would think that it did. 'By a head' is not an answer to 'why is he taller?' but to 'how much taller is he?' (96d8–e1). The same *might* be said of his next examples, that ten is larger than eight 'because it has an extra two', and that two cubits is larger than one cubit because the latter is half the former (96e1–4). But here we should add that at least there is a possible question for the scientist in 'why is one man (or horse) ever taller than another?', whereas we obviously do not look to the *scientist* (the man engaged in the enquiry into nature, ἡ περὶ φύσεως ἱστορία) to tell us why ten is larger than eight, or two than one. If anything, this is a problem for the philosopher or logician. The same is true of the next problem raised: when one is added to one, *what* is it that becomes two (96e6–97a5)? (And the answer to the question must be that nothing does. We can say that when one bit of chalk is added to another, i.e. put next to it, then they—the pair of them—become *two bits together*. But they do not become *two bits of chalk*, for—as Socrates rightly says—they were that already.) But the problem anyway seems to be something of an aside. It is not explicitly a problem about a reason, and it does not recur in the second treatment of these examples at 100e8–101c9. Finally, the examples end with the question why one comes to be, which is a question so vaguely posed that it is difficult to say what kind of answer it looks for (97b3–4).

There seems, then, to be no uniformity in the questions Socrates raises. Some can indeed be seen as questions for the scientist, but others are ordinary everyday questions (with apparently perfectly good ordinary everyday answers), and others are more like puzzles for the philosopher. Moreover, although I said earlier that at first glance Socrates seems right to ask for *general* laws from the scientist, this approval must evaporate when we observe just how general he seems to want the scientist's answer to be. A scientist might hope to give a properly general explanation of why men grow. He might then hope to extend this to a general explanation of why any animal grows, i.e. becomes larger. Conceivably he might use this to give an explanation of why any animal is larger than any other. But that must surely be the limit of his hopes. He could not possibly suppose that the *same* explanation will explain why *anything* gets larger (including mountains, for example), still less that it will explain why anything *is* larger than anything else (including the fact that ten is larger than eight). This ideal of such extreme generality is totally quixotic from the scientist's point of view. The same could obviously be said of the desire to find some *one* explanation of why there ever are, or come to be, two of anything anywhere. Scientists can only hope to find necessary and sufficient conditions for effects which are reasonably narrowly described, and what Socrates seems to be asking for is something they could not possibly supply. This is no doubt why he abandoned science. This 'defect' in natural science he evidently thought was something to do with its *method* (97b6), but he does not here explain what he has in mind. I shall return to the point when we have looked at the other kinds of causes he discusses.

B. MIND AS CAUSE (97b8–99d2)

The kind of reasons we have just been speaking of do not mention the *point* or *purpose* of a thing, though this is just what we mean when we talk of a *person*'s reasons for acting. We explain why he acted as he did by giving his reasons, i.e. his purpose, namely what he was trying to achieve, and why he thought that his present actions would further that purpose. Of course men have purposes because they have minds (or because they have Intelligence, as Gallop prefers to say), and Socrates seems to think that a man's purpose will always be to achieve what seems best to him.[5] This is somewhat over-optimistic. Ordinary human minds are liable to succumb to temptation, or to give way to fears and other emotions, and so to decide to do things which they know are not for the best. Besides, men often make decisions for no very good reason. So the proposition that minds always try to achieve what seems best to them must be regarded as somewhat dubious. But for our present purposes we can set that doubt aside as not very important. For the hypothesis that Socrates next goes on to consider is the hypothesis that a divine mind is responsible for everything's being as it is. Divine minds presumably do not succumb to temptation, and do not act without good reason, and so always will do what seems best to them. Moreover, as they are divine, what seems best to them will actually be best. Hence, if the universe is ordered by a divine mind, everything in it will be as it is because it is best so, and this gives quite a different sort of explanation of why things are as they are. Socrates tells us that he was pleased to discover that Anaxagoras had adopted the hypothesis that a divine mind was responsible for everything, precisely because it would have the consequence that we could always give, as the reason for anything, that it was best so. He eagerly took up Anaxagoras' book, hoping to find the shape of the earth, the movements of the heavens, and so on, all explained in this way. Not surprisingly, he was disappointed.

Of course it may be that the divine mind has ordered everything for the best, and that there are these for-the-best explanations for the astronomical phenomena Socrates mentions, even though we have not so far been clever enough to find them. But we should also notice this possibility: it may be that the universe is ordered by a divine mind, as Anaxagoras promised, but not ordered for the best. By this I do not mean to suggest that the divine mind may not be a benevolent mind after all—though indeed that does seem to be a possibility—but rather that there may be no *best*. Let me remind you of Buridan's ass. This animal was in a way supremely rational, but in another way remarkably stupid. It was placed equidistant between two equally luscious piles of hay, and was hungry. But unfortunately it could see no reason to choose one pile of hay in preference to the other, and as I say it was a very

---

[5] This is a prominent theme in the early dialogues. The main passages are *Protagoras* 358b–c, *Gorgias* 467c–468b, *Meno* 77b–78b.

rational ass. So, as it had no reason to move towards one pile rather than the other, it did not move towards either. It remained stuck in the middle, unable to choose, until it starved to death. Well, the moral of this little tale is obvious. A sensible person, faced with a choice between two actions which are equally good, will plump for one of them even though it is no better than the other.

This objection is no mere academic quibble. For suppose, as used to be very generally believed, that God created the world in a way that was as good as possible for the human beings in it. Then it seems reasonably to say that, so far as human beings are concerned, the world would be no worse if the sun and the stars were a bit nearer and smaller, or a bit further away and bigger. If so, then we cannot explain why the sun is the distance away from · us that it is by the fact that that is the best distance for it to be: there is no best distance for it to be. Similar considerations no doubt apply to the precise shape of the earth. More generally, I think those who believe that God created the world to be as good as possible—whether specifically good for human beings or good in some other way—would usually admit that some features of the world are irrelevant to its goodness: they could be different, and the world would be no worse. But in that case these features do not have for-the-best explanations of the kind that Socrates desires, and this is a point that he seems to have overlooked. (Besides this objection, one might also ask whether it even makes sense to talk of the goodness of the universe, as we have so little idea of what might count as an argument for or against its goodness. But that doubt at once raises very fundamental issues about the nature of goodness, which I cannot discuss here.)

I add two footnotes to this little discussion of for-the-best explanations. First, notice that in Plato's view these explanations will be available only if we are dealing with the work of a mind. One might wonder whether this limitation is actually necessary. For example, if asked to explain why men have hearts, one might well reply that the *purpose* of the heart, its role or function, is to pump the blood round (and the *point* of this in turn is to circulate oxygen and food and other things, and that in turn is *in order to* keep the muscles and organs of the body supplied, and so on). This explanation apparently presupposes that it is in some way *good* that the blood should be pumped round, for we are not *just* saying that this is what the heart does when we call this its purpose. (If we were, then we should equally say that the purpose of the appendix is to give one appendicitis, for that is about the only thing it does. But we do not say this, because giving one appendicitis is not a good thing. We say rather that the appendix now serves no purpose.) But at first sight it seems that we can in this way explain why we have hearts by citing their purpose, the good that they achieve, even though we do not suppose that the heart was designed and created by any mind. Aristotle took this line of thought yet further. Though he did not suppose that the world was created by any divine mind, he still thought it reasonable to assume that practically everything in it had a purpose or function, which it was good that it should achieve. In fact his whole system of ethics is based on the premiss that there is such a thing as the purpose (or function) of man. Here it may well seem reasonable to side with Plato: surely it makes no sense to suppose that man has a purpose, and that the good man is the one who fulfils that purpose, unless we also suppose that the purpose really belongs in some mind that designed and created man with a particular end in view. (That, after all, is why we speak of tools and implements as having a purpose, and being good tools when they fulfil that purpose.) But then if we do think this, how are we to explain the fact that even atheists are happy to talk of the purpose of the heart, the lungs, or the liver? I leave this question to the reader.

Second, one may very well sympathize with the point Socrates makes at 98c2–99b6. When we are dealing with a human action which does have a purpose, an explanation of that action which simply omits its purpose certainly strikes us as inadequate. You might suggest that this is because such an explanation will not have traced the causes of the action back far enough. If a man sits down, then perhaps it is all right to say that he sits down because his muscles contract in various ways, but we can still ask what made the muscles behave in that way. Here one imagines that the further story will talk in more familiar terms about what went on in his mind: he decided to sit down, and his reasons for that decision were . . . But suppose the further story does not mention such things as decisions or reasons or purposes or goals at all, but goes on in the same physical and mechanistic way: impulses were sent out by the brain, and this was because the brain was in such and such an electrical state, which in turn arose because . . . (and we go on, speaking *just* of the physical states of the brain, and other bodily organs, for as far back as is desired). If such an explanation is possible, complete in its own terms and leaving no unexplained gaps, what should we say then? For the materialist whom we discussed in the last chapter, the answer is relatively straight-forward. In his view the mind's decisions, reasons, purposes, and so on, just *are* states or events in the brain, so our explanation has mentioned them, but under another name. However, for one who believes that the mind is immaterial, and quite different from the brain, this answer is not available. He may say that no mechanistic explanation of the kind we are envisaging ever will be complete: it is bound to contain a gap where the mind has stepped in and somehow begun a train of events in the brain. This theory, known as 'interactionism', makes a prediction about the lack of complete mechanistic explanations which seems to many rather rash, and it does nothing to make it easier to understand how an immaterial thing could act upon a material thing. Alternatively he may try to allow that *each* kind of explanation is complete in its own way, and though they do not tie up with one another at all we may still perfectly well accept both of them. Since they are each explanations of the same effect, the sitting down, this has always seemed a very difficult view to accept. Yet attempts to make the two explanations tie up with one another, while still saying that one concerns an immaterial mind and the other a material brain, also run into difficulties. For example, if the happenings in the brain cause corresponding happenings in the mind ('epiphenomenalism'), then the happenings in the mind are not after all the causes of the action, as we thought they were. Alternatively, if there is no causal connection between the two, but they still run in some way parallel to one another ('parallellism'), then this parallel itself is a mystery with no explanation.

We see, then, that Socrates has actually raised here a question which produces some considerable difficulty for the theory that the mind is an immaterial thing. But again I cannot here discuss this major issue any further.

C. FORMS AS CAUSES (99d4–102a2)

Having rejected the method which physical scientists used in their search for causes (ostensibly because it muddled him), and despairing of ever finding those for-the-best explanations that Anaxagoras had seemed to promise, Socrates goes on to describe what he calls his Second Voyage in search of reasons (99c9–d2). It is what he has earlier called, somewhat ironically, 'a different method, a jumble of my own' (97b6–7). The positive characterization of this new method presents several problems, which I postpone to the next chapter. But one negative feature stands out clearly enough: it is a method which does not make use of the senses. Socrates seems to imply that his previous enquiries *had* relied upon the senses ('I was afraid I might be completely blinded in my soul, by looking at objects with my eyes and trying to lay hold of them with each of my senses', 99e2–4). Anyway, the new method is supposed to be one that does not rely on the senses: it is meant to proceed wholly a priori and without the benefit of any lessons from experience. We can also be quite confident about the result which the method leads to, namely the claim that there are such things as forms, and that the only proper reason why any thing has any property is that it participates in the relevant form. (Socrates is careful not to commit himself to any exact account of the relationship between particular and form (100d5–7), but he quite often uses the word 'participate', and I shall do so too.) For example, if a thing is beautiful, that must be because it participates in beauty. That, and apparently only that, counts as a proper explanation. But on the face of it it seems to be no explanation at all. How should we understand this surprising remark?

Commentators have been strongly tempted to approach this question with Aristotle's account of causes in mind. (Indeed it seems quite probable that Aristotle's account was itself worked out with the *Phaedo*'s discussion in mind). Anyway, Aristotle's account is very roughly this (the *locus classicus* is *Physics* ii. ch.3). He distinguishes four different kinds of causes (or reasons, or explanation, etc), which are known as the *efficient* cause, the *final* cause, the *material* cause, and the *formal* cause. The *efficient* cause of an object or event is the further object or preceding event that brought it into existence: for example the efficient cause of a statue is the sculptor who made it. If we say that the main idea here is that the efficient cause of something explains it by explaining how it was brought about, or brought into existence, then there may well seem to be a fair similarity between what Aristotle calls an efficient cause and what Plato has in mind under the heading 'causes enquired into by natural science'. The *final* cause of an object or event is the purpose for which it exists or for which it happened, and this has obvious similarities with what Plato has to say about mind as a cause, and the availability of for-the-best explanations. The *material* cause of an object is simply the matter out of which it is made, and this has no analogue in Plato's discussion. (Indeed Aristotle's 'material cause' does not seem to be the answer to a 'why?' question at all.) Finally, the *formal* cause of an object is what is stated in its definition: for example the formal cause of a man would be (to use a traditional definition) that he is a rational animal; the formal cause of a statue would be that it has a shape of a certain kind; the formal cause of a threshold would be that it has a position of a certain kind; and so on. That is, when giving the 'formal cause' of a so and so, we state the reason why the thing is *called* a so and so, what it is about it that entitles us to apply the word 'so and so' to it. In effect, then, what we are doing is giving an explanation of the *concept* of being a so and so, an elucidation and clarification of what the word 'so and so' *means*, which will amount to a definition if it is a complete explanation. (It will, in fact, be a properly 'philosophic' answer to a Socratic 'what is *X*?' question). According to this line of interpretation, then, the new kinds of 'causes' introduced in the Second Voyage are explanations of concepts, and it is these 'causes', and only these, that Plato admits as satisfactory.

Let us begin by noting two points in favour of this interpretation. First, a proper definition must be completely general: if we are explaining what it is to be a man, our explanation must apply to *all* the things that are men, and it must apply *only* to things that are men, which is to say that it must state a condition that is both necessary and sufficient for being a man. We observed that Socrates seemed to require this of any proper 'cause' during his discussion of physical causes. Second, a proper definition must state an a priori truth, one that can be seen to be true independently of how the world is. This is because what we can find out about the world from experience is never enough to establish the correctness of a definition. To illustrate this, let us observe that the traditional definition of man as a rational animal is in fact quite obviously an incorrect definition. So far as our experience can tell us, it is no doubt perfectly correct to claim that all rational animals are men (provided we pitch the standard of rationality high enough to exclude dolphins, apes, and so forth). But this is not a logically necessary truth: as any piece of science fiction will show, there is no *contradiction* in the hypothesis that there are things, e.g. Martians, which are rational animals but not men. It follows that 'man' cannot *mean* 'rational animal', for if it did the hypothesis would be contradictory. Definitions, then, cannot be certified correct by relying on experience, and so if we ever can tell that a proposed definition is correct we must be able to do so a priori.

So far, then, the interpretation looks promising. It will explain why, in the Second Voyage, Socrates determines not to use the evidence of the senses, and it will explain why he finds inadequate all those explanations discussed under the heading 'physical causes'. None of them were even attempting to be explanations of the concepts involved, i.e. of the concept of being or becoming larger, or of the concept of being or becoming two. Admittedly this interpretation does not explain why he says, concerning those for-the-best explanations that he had hoped to find in Anaxagoras, that they *would* be satisfactory if only we could find them. One might perhaps argue that these explanations, if only we could find them, would have to be a priori. For the complete set of these explanations would in effect be a complete reconstruction of God's reasons for creating the world as he did, and clearly God must have worked it out a priori. But that is not enough for the present interpretation. There still seems no obvious reason to suppose that for-the-best explanations would be, or would necessarily include, explanations of the concepts involved. (But perhaps Plato would disagree. At any rate in *Republic* vi. 509b, he does seem rather obscurely to suggest that the full explanation of any concept will relate it somehow to the concept of goodness.) However, even if this objection is admitted, it may not seem very serious. Perhaps for-the-best explanations, if we could find them, would be satisfactory for some *other* reason, and not because they were explanations of concepts. The main claim is that the only satisfactory explanations that we *can* find are explanations of concepts. I come, therefore, to a more direct attack upon this claim: it simply does not fit what we are told about explanations in the course of the Second Voyage.

First, it apparently does not fit even that 'safe' and 'simple-minded' explanation with which the Second Voyage begins, that if a thing is P that is always because it participates in P–hood (100b–e). This so-called explanation apparently offers us *no* elucidation or clarification of the concept of being P, just because you can say exactly the same of any concept whatever.[6] If Plato had wished to show us that, in the Second Voyage, what he counts as a proper explanation of being P must be a proper answer to the Socratic question 'what is P–hood?', then this formula is quite inadequate for his purpose. No one who had been subjected to Socratic questioning would think that this formula was going to get him anywhere. Perhaps it will be replied that the 'safe' and 'simple-minded' explanations with which we begin are intended only as a very small first step towards the kind of explanations that are ultimately wanted, and we should wait to see how Plato elaborates his ideas as the discussion proceeds. But when we do turn to the later elaboration we find that in fact the suggested interpretation breaks down entirely.

The 'more subtle' causes introduced in 103c10–105c8 are quite clearly *not* elucidations of the relevant concepts in the way that this interpretation requires. When fire is said to be a cause of heat, and snow of cold, and threeness of oddness, this is evidently not because fire, snow, and threeness provide adequate definitions of heat, cold, and oddness. Nor are they even partial definitions: in giving an account of the concepts of heat, cold, or oddness, one would not have to mention that fire is hot, that snow is cold, or that three is odd. Rather if there is a conceptual connection here, it is the other way round. At best, it is part of the definition of fire that it is hot, and part of the definition of snow that it is cold, but not conversely. (In fact, I think that even this would be a mistake: I see no *contradiction* in the supposition that there could be a fire that was not hot, or a lump of snow that was not cold. But I imagine that Plato would not have agreed on this point, and he would have thought that we can tell a priori that fire is hot and snow cold. That, however, is rather by the way.) To take just the clearest example, Plato evidently could not have thought that a proper answer to 'what is oddness?' would have to mention the various odd numbers: three, five, seven, and so on. He was always quite clear upon the point that a list of examples is not a definition, and anyway it is in this case easy to provide a definition which

---

[6] Or can you say this *only* when there is such a thing as the form of P–hood? If so, when is that? I take up this question in my last chapter (pp. 196–201).

mentions no examples: an odd number is a (whole) number which is not divisible by two.

I conclude that, despite its attractive link with Aristotle's discussion of causes, this interpretation will not do. We cannot explain the difference between the causes that Plato accepts and the causes the he rejects as being that the ones he accepts are all (like Aristotle's 'formal causes') explanations of the concepts in question. In that case, what *is* the difference? Why exactly does Plato reject the causes he does reject, and accept the causes he does accept? Notice that it will not do to say simply that he accepts those explanations which are true a priori and rejects those which are not. Again we have a difficulty for this view with the 'more subtle' causes, for although it may possibly be a priori true that fire *is* hot, and snow *is* cold, still it does not follow from this that fire also makes *other* things hot, and snow makes *other* things cold. These latter claims are surely not a priori, but known only through the evidence of the senses. (Still, it is possible that Plato overlooked this point.) What is more awkward is that some of the explanations that Plato rejects are true a priori, for example that ten is greater than eight because it has an extra two (96e2–3). Plato may well be right to say that this is not a proper explanation, but if so that is not because it is not true a priori, for it is.

Unfortunately, I see no satisfying answer to the question I have just raised. The only reason that can be extracted from the text seem to be the three principles I mentioned at the beginning (p. 137), namely:

> (i)   Two opposite causes cannot have the same effect.
> (ii)   The same cause cannot have opposite effects.
> (iii)   A cause cannot be the opposite to the effect it has.

We observed that it is tempting to generalize the first two of these to, respectively,

> (i)'   A cause is a necessary condition of its effect.
> (ii)'   A cause is a sufficient condition of its effect.

(But the 'more subtle' causes do not obey the generalized principle (i)', though they do obey the generalized principle (ii)'.) The difficulty, however, is to see *why* it is reasonable to impose these three conditions. It is true that the explanations which Plato rejects do not satisfy them (at any rate if we extend (ii) to (ii)'). It is also true that the explanations which he accepts in his Second Voyage do satisfy them (at any rate if we keep to (i) and do not extend it to (i)'). Thus according to the 'safe' and 'simple-minded' explanation the cause of a thing's being P is always (its participation in) the form of P-hood. Since a thing is P if and only if it participates in this form, the cause is both a necessary and a sufficient condition of its effect, so both (i)' and (ii)' are satisfied (and therefore also (i) and (ii)). Moreover, according to Plato the form of P-hood must itself be P, and cannot also be the opposite to being P, since it has to function as an unambiguous paradigm of a thing that is P. Hence condition (iii) is satisfied also. The 'more subtle' explanations also satisfy these conditions. They satisfy condition (i) 'vacuously', since we are told that the causes in question are ones which have no opposites (104b8, e7); Plato evidently supposes that they also satisfy (ii), and indeed (ii)'—for example, whatever fire has occupied must become hot; and he is at pains to point out that they satisfy (iii) as well. So it is quite fair to say that these three conditions govern his entire discussion (except that, once again, it is not clear how they would apply to the desired for-the-best explanations). But this still does not answer the question: *why* is it reasonable to claim that all proper causes must satisfy these three conditions?

In fact it will turn out that the only one of these three conditions that will be important for the final proof of immortality is condition (iii), which we may restate thus

> The cause of a thing's being P must itself be P, and cannot be the opposite to being P.

In the final argument we will begin with the premiss that the soul is the cause of life, and then use this principle to infer that the soul must therefore be alive itself, and cannot admit the opposite to life, namely death. Since this is the only claim made during the present discussion of causes that is used later, I shall henceforth confine attention to it. We might perhaps call it 'Plato's principle of causation', and we might note that it has been extremely influential.[7] But why should we agree that this principle does hold of all 'proper' causes? Plato's own discussion seems to provide no

---

[7] It was a central feature of Aristotle's doctrine of causation, and persisted through all further Greek and Mediaeval philosophy. It is still to be found in Descartes (*Meditation*, III).

argument for it at all. Moreover the truth is that this principle is plainly false, and could only *seem* to be true as the result of a conceptual muddle. I argue this in the next section.

D. FACTS, EVENTS, AND OBJECTS

Any proper 'why'–question can be put in the form 'why is it that so-and-so?', where 'so-and-so' is some complete sentence. Further, the question is only appropriate if it is true that so-and-so, i.e. if that sentence states a fact. Since explanations (or reasons, or causes) are offered in answer to 'why'–questions, we may therefore say that what is explained is always a *fact*, meaning by this simply that it is the kind of thing that can be stated in a complete, true, sentence. Moreover, the same is true of the answers to 'why'–questions. These answers can always be expressed by beginning with the word 'because' and continuing with a complete sentence (or perhaps several sentences). Further, the sentences following the 'because' must be true if the answer is to be a correct one. So again we may say that what explains a fact must itself be a fact, or perhaps several facts. It is facts that explain, and facts that are explained. Similarly a reason for something is always a fact (or facts), and what it is a reason for is always a fact. The same must equally hold for causes, if indeed causes are like reasons and explanations in providing answers to 'why'–questions. The point is just that the answers to 'why'–questions, when fully expressed, must take the form of one or more complete sentences. So a causal statement can always in principle be expressed in some such form as this: 'the fact (or facts) that such-and-such was the cause of the fact that so-and-so'.[8]

Obviously we do not in practice use such a long-winded form of expression, but abbreviate in various ways. For example, if I dropped a glass because I was startled by a flash of lightning, then we quite often say that I dropped the glass *because of* the flash of lightning. We can equally say that that flash of lightning explains why I dropped the glass, that it was the reason for my dropping the glass, or that it caused me to drop the glass. That is, we do not cite

[8] Obviously I am concerned here only with *singular* causal statements (and, more generally, with *singular* 'why'–questions and their 'because'–answers). A corresponding account of causal generalizations, such as 'taking arsenic causes death', would require more sophisticated logical apparatus than it is proper to develop here.

as cause, reason, or explanation the full fact (that I was startled by a flash of lightning), but just its 'salient ingredient', the flash of lightning. We leave the rest to be understood. But the rest must *be* understood if what we cite as cause, reason, or explanation is to furnish an answer to the question 'why did I drop the glass?'

Now the verb 'to cause' is perhaps a trifle more natural than its alternatives in these abbreviated locutions, and it very often happens (as with my example) that the 'salient ingredient' picked out is an event. This, I think, has helped[9] to lead to the modern dogma that causes are always events (and that what is caused is also an event). But there is no good basis for the dogma in this phenomenon, for the 'salient ingredient' picked out does not have to be an event: it can perfectly well be an object. Thus if the window broke because a large stone was thrown at it with some force, we may, speaking in the abbreviated fashion, say simply that that stone caused the window to break. Similarly we say simply that it was the pot-hole that caused the puncture, the oysters that caused the sickness, the clown that caused the laughter, and so on. It is obvious on reflection that this is an abbreviated way of talking, and I think the same is no less true when we cite events as causes. But since this point is somewhat controversial, and unnecessary for my present argument, I am content to leave it here unresolved. At least it is clear that mentioning an object, or an event, cannot by itself be the full and complete answer to any 'why'–question, for a 'why'–question requires a whole sentence as answer. Some may say (implausibly, in my view) that we sometimes talk of causes when we do not have in mind the answers to 'why'–questions, but if that is so we can set it aside as irrelevant. Our topic *is* the topic of how to answer 'why'–questions. That is how Plato introduces it at 96a9–10.

Now the point of this little excursus into our linguistic habits is that Plato himself very clearly tends to prefer the abbreviated way of talking, which makes it seem as though it is *objects* that are causes (or reasons, or explanations). (So, incidentally, does Aristotle. Perhaps Greek idiom encourages this more than English, for the Greek for 'why?' is more literally 'on account of

---

[9] There are other sources of this dogma, for example a failure to distinguish between expressions related as 'my dropping the glass' and 'my dropping of the glass'. We can very often use the former to express a cause, reason, or explanation; but only the latter should be regarded as referring to an event.

what?' (διὰ τί), which can more naturally be seen as inviting the answer 'on account of this *object*'.) But if one does take this idiom seriously, and supposes that a cause is always an object, the following line of thought can be very tempting. An object A, let us imagine, causes some other object B to have a certain property. If so, then it seems natural to assume that the object A must *act* in some way, and a consequence of this action is that B now has the property, which it did not have before. But that seems much the same as to say that A's action must amount to an action whereby A *gives* B the property. Thus, causing B to have some property must essentially be the matter of *giving* B the property. The crucial thought is then this: you cannot *give* what you do not *have*. So if A can give B some property, then A must itself *have* the property. In other words, if A causes B to be *P*, then A must itself be *P*, for if it were not it could not *pass on* this property to B.

A moment's reflection will show that this line of thought has led to an obviously absurd result. For example, if a stone causes a window to break, we can hardly conclude that the stone was itself breaking; if a loud noise overhead causes me to look up, that is not because the loud noise was itself looking up; or, to use an example that Plato carelessly mentions himself, if a fever causes me to be ill, that is not because the fever is itself ill (105c2–4). There are many, many obvious counter-examples to the principle, and it is really rather difficult to see how Plato could have overlooked them. Perhaps the explanation is that he tended to dismiss them as not the right kind of 'cause' because they also suffer from the other defects that he professed to find in physical causes, namely that they are not sufficiently general, and can anyway be discovered only by using the senses. Then, since his paradigm case of a really satisfactory cause was of forms as causes, and since this case really does seem to satisfy the principle, he felt entitled to adopt it as a requirement for all genuine causes. But I imagine that he must *also* have been drawn by some such line of thought as I have sketched in favour of the principle, which made it look as if the principle were in itself a very plausible one.

The truth is that the principle could not even have *looked* plausible without the initial step of taking causes to be *objects*. To see this, let us just consider Plato's own favoured case of forms as causes. According to the 'safe' and 'simple-minded' hypothesis, the question of why this or that thing is beautiful is always to be answered in the same way: 'it is by the beautiful that beautiful things are beautiful' (τῷ καλῷ τὰ καλὰ καλά, 100e2–3). This appears to cite an object, 'the beautiful', i.e. the form of beauty, as the cause of beauty in other objects. But evidently this is an abbreviated way of talking, for the question 'why is this beautiful?' is not fully answered just by naming the form of beauty. The full answer intended is something like 'because *it participates in* the form of beauty'. Hence our formula might be filled out to 'it is by *participating in* the form of beauty that beautiful things are beautiful'—or, in my yet longer version, 'if anything is beautiful, the explanation/reason/cause for that fact is always (the fact) *that it participates in* the form of beauty.' But now it is clear that when the cause is thus expressed more fully, it is not itself the right kind of thing to be beautiful: participating in the form of beauty—or, (the fact) that it participates in the form of beauty—is not itself a beautiful thing, even if the form of beauty is. Similarly, it is completely nonsensical to say: participating in the form of largeness—or, (the fact) that it participates in the form of largeness—is itself a large thing. This is nonsensical, even granting that the form of largeness *is* a large thing. Generally, the cause of a thing's being *P* cannot itself be *P*, since it is not an entity of the right kind. It can only seem that this is possible if one refers to the cause in an abbreviated way of talking.

VIII

THE METHOD OF HYPOTHESIS
(99d–100a, 101d–e)

AFTER telling us he was confused by this investigation of physical causes, and disappointed of his hope to be able to explain that things are as they are because that is the best way for them to be, Socrates comes to describe his 'second voyage in quest of the reason' in 99d. He represents this as involving the adoption of a new *method*, using hypotheses. The metaphor of the 'second voyage' apparently derives from having to take to the oars when the wind has failed, which is a second-best method of proceeding. But here at any rate it seems to be envisaged as a second-best way of reaching the same destination, for Socrates tells us that he was still 'in quest of the reason'.[1] However, he also tells us that he now applies the new method in other enquiries too (100a6), and it is evidently intended to be of quite general application. We must ask what the method is, and whether it is likely to succeed in its aim.

A. WHAT THE METHOD IS

I shall take the description of the method in three parts: 99d4–100a3, 100a3–7, and 101d3–e3.

(i) *99d4–100a3*. Socrates begins by explaining why he changed his method. His previous attempts had proved unsuccessful, and he thought that this might be because he was trying to proceed too directly. Just as people are blinded if they try to observe an eclipse of the sun directly, and the sensible procedure is to study an image or reflection of it, so he thought that he too was perhaps being 'blinded in his soul' because he was trying to grasp things[2] by his

---

[1] The singular expression 'the reason' is slightly unexpected. It seems that Socrates is still thinking of that single reason, the good, which ensures that everything is organized for the best. If so, then the destination has apparently changed to some extent, for the new method does not reveal any *one* reason as the reason for everything.

[2] Gallop translates τὰ ὄντα as 'the things that are' throughout this passage. This seems to me to put overmuch emphasis on what is quite an ordinary Greek expression, and I shall speak simply of 'things'. The expression gives no clue as to what kind of things are in question.

senses, and it would be better if he too approached more indirectly. Accordingly he determined to study things in *logoi*—a word I shall leave untranslated for the moment—for *logoi* are images of things. But, having introduced this simile, Socrates at once withdraws it: he does not actually admit that studying things in *logoi* is any more an indirect method than studying them 'in concrete',[3] for each is really a case of studying things in images. (That is, Socrates is presumably not withdrawing the claim that the study of things in *logoi* is indirect—for that seems to be the main point of the passage—but is rather withdrawing the claim that the study of things by the senses is direct.)

At least this much is clear. The previous method that is being talked of here is primarily the method employed in the study of physical causes. This Socrates regards as relying on the senses, and he has earlier told us that it did indeed 'blind' him (96c5). Presumably it proceeds by investigation of physical objects, and that is what he must mean by studying things 'in concrete'. But now we must ask why, when he withdraws the opening simile, Socrates says that this is, after all, an equally indirect method: it too is a case of studying things in images. What, then, are the real objects of study of which physical objects are mere images? To anyone familiar with Plato's later writings there can only be one answer: it is standard Platonic doctrine that physical objects are images of forms. But, as I have earlier observed, this doctrine is nowhere explicitly stated in the text of the *Phaedo* itself (pp. 90–2). This leaves us in something of a dilemma. On the one hand we can say that the remark in which Socrates withdraws his simile is clearly an aside, and one that the reader could hardly be expected to understand, so we should not build too much upon it. It will be better to ignore it when seeking an interpretation of the whole passage. On the other hand we can say that even though the remark is an aside it gives us a valuable insight into Plato's meaning, for *we* can understand it even though the contemporary reader of the *Phaedo* could not. And what it tell us is that the images Plato is talking of in this passage are images *of forms*; at least, that is what physical objects are images of, so one would

---

[3] ἐν ἔργοις. The phrase is slightly surprising, and seems designed to recall the well-known antithesis λόγῳ μεν . . . ἔργῳ δε . . . , i.e. 'in theory . . . but in reality . . .'. But if so then it recalls it only to reject its usual implications: Socrates claims that 'reality' is no less an image than 'theory'.

certainly expect the *logoi* in question to be images of forms as well. With this in mind, let us turn to the question of what these *logoi* are.

The Greek word *logos* (plural *logoi*) has a very wide range of meanings. The ones that may be relevant here are all connected with the root idea that a *logos* is something that can be *said*. Thus a *logos* may be a phrase (but not usually a single word), or a sentence, or a paragraph, or a whole speech; equally it can be the thought expressed by any of these sayings. In a more specialized use, a *logos* is often specifically an argument, in the sense of a piece of reasoning, and the word is used in this meaning throughout the section on 'mistrust of arguments' in 89d–91c. In another specialized use, to give a *logos* of something is to give an account of it, and more specifically a definition of it, and so another meaning is 'definition'. From what we have had so far, it would seem a very plausible conjecture that this is its meaning here. After all, Socrates is professing to give us an account of his own intellectual history, and the actual Socrates was much concerned with definitions. Moreover, the *logoi* we are here concerned with are said to be images of something, and if we take seriously the hint discussed in my last paragraph we can say that they are images of forms. But it is good Platonic doctrine that the things that have definitions are forms, and it is not at all surprising to find a definition called an image of the thing it is a definition of. On this interpretation, then, Socrates says that he decided to stop trying to study forms via their sensible instances, and instead to study them via their definitions.

Unfortunately the interpretation breaks down as soon as we continue. Having told us of his decision to work with *logoi*, Socrates explains that his procedure is to hypothesize whatever *logos* seems strongest (100a3–4), and to help us understand he at once proceeds to offer an example. He hypothesizes that there are such things as forms (100b4–7), and goes on to add, as something that comes next, that ordinary things are what they are by participating in the relevant forms and for no other reason (100c3–6). (It is actually the latter which is referred to as the hypothesis at 101d1.[4]) One or both of these propositions are clearly meant as an

---

[4] More exactly, it is referred to as 'that safe thing [perhaps that safe *part*] of the hypothesis' (ἐκείνου τοῦ ἀσφαλοῦς τῆς ὑποθέσεως). Perhaps the idea is that it is risky to suppose that there are forms, but, if this is granted, it is then safe to go on to add that things are what they are by participating in the forms. The addition is the safe part of the whole hypothesis.

example of a *logos* that is hypothesized, but neither of them could possibly be regarded as a definition of anything. We must conclude that *logos* does not here mean 'definition' after all, and apparently it just bears its general meaning of 'statement' or 'proposition' (or, as Gallop prefers to say, 'theory'). It apparently covers any kind of view that may be advanced, and not only views about definitions. But in that case how are we to explain Socrates' idea that a *logos* is always an image of something (and, perhaps, of a form)?

It may seem tempting to seek elucidation from another dialogue, the *Cratylus*, though there is no strong reason to suppose that it is at all close in date to the *Phaedo*. (In my opinion, it is towards the *end* of Plato's 'middle' period.) In the *Cratylus* Plato apparently argues that a name, when rightly framed, will fit the thing it is a name of, by resembling it or being an image of it (430b–434b). Moreover, the resemblance must be to the true nature of the thing, which is to say to those features of it which make it an image of the relevant form (423d–424a; cf. 389a–390e). This tells us that both the thing and its name, when rightly framed, will resemble the form. But also Plato twice suggests in passing that what holds for names will also hold for verbs, and hence for the combinations of names and verbs which constitute propositions (431a–b, 432e; cf. 385b–c). From this one might infer that a proposition will be an image of some complex of forms, and perhaps we can add that a suitable complex of physical objects will be an image of the same complex of forms. One of the arguments used, 432a–433a, would apparently entitle us to say that even false propositions are in this way images of genuine form-complexes, but not very good images of them. However, it is not even clear that this (rather confused) line of thought was Plato's own view at the time when he wrote the *Cratylus*. This is partly because the dialogue goes on to reject the premiss that names need to be rightly framed (434c–435c), and partly because there are evidently many things in that dialogue that Plato is not very serious about, and the way the argument is extended from names to propositions may well be one of them.[5] It is therefore doubly hazardous to infer that this line of thought in the *Cratylus* lies behind the claim in the *Phaedo*.

[5] If Plato *is* serious about this extension, then the *Cratylus* ends by rejecting the *Phaedo*'s proposal to investigate reality via propositions. For it certainly ends by arguing that it must be possible, and indeed preferable, to investigate things directly, and not via their *names* (435d–439b).

I am more inclined to think that, when he wrote the *Phaedo*, Plato had no properly elaborated view of how exactly propositions are images, or of what it is that they image. I suspect that he took it to be pretty much a commonplace that language somehow represents reality, and did not stop to enquire more closely. Consequently I think it is probably wrong to put much weight on the remark that propositions and physical objects are equally images; we need not infer that a close parallel is intended. No doubt physical objects are supposed to be images of forms, in the way that the *Republic* explains. But, as the *Phaedo* does not explain this, the remark cannot have been meant to clarify the claim that propositions are images. It is merely an aside, and the claim about propositions is, presumably, not thought of as in need of clarification.

In that case, there is no doubt a qualification to be made. Certainly it is a commonplace thought that language somehow represents reality, and this may seem justification enough for supposing that propositions also must somehow represent reality, but one is not likely to take it as a commonplace that this applies to *false* propositions. One is more likely to say that false propositions do not represent reality but *mis*represent it; they are not images or likenesses (εἰκόνες) of anything, but at best are things that merely seem to be likenesses (φαντάσματα, as they are called at *Sophist* 236b). It would be out of place to pursue here the difficulties involved in these ideas (which gave Plato some trouble in much later dialogues), but the point can anyway be made without relying on the questionable view of propositions as images. If Socrates hopes to study 'the truth of things' (τῶν ὄντων τὴν ἀλήθειαν, 99e6) in propositions he must evidently be wanting *true* propositions, and the method must be designed to show that certain propositions are true. We shall see in a moment how it is meant to do this.

The one thing that we can say already is that the method can only be expected to yield definite results for certain rather special propositions, namely those that can be seen to be true or false a priori. This is simply because the new method is supposed *not* to make any use of the evidence of the senses. It is true that Socrates does not quite say this directly. He does indeed say that his earlier attempts failed because of the way they did make use of the senses, but it would, at first glance, be possible to hold that they went wrong because they used the senses in the wrong way, i.e. too 'directly'. Perhaps the new method is permitted to make some use of the senses, but a more 'indirect' use? But I think it most unlikely that this was Plato's own view of the matter. In the earlier part of the dialogue it has been stressed over and over again that the soul can think properly only when it pays *no attention whatever* to the senses (e.g. 65a9–66a10, 79c2–d8, 82d9–83b4), and the new method is surely meant to be a proper method of thinking. Indeed it is the only information in the *Phaedo* on how one can think without relying on the senses. Admittedly, it is a consequence of the Recollection Argument that the senses must be assigned *some* role: though they do not *give* us our understanding of the concepts which we employ in thinking, still they are needed to reawaken that understanding. But once we do understand the relevant concepts, then we are supposed to be able to employ Plato's new method without paying any further attention to what the senses can tell us.

How, then, do we proceed? Once the relevant concepts have been (re)acquired so that we do at least understand the propositions in question, how can we find out anything about their truth without resorting to perception? In broad outline, Plato's answer is 'by reasoning', for valid reasoning is indeed a priori: we do not need the senses to tell us that one proposition follows logically from another. So let us now look more closely at just how Plato thinks that pure reasoning might by itself establish the truth or falsehood of some propositions.

(ii) *100a3–7.* The initial account in 100a is merely a preliminary sketch. In effect it tells us that we are to proceed by setting up hypotheses and seeing what follows from them, but it does not yet show how this procedure can determine the truth or falsehood of any propositions. Even so, there are still some points about this initial account that require clarification. What Socrates says is that he hypothesizes on each occasion the theory (*logos*) that he judges strongest, and puts down as true whatever seems to him to accord with it, and as false whatever does not accord with it. What does he mean by 'strongest', and what does he mean by 'accord'? I take the second question first.

Whatever 'accord' means, Socrates cannot have said quite what he intended when he recommends a different treatment for the things which 'accord' and 'do not accord' with the hypothesis. The difficulty emerges when we consider propositions totally irrelevant to the hypothesis adopted. For example, suppose we have adopted the hypothesis that there are forms, and we are now faced with the question of how to treat the proposition that it will rain tomorrow. It must, presumably, either accord with our hypothesis or not, but if we say that it accords then apparently we must set it down as true, while if we say that it does not accord then apparently we must set it down as false, and it is obvious that either of these would be stupid. The hypothesis simply has no implications at all for the proposition that it will rain tomorrow, and does not affect the question either way. The reasonable procedure, of course, is to set down as true what *follows* from the hypothesis, and to set down as false what *conflicts* with the hypothesis, i.e. what is *not consistent* with it; and this, or something like this,[6] must be what Socrates has in mind. But since following from is not the same as being consistent with, there will be some propositions that neither follow from our hypothesis nor conflict with it, and these we should simply leave undetermined by the hypothesis. This, then, was a slip on Socrates' part, but since it is easily corrected I shall not fuss about it any further.

A more interesting question is what Socrates means when he recommends us to adopt the 'strongest' hypothesis. It seems very probable that what he has in mind is similar to what Simmias had in mind in 85c, when he said that, if the truth seems not to be discoverable, then one should 'adopt the best and least refutable of human doctrines (*logoi*)'. Here Simmias explains the *best* available theory as the one which is least open to refutation, and that could equally be called the *strongest* theory. (We shall learn more of what it is to refute a hypothesis from the next passage.) But there is another question worth raising here. It would be natural to suppose that there can only be one hypothesis that is 'the strongest', i.e. stronger than all others, and if so it should apparently be that one that Socrates adopts on all occasions. That is to say, we should expect him always to adopt the *same* hypothesis, presumably the hypothesis that there are forms. But again I think the truth is that he has not quite said exactly what he intended.

The later passage at 101d–e shows clearly enough that Socrates does not really suppose that only one hypothesis is ever available.

[6] I turn later to the question whether it is exactly the strictly logical notions of following from, and being inconsistent with, that Plato intends.

We are told there that when the time comes for you to give an account of your hypothesis you should do so 'in the same way, once again hypothesizing another hypothesis, whichever seems best of those above' (101d5–7). But I think we can extract more from this passage than just the admission that more than one hypothesis is possible. Socrates says that when you put forward your second hypothesis you will be proceeding *in the same way*, which presumably means in the same way as when you set up your first hypothesis. But on the second occasion you do not choose the best (i.e. strongest) hypothesis absolutely; you choose the best *of those above* (i.e. above the first hypothesis). This is because you are here concerned with a particular problem, the problem of giving some justification (account, *logos*) of your first hypothesis. So the 'higher' hypothesis should be one which does this; it should provide a reason for supposing that the first hypothesis was true. That is, you do not look for the 'strongest' hypothesis absolutely, because that may not be of any use for the problem in hand; you limit your attention to 'those above', because they are the ones that will resolve your problem. Since this is said to be proceeding 'in the same way', it seems reasonable to infer that the same constraint applies to your original choice of the first hypothesis. There too you will have had some particular proposition to be proved, or some particular problem to be investigated, and so you will choose what seems to you to be the strongest hypothesis that is useful for that purpose. Different problems will naturally lead us to begin with different hypotheses, for a 'strong' hypothesis on one topic may be of no help with another topic.

There are in fact two different hypotheses about forms that are set up in our dialogue. The present passage introduces the hypothesis that there are forms *and they are causes*; the Recollection Argument makes use of the hypothesis that there are forms *and we know them*. The first is of use when our problem is to say what kind of a thing a true 'cause' must be, and in particular when we wish to substantiate the claim that the cause of a thing's being *P* must itself be *P* and cannot be not–*P*. The second is of use when our problem is to explain how we understand language, and in particular when we wish to show that this understanding is recollection. It is not absolutely clear that Plato realized that these were two different hypotheses, for in both places he has a tendency to write as though the only hypothesis being invoked were the simple hypothesis that there are forms. On the other hand when he concludes his whole series of arguments at 107b, he warns us that 'the initial hypotheses' still need to be examined more clearly, and the plural shows that he does think more than one hypothesis was used. This *may* be because he also has in mind some quite different hypothesis, e.g. the principle of the Cyclical Argument that opposites come from opposites, but I am more inclined to think that that argument has dropped out of consideration by now. However that may be, the concluding passage certainly confirms my view that there is no *one* hypothesis that Socrates always begins with, whatever the tasks in hand. Further confirmation may be drawn from other dialogues, and it will be worth our while to look briefly at what happens in the *Meno*, where we first hear about how to use hypotheses.

In the *Meno* the topic is virtue (ἀρετή). Meno has opened with the question whether virtue can be taught, and at first Socrates insists in his usual manner that that question must be postponed until they have first discovered what virtue is (70a–71b). Meno, who thinks that is a simple problem, is soon shown that it is not, and reduced to perplexity (71e–80b). He asks Socrates how they could hope to succeed in this question of what virtue is, and in reply Socrates expounds the theory that what is needed is recollection of what we once knew perfectly well, and goes on to demonstrate that such recollection is possible (80d–86b, discussed earlier pp. 110–15). Nevertheless they do not in fact continue the search for what virtue is, and Socrates agrees to consider instead whether virtue can be taught, provided he may do so with the help of a hypothesis (86c–87a). It is then agreed that if virtue is knowledge it is teachable, and if it is not knowledge it is not teachable, which apparently introduces the hypothesis Socrates had asked for (87b–c; cf 89c–d).[7] So the question has now become the question whether virtue is knowledge. Socrates proceeds to tackle this by introducing the further assumption that virtue is good, commenting that that is a hypothesis which they will not abandon (αὕτη ἡ ὑπόθεσις μένει ἡμῖν, 87d3). There then follows

---

[7] The text is not very clear about just which proposition is the one called the hypothesis. To conform with the *Phaedo*'s terminology it should be the proposition that virtue is knowledge, but on two occasions it seems rather to be the conditional proposition that if virtue is knowledge it is teachable (89c3–4, 89d3–5).

an argument that is meant to show that if virtue is good it must be knowledge (87d–89c), but Socrates later finds a mistake in this argument (97a–98b), and the dialogue ends with the position that virtue is good, but is not knowledge, and is not teachable.

Four points are here worth noting. First, Socrates is using the technique described—but not used—in the *Phaedo* of (attempting to) defend one hypothesis by recourse to another 'higher' hypothesis. The first hypothesis is that virtue is knowledge, and the higher hypothesis is that virtue is good. The idea is that the first hypothesis should *follow from* the second higher hypothesis (although in the end it turns out with this example that it does not). Second, the hypotheses here have nothing directly to do with forms, and obviously do not pretend to be hypotheses that can resolve *all* problems; they are relevant to the *Meno*'s topic, but would not have been of any use in the *Phaedo*. Third, the method of hypothesis is apparently regarded even in the *Meno* as a second-best method. The really satisfactory procedure would have been to concentrate first on the question what virtue is, and the answer to that question would have shown whether it is teachable or not. But, despite Socrates' defence of 'what is *X*?' questions, he does not actually proceed in that way. One may speculate that Plato (like Meno) had become somewhat perplexed as to how a positive answer to such a question could ever be obtained, and the technique of arguing from a hypothesis was perhaps introduced as a way of getting some worthwhile results while avoiding that apparently unanswerable challenge. Finally, it is worth observing that Plato's earlier dialogues are full of *refutations*: time and again an answer suggested by some disputant is proved to be *wrong*. But here Plato is, perhaps for the first time, asking how any thesis might be proved *right*. The *Meno* offers the suggestion that a thesis can sometimes be proved if an initial hypothesis is granted, but naturally we shall now want to know why that hypothesis itself is worthy of acceptance. This brings us back to the discussion in the *Phaedo*.

(iii) *101d3–e3*. This passage is perplexing in several ways. I first give what I take to be orthodox interpretation (which is mainly due to Robinson (1953), ch. ix), and then notice some of its difficulties. We may split the passage into three sections.

(*a*) 'If anyone hung on to the hypothesis itself, you would dismiss him, and you wouldn't answer till you should have examined its consequences,[8] to see if, in your view, they are in accord or discord with each other.' According to the orthodox view, the situation envisaged here is that someone *attacks* your hypothesis, claiming that it is false or anyway unwarranted. Your reaction is to pay him no attention until you have satisfied yourself that the hypothesis does pass its first test, namely that its consequences are in accord with one another and not discordant. This means that the consequences are *consistent* with one another. Presumably a hypothesis that fails this test has shown itself open to refutation, and therefore not sufficiently 'strong'.

(*b*) 'When you had to give an account of the hypothesis itself, you would give it in the same way, once again hypothesizing another hypothesis, whichever should seem best of those above, till you came to something adequate.' Apparently the time comes for you to give an account of the hypothesis itself when you have completed stage (*a*) and satisfied yourself that its consequences are consistent. We can perhaps add that your hypothesis would have been first introduced in order to give an account of something, and that is why the phrasing suggests that you now turn to a *new* giving of account, an account of the hypothesis itself. This is to be done, as I have already said, by finding a new hypothesis from which the original hypothesis follows. But the new hypothesis may equally be attacked, in which case you repeat the procedure, first checking its consequences for inconsistency and then looking for a yet higher hypothesis from which it will follow. You continue in this way until you come to something 'adequate'. We are not told what this would be, but presumably it must be something which is not in its turn open to a similar attack.

(*c*) 'You wouldn't jumble things as the contradiction-mongers do, by discussing the starting-point and its consequences at the same time, if, that is, you wanted to discover anything.' Here we are to understand the starting point (ἀρχή) as the hypothesis, and stage (*b*) is counted as 'discussing the starting-point' while stage (*a*) is counted as 'discussing its consequences'. The advice is to see that these two stages are kept separate. (But it is not very clear

---

[8] ὁρμηθέντα, i.e. the things that proceed from the hypothesis. The word is somewhat vaguer than the translation 'consequence' may suggest. For example, it is possible that it is meant to cover the step from the hypothesis that there are forms to 'what comes next', viz. that they are the only true causes (100c3).

why the mistake of muddling them together should be thought especially characteristic of 'the contradiction-mongers'.[9])

The main difficulties with this interpretation concern stage (*a*). First, it is doubtful whether the phrase translated as 'hanging on to' the hypothesis in 101d3 could possibly mean adopting a *hostile* attitude to it, as this interpretation says. The difficulty is especially acute as the same phrase has occurred only two lines earlier in the opposite sense of continuing to hold the hypothesis *true* (101d1–2; cf. 100d9). The abrupt change of sense is very startling. Second, the procedure recommended seems so very odd. One would suppose that a hypothesis which had inconsistent consequences would never have appealed to you as a 'strongest' hypothesis in the first place. Moreover, if this test is a serious one, then one would suppose that it should be carried out before the hypothesis is even proposed. It is strange to find that you should undertake it only when someone attacks the hypothesis, and stranger still to find that when that does happen you should at first simply dismiss the attack, in order to carry out your test, apparently in the contemptuous way that Socrates has just said he will dismiss the 'subtleties' of physical causes (101c7–9). This seems very bad manners. Third, when at the end we are told not to muddle stages (*a*) and (*b*) together, stage (*a*) is described as discussing the consequences of the hypothesis and *not* the hypothesis itself. But according to this interpretation stage (*a*) is intended as a test of the hypothesis, and so surely *is* a way of discussing the hypothesis itself.

In the light of these difficulties one naturally looks for an alternative interpretation, and a tempting suggestion is this. A perfectly appropriate thing to say about arguing from a hypothesis is that one should separate these two questions. (i) Does the conclusion we are aiming for really follow from the hypothesis introduced? (ii) Is there any reason to accept the hypothesis? In other words: (i) is the argument valid, and (ii) is the premiss true? (It was the first of these that went wrong in the *Meno*: the conclusion that virtue is knowledge did not actually follow from the hypothesis that virtue is good). If stage (*a*) in our text is supposed to represent this first question, then it is not after all

---

[9] οἱ ἀντιλογικοί. These people are no doubt to be identified with the people 'bent on victory' who are referred to at 91a2–6 as caring nothing for the truth. Plato gives us a portrait of them in his *Euthydemus*.

meant as a test of the hypothesis and can quite properly be described as a discussion of its consequences and not of it. Perhaps this is what Plato means? Could we perhaps understand our text along these lines: 'If someone else[10] hung on to the hypothesis (i.e. accepted it, as you do), then you would dismiss it (the hypothesis, i.e. the question whether it is true) and would not answer (that question) until you had examined its consequences . . .'?

But this suggestion cannot be carried through. The alternative reading proposed so far is already somewhat forced, and the continuation of our sentence must destroy it. For it says that you are to examine the consequences 'to see if, in your view, they are in accord or discord with each other', and this cannot be reconciled with the suggested interpretation. Admittedly in 100a when Socrates speaks of things which 'accord' (συμφωνεῖ) with the hypothesis he seems to have in mind things which follow from it (though also when he speaks of things which 'do not accord' he seems to have in mind things which are not consistent with it). But it is altogether too much to suppose that the phrase 'accord or discord' (συμφωνεῖ ἢ διαφωνεῖ) could be used to mean the things that follow or do not follow. Propositions which are in discord with one another must evidently be in disagreement, in conflict: it is not enough if they simply fail to follow from one another. Besides, the relevant question (on this interpretation) is whether the desired consequences follow or do not follow *from the hypothesis*, not whether they follow or do not follow *from the another*, which is simply irrelevant. I conclude that this alternative interpretation collapses, and I have no other alternatives to suggest. The crucial point is that Plato must be envisaging a situation in which the various consequences of our hypothesis disagree with one another, and surely he intends that in that situation the hypothesis should be rejected. There seems no avoiding the conclusion that stage (*a*) is meant as a test of the hypothesis, and that is the main feature of what I called the orthodox interpretation.

I think, therefore, that the orthodox interpretation must in fact be accepted, and we simply have to swallow the difficulties that it

---

[10] The suggested construction seems to require reading ἄλλος for αὐτῆς in 101d3. (Alternatively we might retain αὐτῆς and explain: 'if someone hung on to the hypothesis itself (as you are hanging on to the safe part of it)'. Cf. p. 159 n. 4 above.)

involves.[11] In this passage, then, Plato is telling us of two different ways of testing a hypothesis, or defending it against attack. The first is to examine its consequences, and make sure that they do not disagree with one another. If a hypothesis passes that test, then we should try to find a higher hypothesis from which it follows (and which also passes the first test, presumably). This should be continued until you come to something 'adequate', which must at least mean something that finally blocks the attack. How should we react to this? Does it really show us how some truths can be established without relying on the evidence of the senses?

B. CRITICISM OF THE METHOD

It seems improbable that a single hypothesis should of itself give rise to consequences which are inconsistent with one another. As a matter of fact it is not impossible. To take a famous example, Frege adopted the 'hypothesis' that for any predicate there is always a class which has as members just those things that the predicate is true of. Considering, then, the predicate '. . . is not a member of itself', we deduce that there is a class which has as members just the things that are not members of themselves. It then follows that this very class is a member of itself if and only if it is not a member of itself, which is a contradiction. For if it is a member of itself then it is also not a member of itself, and if it is not a member of itself then it also is a member of itself. Either way, it both is and is not a member of itself. That is to say, our single hypothesis has consequences which contradict one another. But although this can happen, it is evidently very unusual. Indeed if we use the word 'consequence' strictly, to mean what follows by logic alone, then most hypotheses—taken just by themselves—have no interesting consequences at all.

What we normally have in mind when we speak of the consequences of a hypothesis are not strictly consequences of that hypothesis by itself, but consequences which follow from it together with other things that we believe anyway. For example, one would no doubt count the hypothesis that God created

---

[11] As is often noted, the first difficulty, concerning the meaning of 'hang on to', could be avoided by supposing that our manuscripts, contain the wrong word and need a small correction (ἐφοῖτο for ἔχοιτο in 101d3). The other two remain.

everything as having the consequence that God created men, but not as having the consequence that God created unicorns. This of course is because we believe anyway that there are such things as men, but do not believe that there are such things as unicorns. Again, this same hypothesis presumably has as a consequence that God created himself, which is a perfectly good ground for rejecting it, because it is surely impossible for anything to create itself. In fact one would be likely to say that, because of this consequence, the hypothesis is *self*-contradictory, although the truth is that it contradicts, not itself, but a different claim about creating which we feel very sure of. In general, we do not in practice use the notions of 'consequence' and 'contradiction' in quite the strict way that a modern logician would desire.

Bearing this in mind, we can see that Plato's first test is not unreasonable. For example, Plato evidently thinks that this first test rules out various rival hypotheses about causes, and it is fairly clear why he thinks this. To take just one instance, he thinks that the hypothesis that a head may be the cause of one thing's being larger than another can be ruled out in this way, because it meets the 'contradiction' (ἐναντίος λόγος) that the same thing may cause both largeness and smallness (101a5–8). Now the hypothesis that a head may cause largeness does not by itself strictly imply that a head may also cause smallness, though it is quite natural to write as though it did, since anyone who accepts the first is very likely to accept the second too, as the cases are entirely similar. Again the two claims that a head causes largeness, and that it causes smallness, do not actually contradict one another, though they do together contradict the claim that the same cause cannot have opposite effects (granted also that largeness and smallness are opposites, as we ought strictly to add). So if, like Plato, you take it to be an obvious truth that the same cause cannot have opposite effects, then the two claims about the head will present themselves to you as conflicting with one another. If this is on the right lines, then we can say that what Plato's first test in fact comes down to just this: examine whether your hypothesis is consistent with all the other beliefs that you already have. Several quite interesting hypotheses, and not just the rather silly example discussed here, might fail this test.

But when we do put the first test in this way, it reveals a difficulty: it is now not at all clear that a hypothesis which fails this test ought to be rejected. Certainly, whenever we find a contradiction we know that at least one of the premises that led to it must be rejected, for contradictions cannot be true. But we do not necessarily know *which* of the premises should be blamed. It may indeed be the new hypothesis which is wrong, but it may also be that the new hypothesis is perfectly correct, and that some other belief we held, and relied upon in deriving the contradiction, is mistaken. This is apt to be concealed from us if we think of the contradiction, as Plato does, as coming *just* from the hypothesis in question. Indeed, as Robinson has pointed out (op. cit., ch. iii), Plato has a tendency to think of *all* refutations as arguments which show that some thesis contradicts *itself*. But this is somewhat loose logic, and when we look more strictly we see that the first test is not nearly so conclusive as it might at first seem: when a hypothesis appears to give rise to a contradiction there will nearly always, when we look more strictly, be other premises involved too, and the fault may in fact lie in them, and not in the hypothesis under test.[12]

Anyway, suppose our hypothesis passes the first test, and is consistent with everything else we know or firmly believe. It clearly does not follow that it is true. As Plato himself remarks elsewhere, mere consistency is not by itself a guarantee of truth (*Republic* 533c, *Cratylus* 436d). For example the hypothesis that there is life elsewhere in the universe is consistent with everything we know or firmly believe, but so also is the hypothesis that there is life only on this earth, and they cannot both be true. This is presumably where the second stage of the method is supposed to help: we are to seek for a 'higher' hypothesis from which the original will follow, and then if necessary for one still higher, and so on until we reach something 'adequate'. But, even supposing we could always do this, how would it help? On the face of it, even a successful advance to a higher hypothesis would still leave us with mere consistency, and no better guarantee of truth.

In fact, something will have been gained by a successful advance. The higher hypothesis to which we ascend will presumably be a more general hypothesis, and so will have many *extra* consequences which the original did not have. So the first test will need to be applied again, and as we now have more consequences

---

[12] *One* way of understanding the second part of the *Parmenides* is that it is meant as a protracted illustration of exactly this point.

to consider there will naturally be more chance of our new hypothesis failing on the first test if it is mistaken. Consequently, if it does not fail, our confidence can reasonably be increased. There are many examples of this from the history of science. For instance, Galileo put forward a hypothesis about how bodies move when they are falling freely near the surface of the earth, namely that they move downwards with a constant acceleration, and that the rate of acceleration is the same for all bodies. He showed that his hypothesis was consistent with all the evidence he obtained from some highly relevant experiments. But later Newton put forward a much more general theory, his theory of gravitation, from which Galileo's laws about falling bodies followed as a special case. But Newton's theory, being more general, also had many other consequences, e.g. that the planets moved round the sun in ellipses, that the motion of the moon round the earth would cause tides, and so on. Because this was a much 'higher' hypothesis it was much more open to falsification by the evidence, and yet—so far as anyone could see—it was not in fact falsified. This naturally increased people's confidence a great deal. In fact Newton's theory had so many consequences, none of them conflicting with the available evidence, that people came to look on it as pretty well certain truth.

However, that was over-confidence. What one can reasonably say is that Newton's theory was *more probable* then Galileo's, because it was so much more general, and therefore so much more open to falsification, and yet not falsified. But it was a mistake to regard it as certain; we now know (due to Einstein) that it is not quite right after all. Generalizing, then, we may say that a successful advance to a higher hypothesis, which has more consequences but is still consistent with all our evidence, can reasonably be said to increase probability. But it cannot ensure certainty. Indeed it is a truism nowadays that science, which employs something very like Plato's method, can never attain certainty. Whatever theories we currently adopt, there is always the possibility that new evidence may overthrow them. In Plato's terminology, this seems to be a way of saying that science can never succeed in reaching 'something adequate'. Of course this need not be taken as a criticism of Plato's own position, for he could no doubt reply that his own concern is with philosophy and not science. But it leads us naturally to the question of how he proposes to reach 'something adequate', and what he means by this. Was I in fact right to suggest just now that what he means is 'something absolutely certain'?

The one thing he says about it himself would leave it open to us to adopt a much less demanding interpretation. He is speaking of what to do when your hypothesis is attacked, and in that context a satisfactory reply might well be to show that it follows from another hypothesis which the man attacking you agrees to. In other words, an 'adequate' hypothesis might simply be one that your present antagonist accepts: it is adequate *ad hominem*. Now certainly Socrates does sometimes speak as though an argument that is adequate *ad hominem* is what he mainly requires (e.g. *Gorgias* 474a; cf. 471e–472c), but it is almost always coupled with the idea of an argument that genuinely reaches truth (ibid.), and he is always scornful of those who argue for victory and not for truth. He says this clearly in our dialogue at 91a–b, where he also connects the notion of truth with what satisfies him, and not just his audience. From this we can at least infer that an 'adequate' hypothesis must be one that you accept yourself, as well as one that your present antagonist accepts, and I think it reasonable to go on to add that it should be one that *all* possible antagonists would accept, and not merely the one presently confronting you. Otherwise it would be more or less an accident that a hypothesis happened to prove 'adequate' on this or that particular occasion, and it does not seem to me likely that this is what Plato means. But the idea of something that would satisfy all antagonists seems much the same as the idea of something absolutely certain: no rational man could object to it.

This suggestion at least fits the discussion of the *Meno*, where the highest hypothesis put forward is that virtue is good. Plato does seem to imply that this hypothesis is 'adequate' when he says that it is one we shall not abandon (87d). Why not? Well, a natural suggestion would be that it is regarded as evident a priori, or 'self-evident'. It is not supposed to depend on our observations of virtuous people, observations that might at some future time be upset by further observations. Rather, we know before we start that anything *properly* called a virtue must be good, because that is part of what 'virtue' means. But that implies that any rational person will accept this 'hypothesis'; if you do not accept it you simply show that you do not understand what you are talking about. It is true that if we take a broader view of the whole structure of the *Meno* we may be tempted to place a further condition on what would count as a *really* adequate hypothesis about virtue: it should ideally be one that answers the Socratic question 'what is virtue?' If we look ahead to the *Republic* (507–17) we shall suggest that in the end there is only one 'hypothesis' that is completely satisfactory, and that is the one that answers the Socratic question 'what is goodness?' But these are extra requirements that receive no support from the *Phaedo*, and they cannot replace the main requirement, which is that an adequate hypothesis is one that no rational man can object to. It must be 'self-evident'.

Philosophers since Plato have often hankered after ultimate premises that are self-evident, because if the premises are admitted to be doubtful then it seems that the conclusions drawn from them must be equally doubtful, and all their doctrines will be without adequate foundation. But it is interesting to notice that Plato's own theory of method is less extreme on this issue than is, for example, Descartes' theory.[13] Descartes held that the proper method of philosophizing is never to admit any premises that are not self-evident, and to proceed always by self-evident steps of reasoning from these self-evident premises. By contrast, Plato allows us to begin by reasoning from hypotheses that are not self-evident, but we hope eventually to reduce these to more ultimate hypotheses that are self-evident. Of course if Plato's desired reduction could be achieved, then that would show that Descartes' method was equally applicable. But Plato at least allows us to get started without insisting that we complete the reduction first. In fact Plato would never have claimed that he had himself accomplished this reduction. It remained for him an ideal demanded by theory but never in practice achieved.

After all this, what are we to say about Plato's theory on the correct method of philosophizing? First, given the questions that Plato regarded as falling under philosophy—e.g. the question whether the soul is immortal—it would seem to be a vain hope that these could eventually be settled by appeal to purely self-evident premises. However, the point is difficult to argue, because the

---

[13] I have in mind mainly Descartes' *Meditations*, not his *Discourse on Method*. Even so, what I say is something of an over-simplification.

notion of a self-evident truth proves to be a very difficult one. In fact some philosophers have denied that there are any truths at all that deserve to be called self-evident. Others have admitted that there are some, but claimed that they cannot tell us anything important, since they merely reflect our own decisions about what our own language is to mean. For example, if it is indeed a self-evident truth that virtue is good—something that we can see at once to be true independently of observation—then that can only be because it is our decision that this shall be part of what the word 'virtue' means. If we take this view of all self-evident truths, then an enquiry which proceeds from self-evident premises by self-evident steps of argument can never do more than tell us about our own language, which is certainly not what Plato wanted to know about. But on the other hand it is very doubtful whether this view can give any adequate explanation of our ability to discover new truths in logic and mathematics, where it certainly appears that we do proceed a priori but are not just discovering our own linguistic habits. Since these issues become very complicated, I shall not attempt to say more about them here, but must leave this question open. What we can say, however, is that Plato himself never claimed to have reached the ultimate reduction to purely self-evident premises, and for our purpose it will be enough to concentrate on the earlier stages of his method, which he did profess to be able to carry out.

Here we can make one simple and important criticism: in its earlier stages the method is *not* independent of perception, as Plato apparently thought that it was. This becomes clear when we bear in mind my earlier observation that when a contradiction is deduced from some hypothesis many *other* premises will be employed besides the hypothesis itself. These other premises will be propositions we know or believe on other grounds, and very often the ground will be perception. The point can perfectly well be illustrated from the *Phaedo* itself, where Plato offers a refutation of the hypothesis that the soul is an attunement. (This is explictly called a hypothesis at 94b, and contrasted with the hypothesis of the Recollection Argument at 92d6.) According to his own argument, that hypothesis should be rejected because it has the consequences that all souls are equally good, and that reason never does control desires and emotions. But how are we supposed to know that these consequences are false? No doubt it is a matter of 'common sense' that they are false, but 'common sense' is here evidently relying on 'common observation'.

In fact, as I remarked earlier, Plato's recommended method for philosophizing has many similarities with what is now a well-known view of the proper method for empirical science, the so-called 'hypothetico-deductive' method. But this is a sensible method for science because its hypotheses have to fit the data obtained from experiments, and without this test any hypothesis would seem to be as good as any other. Plato sees well enough that our hypotheses must somehow be tested, but it is a mistake to suppose that this can be done by pure reason alone, and without any help from observation and experiment to supply the 'extra' premisses that reason needs.

IX

THE FINAL ARGUMENT
(102b–106e)

THE little interlude at 102a, when Echecrates breaks in to express his approval of Socrates' exposition of the method of hypothesis, evidently marks a break in the argument. When we come back to our topic at 102b we begin upon the final argument for the immortality of the soul, which Plato thinks will clinch the matter. The first stretch of this argument aims to introduce a more interesting kind of cause than that which the 'safe and simple-minded' answer provides. In fact, though Plato does not draw attention to this, part of the 'safe and simple-minded' view will actually be abandoned: we shall no longer say that the *only* cause of a thing's being *P* is its participation in the form of *P*–hood, but will allow ourselves to cite other 'more subtle' causes as well. We then bring this discussion to bear on our target by applying it to the cause of *life*. The idea is that we are now no longer confined to saying that the reason why a thing is alive is simply that it participates in life, but can say instead that the reason is that it has a soul, for the soul always brings life with it. The soul, then, is the 'more subtle' cause of life, but—like all causes—the cause of a thing's being alive must itself be alive, and cannot admit the opposite of life, death. That is to say that the soul, as cause of life, cannot be dead, and must therefore be deathless, and hence immortal.

That is the overall tactic of this argument. We begin, then, by explaining the 'more subtle' kind of cause, being careful to preserve the principle that the cause of a thing's being *P* must itself be *P*, for that is going to be the crucial point when we come to apply these considerations to the soul.

A. 'MORE SUBTLE' CAUSES (102b–105c)

The strategy of the argument is only gradually revealed, and the fact that we have now discovered some 'more subtle' causes to take over from the original 'safe and simple-minded' causes is not announced until the end of this section (105c1–2). At the beginning the general drift of the argument is left somewhat unclear.

(i) *A 'form-in-something' as cause* (102b–103c)

Plato begins by introducing what I shall call a 'form-in-something'. He distinguishes between the form largeness itself and the largeness in Simmias (for example), and he says that his point is that both are alike in not admitting the opposite form, smallness. Largeness itself cannot be small, and the largeness in Simmias cannot be small either (102d5–103a3). They thus contrast with Simmias himself, who admits both largeness and smallness, since he is both larger than Socrates and smaller than Phaedo. This is to be explained by the fact that it is not 'by virtue of being Simmias', or 'because he is Simmias', that Simmias is large (larger than Socrates) (102c1–8). Presumably the point is that whereas Simmias is not large 'by virtue of his own nature', the largeness in him—like largeness itself—*is* large 'by virtue of its own nature'. But how are we to understand this phrase?

It would help if we could get clear why it would be wrong to say that Simmias is large 'by being Simmias'. Plato indeed seems to think that it is not strictly correct even to say 'Simmias is larger[1] than Socrates', but that is surely an exaggeration on his part. He no doubt believes that the word 'large' applies to Simmias only because of the largeness in him, i.e. only because Simmias participates in 'the large itself', and that the word 'large' applies in a more basic and fundamental way to the form, and only derivatively to the things that participate in that form (102b1–2, 103b6–8; c.f. 78e2). But still, it surely *does* apply to these things too, and it is not actually wrong to call Simmias 'large' or 'larger than Socrates'. What would be wrong would be to say that he is large, or larger than Socrates, 'by being Simmias'. But why would that be wrong?

A suggestion that may seem appealing is this: perhaps the point is that being larger than is a relation, and it takes *two* things to stand in a relation. Thus if Simmias is larger than Socrates that is not just because of the way Simmias is; it is also important that Socrates should be the way *he* is. Without any change in himself,

---

[1] I translate the verb ὑπερέχειν in the natural way, as 'be larger than'. Gallop prefers to use 'overtop'.

Simmias could cease to be larger than Socrates if Socrates grew somewhat taller. But although that is a perfectly sensible suggestion, it seems that it cannot be what Plato is thinking of, for the same point would apply not only to Simmias himself but also to the largeness in him. *It* could not be larger than the smallness in Socrates without some co-operation from the smallness in Socrates. It is true that Plato apparently thinks that the form, largeness itself, is large without being larger *than* anything (for it is large 'without qualification'). So he might perhaps think that the largeness in Simmias also manages to be large without being larger than anything. But that cannot be the point he is wanting to make here because he does permit himself to say that it is larger than the smallness of Socrates, in the twisted sentence at 102c10–d2. We may conclude that, whatever Plato's point is, it is not that largeness is a relation.

In that case, the point must presumably be that the property of being large, or larger than Socrates, is not an *essential* property of Simmias, which just means that he *could* lose this property while still remaining Simmias. We are going to be told shortly that being hot is an essential property of fire, and being cold of snow, and being odd of three. That is, fire (for example) cannot lose the property of being hot and still remain fire. Similarly, largeness is an essential property of the largeness in Simmias, but not of Simmias himself: he could exist—and could still be Simmias—without being large, but it could not. And that, Plato thinks, is the reason why we cannot say that Simmias is large (or larger than Socrates) 'by being Simmias' although we can say that he is large (or larger than Socrates) 'by the largeness in him': it is because the largeness in Simmias must necessarily be large (if it exists), though Simmias himself might not be. Thus, if we may add a point that is not quite in the text, the largeness in Simmias is eligible to be the *cause* of Simmias' being larger than this or that other thing, since it has to be large (so long as it exists) and cannot admit smallness. That is to say, it satisfies the principle that the cause of a thing's being *P* is itself *P*, and must be incapable of being not–*P*.[2] So here is our first example of a new and 'more subtle' kind of cause.

---

[2] There is a subtle shift here. 'Plato's principle of causation', as I stated it on p. 152, was in effect the principle that

It is necessary that: if anything *x* is the cause of a thing's being *P*, then *x* is *P*.

But the principle now under discussion is actually this more complicated principle:

Supposing this to be Plato's doctrine, what shall we say of it? I would say: first, that the doctrine very probably rests on the same mistaken way of construing causal statements that we have mentioned already (pp. 153–6); second, that the doctrine is awkwardly ambiguous; and third, that however we resolve the ambiguity it is a terrible muddle. I take these points in order.

Suppose that, faced with the question why Simmias is larger than Socrates, we offer the answer 'because of the largeness in him'. This answer seems at first glance to come to very much the same as the answer 'because *there is* largeness in him', which in turn is to say, in Plato's language, 'because he participates in largeness'. If this is right, then the answer does not really mention a *new entity*, the largeness in Simmias, but cites in an abbreviated way the same old *fact*, that Simmias participates in largeness. This fact concerns the familiar entities, Simmias and the form of largeness, and does not introduce a new entity at all. But perhaps this is being unfair. It may be said that the answer 'because of the largeness in him' does not mean to point just to the fact that there is *some* largeness in Simmias, but wishes instead to draw our attention to the 'particular' largeness that is in him, one that is larger than what is in Socrates. How, then, shall we construe this 'particular' largeness?

A natural answer would be that we are trying to talk of the particular *degree* of largeness that Simmias has, i.e. of his *size*—or, in this context, of his height, say 5ft. 11 in. Now a height such as 5ft. 11 in. is a universal, in that many things can all have the same height. On one way of construing Plato's forms, then, a height is itself a form. It is a *specific* form, falling under the more general form of largeness in much the same way as the specific virtues— justice, courage and so on—fall under the general form of virtue. On this account, then, the explanation does mention a new entity, Simmias' specific height, but this entity is simply another form—or anyway a universal[3]—like largeness. On the other hand philosophers from Aristotle onwards (*Categories*, 1a23–9) have perpetu-

It is necessary that: if anything x is the cause of a thing's being P, then it is necessary that if x exists x is P.

The second and more complicated principle does not follow from the first, but the first follows from the second. Since it seems in fact to be the second and stronger principle that Plato subscribes to, perhaps it has a better title to be called 'Plato's principle of causation'.

[3] I take up the question whether all universals are forms on pp. 196–201.

ally been tempted to suppose that the 'particular' largeness that is in Simmias is supposed to be 'particular' in the sense that it is *peculiar* to Simmias: it is *his* largeness, found in him and found nowhere else. On this view it is not a universal, but some kind of 'instance' of the universal; other people may have heights which *match* Simmias' height, but the heights which they have cannot be the *same* as Simmias' height, since it is to be understood as something found only in him. (Admittedly this does not seem to me a very natural way of construing the phrase, but for the sake of argument let us admit that it is a possible way.)

In both of these explanations, the largeness in Simmias could equally well be called Simmias' height, whether this phrase is then taken straightforwardly as mentioning the universal height which Simmias shares with others, or unexpectedly as referring to the 'instance' of this height which is found in Simmias and nowhere else. But this shows that neither explanation will fit what Plato says, for they each commit us to saying that the largeness in Simmias is exactly the same thing as the smallness in Simmias, since both expressions will equally refer to Simmias' height. Plato, however, claims that the largeness in Simmias is large and cannot be small, while the smallness in Simmias is small and cannot be large, in which case they evidently cannot be the same thing. No doubt it is perfectly in order to speak of heights as larger or smaller than one another (though *we* more naturally use the pair 'greater' and 'less' here). But just as Simmias is at once smaller than Phaedo and larger than Socrates, so also his height is both smaller than Phaedo's and larger than Socrates'. Apparently this cannot be what Plato was thinking of.

What, then, was he thinking? I fear that he was probably thinking in this way. If Simmias participates in the form of largeness, then some *chunk* of the form is lodged within him. Equally, if he participates in smallness, then some *chunk* of that form is lodged in him also. Since they are chunks of different forms they must be different from one another, though both dwell in Simmias. Moreover, the only character which the form of largeness has is that it is large, and the same character will therefore belong to any part of it. Similarly, any part of the form of smallness must be small, because again the form of smallness has no other property to pass on to it. Of course all this is totally absurd, and it is easy to make fun of it. The reason why I am inclined to think that it was nevertheless roughly how Plato was thinking is precisely that he himself later realized that it was absurd and did make fun of it. In the first part of his dialogue *Parmenides* he raises several objections to the theory of forms as we find it in the *Phaedo*, and one of them is precisely an objection to the way of thinking here sketched (*Parmenides* 131a–e). It is not unreasonable to conjecture that he thought it worth while to show that this way of thinking will not do because it was a way in which he had once thought himself. But whether this conjecture is right or not, still I think the only conclusion we can come to about this passage on forms-in-us is that it is simply a muddle. The main cause of the muddle is clearly the same misunderstanding of relations as we have noticed earlier (p. 105).

Before leaving this section, I add one further note on the idea of 'retreating' or 'perishing' (102d9), which is going to play some role in what follows. Under what circumstances does the largeness in Simmias retreat, and under what circumstances does it perish? Well, if what we are concerned with is Simmias' height, construed as a universal, then presumably it never perishes. It will remain in Simmias so long as he has that height, and will retreat from Simmias when Simmias changes in height, but may still go on being in other things. On the other hand, if we are supposed to be considering that particular 'instance' of largeness which is in Simmias and therefore *not* in anyone else, then it seems impossible for it ever to retreat: it cannot go anywhere *else* while remaining the particular instance that it is, for in order for it to be that same instance it must still be Simmias who has it. It therefore remains intact while Simmias stays the same height, and simply perishes when he loses that height. Much the same seems to apply if we construe the largeness in Simmias as the 'piece' of the form that is to be found in him, except that one might say instead that that 'piece' stays with him so long as he remains large, i.e. larger than something, and it perishes when he is no longer large, i.e. when he is not larger than anything. But again it does not seem possible for it to retreat. Commentators sometimes suggest that it somehow 'comes to the fore' when we compare Simmias with the smaller Socrates, and retreats—i.e. 'takes a back seat'—when we compare Simmias with the larger Phaedo. But (*a*) this seems to overlook the fact that Simmias still *is* larger than Socrates when we are busy comparing him with Phaedo, and besides we may of course make both comparisons simultaneously. Moreover (*b*) there is evidently no answer to the question where it could go *to* when it retreats. So it seems to me that in the case of a form-in-something there are just two alternatives: either it persists or it perishes. Why, then, does Plato bring in the option of retreating? Only, I suggest, because this is a genuine option in the case of *other* 'more subtle' causes. So let us now move on to consider these.

(ii) *Causes that bring opposites with them* (103c–105c)

The main outline of this passage seems reasonably clear. It begins by pointing out that certain things, though not opposites themselves, always and necessarily have one of a pair of opposite characteristics. Thus fire is always hot, snow is always cold, and three is always odd. That is to say, there cannot be such a thing as cold fire, hot snow, or an even-numbered trio. Hence if you do try to cool fire, heat snow, or even up a trio then *either* you will fail because the fire or whatever escapes you—it 'retreats'—*or* you succeed in a sense, i.e. you do cool it down, but then what you are left with is not fire: the fire has 'perished' (103c–104c). The next step introduces the idea that fire, snow, or three can 'occupy' things, or 'get hold of' them (κατέχειν: 104d1, 104d6); in another phrase, they can 'come up to' things (ἰέναι ἐπί τι: 105a3–4; cf. 104d9–10, 104e1); in yet another phrase they can simply 'come to be in' things (ἐγγίγνεσθαι: 105b9, c3, c9). (Those somewhat vague phrases are evidently intended as interchangeable, as is clear from the way they are all subsequently applied to the soul's relation to the body.[4]) When they do this, they bring with them in addition the opposite that always characterizes them, and can thus be called the cause of the thing's having that opposite. For example, if fire gets into a body, then since fire itself is always hot, the body too will become hot, and we can say that fire is the cause of this. As Socrates says, this is a more interesting kind of cause than the 'safe and simple-minded' cause we began with, but he also says that it is still, in its own way 'safe' (105b6–8). He does not explicitly say why, but I do not think his reason can be seriously in doubt: it is 'safe' to cite fire as the cause of something's being hot because fire is itself necessarily hot, and cannot be cold: being hot is an *essential* property of fire.

---

[4] By *coming to be in* a body, the soul makes that body a living body, so whatever the soul *occupies* it always *comes to* it bringing life (105c9–d4).

But although the general outline may be reasonably clear, there are problems with the details. Some commentators have urged that the new and 'more subtle' causes here introduced are still, like the old, intended to be *forms*, while others have denied this. Now one of the examples, namely three (or threeness, or triohood)[5] certainly is a form: we are told so explicitly at 104d6. We have no such explicit statement for fire or snow, but instead we have this general consideration. It was stated in the Recollection Argument that perceptible things always fall short of forms, which we took to mean that they never provide unambiguous examples of forms. So, since there surely are forms of the opposites hotness and coldness,[6] we can apparently infer that no perceptible thing can be unambiguously hot; it must also be, in a way, cold as well. Consequently the fire that is here in question, which we are told *is* always hot and never cold, cannot be a perceptible thing. It must, then, be the *form* of fire that is meant. Similarly, it must be the *form* of snow.

A further argument to the same conclusion might be drawn from the definition of these 'more subtle' causes at 104d1–3. Unfortunately, this is one of the very few places where I cannot accept Gallop's translation, so we must first pause to get this right. Gallop translates:

Would they be these: things that are compelled by whatever occupies them to have not only its own form, but always the form of some opposite as well[7]

According to this translation, the 'subtler causes' are not occupiers but things occupied, which is plainly at variance with the general run of the text (esp. 105d3). Moreover it defines these things occupied as things compelled by *whatever* occupies them to have not only its own form but another in addition. This is clearly nonsense, and it leads at once to an infinite regress of occupying forms. (Say *x* is one of these things, and is occupied by *P*–hood.

---

[5] Since Plato's language does not distinguish the number three from the property of being a trio, I shall equally ignore the distinction.

[6] At 106b6–7 the hotness in the fire is surely meant as an example of a form-in-something.

[7] Ἆρ᾽ οὖν τάδε εἴη ἄν, ἃ ὅτι ἂν κατάσχῃ μὴ μόνον ἀναγκάζει τὴν αὐτοῦ ἰδέαν αὐτὸ ἴσχειν, ἀλλὰ καὶ ἐναντίου [αὐτῷ] ἀεί τινος. On *any* interpretation the bracketed αὐτῷ makes no good sense; it should either be dropped altogether or replaced by τῳ (as Robin).

Then *P*–hood imports another opposite form *Q*–hood, which also occupies *x*. Hence *Q*–hood in turn imports yet another opposite form *R*–hood, which again occupies *x*. And so on.) Add to this that, as Gallop admits, this translation requires a change in the manuscript reading that other translations would avoid,[8] and I think we can fairly conclude that the translation is indefensible.

The obvious alternative translation, which seems to me a far more natural way of taking the Greek, is:

Would they be these: things which compel whatever they occupy to have not only its (or: their) own form but always the form of some opposite as well.

Strict grammar would require the translation 'its own form', but then the thought is somewhat odd: the thing occupied presumably has 'its own form' all by itself; it does not need to be compelled to do so by the thing occupying it. So it is more natural to suppose that the 'subtler causes' are occupiers which compel whatever they occupy to have *their* own form, i.e. the occupier's form. This slight shift in grammar is by no means unusual in Plato,[9] and the thought seems to be exactly what the next sentence illustrates:

Whatever the form of three occupies must be not only three but also odd (104d5–7)

That is, whatever the form of three occupies must not only have the form of three (i.e. the occupiers' form) but always the form of some opposite (namely the odd) as well. If all this is right, then not only are the 'subtler causes' occupiers, but they also compel whatever they occupy to have 'their own' forms (as well as the forms of the opposite they bring with them). This very strongly suggests that the occupiers *are* forms, and the reference to 'their own forms' is simply a reference to 'them'.

But for all that, the conclusion to which these arguments point cannot be correct. One may reasonably doubt whether Plato, at this time, believed that there was a form of fire, or of snow—I shall take up this point later (p. 196–201)—but in any case it is surely not those forms that he is talking of here. One strong indication of this is his use of the alternatives 'retreat or perish'. Presumably no form can ever perish, but an ordinary perceptible fire can certainly

---

[8] αὐτὸ in line 2 must be dropped or changed to αὐτὰ.

[9] A similar shift from neuter plural to neuter singular occurs in our dialogue at 70e5.

be quenched, and an ordinary lump of snow can certainly be melted. But a more crucial point is that this whole section is working up to the final step, by which we recognize that the soul is itself one of the 'more subtle' causes. This simply cannot mean that the *form* of soul is a 'more subtle' cause, for if it did then what Plato would be labouring to prove would be that the *form* of soul is immortal. That is obviously absurd. All forms are automatically immortal, and it is clearly no comfort to *me*, when faced with death, to be told to cheer up because the *form* of soul will not perish. What is of concern to me is my individual soul, and that must be what the argument is meant to be about.

How, then, do we explain the points I have just mentioned as seeming to show that the 'more subtle' causes always are forms? Well, to the first we simply have to say that it is after all the physical stuffs fire and snow which Plato is crediting with essential properties. I suspect that at this stage he had not noticed the apparent tension between this claim and the claim that physical things always 'fall short of' forms. But a position that he adopted in later dialogues would certainly allow him to reconcile the two, for according to this later position fire (for example) would be an inadequate example of heat just because it is not permanent: perhaps it must always be hot, and never cold, so long as it exists, but the trouble is that it is liable to cease existing (cf. e.g. *Timaeus* 48e–51b). That, however, is a speculation going somewhat beyond our text; so far as the *Phaedo* itself is concerned all we can say is that there does seem to be some tension, but we shall get into an impossible position if we try to resolve it by supposing that it is forms and not physical things that are under discussion.

It is less obvious what we should say about the definition of the 'more subtle' causes in 104d1–3. We must, I think, retain the view that these causes are occupiers rather than things occupied, but we cannot accept that they compel the thing occupied to have 'their own form'. No doubt this is all right when the occupier *is* a form, as is the case with the example of threeness, which is what Plato is mainly thinking of here. But where the occupier is not a form this leads to absurd results. For example we should have to say that when fire occupies something that thing becomes fire, when snow occupies something that thing becomes snow, and when the soul occupies something that thing becomes a soul. This is obviously wrong. The body which has a soul in it does not become itself a soul. Yet the alternative of sticking to what grammar strictly requires, viz. that occupiers compel a thing occupied to have 'its own form', is also somewhat strange. It would follow that when a soul occupies a body it compels that body to have 'its own form' (the form of a body?), as well as to be alive. Similarly, when snow seizes upon a patch of mud it compels that mud to have 'its own form' (the form of mud?) as well as to be cold. The thought still seems somewhat odd, for the reason given earlier, and besides it apparently commits Plato to a whole new range of forms which it is not clear that he would have welcomed. At any rate, when later in the *Parmenides* he explicitly raises the question whether there is such a thing as the form of mud, it is clear that Socrates shrinks from an affirmative answer (*Parmenides* 130b–e). As we shall see, this is not without reason (pp. 201–2).

I conclude that Plato *may* have meant to be taken as grammar strictly requires ('its own form'), but in that case he probably has not thought through the implications of what he says. But I think the slightly ungrammatical reading ('their own form') is equally, if not more, probable, and in that case we can only say that his writing is distinctly careless. He is, as the surrounding context shows, thinking of the case where the occupier is a form, and has not noticed that what he says does not fit the case where it is not. But it is essential to his argument that these 'occupiers' do not have to be forms. At least the second attempt at a definition, at 105a, is free of these difficulties.

To sum up, these 'more subtle' causes are a mixed lot. Some of them are forms, e.g. the form of threeness, but others are not. Some of them are forms-in-something, if we were right about the general bearing of that passage, but again others are not. (Notice that at 106b6–7 both fire and the hotness in fire are cited as causes of the 'more subtle' kind.) Some of them are physical stuffs such as fire and snow. We are also given fever as an example (105c3–4), which is something of a different kind again, but as this example seems ill chosen on several grounds it is probably best not to press it.[10] At any rate, the list gives us little guidance on how to conceive of the most important example of these new kinds of causes, namely the soul. No doubt it is intended to be something invisible

---

[10] Fever, understood as the condition of having too much heat in the body, would seem to have an opposite, viz. having too much cold in the body. Moreover both of these opposites can cause illness, and neither does so by being ill itself.

and incorporeal like a form, but also something that is a particular individual like a lump of snow. Some have speculated that it is supposed to be a form-in-something, the idea being that my soul is 'the life in me', but the text lends no support to that idea at all. Whatever it is, Plato thinks that he can now prove that it is immortal, so let us at last come to the final stage of this long argument.

B. THE SOUL AS CAUSE (105c9–106e1)

Socrates begins by securing agreement to the premiss that that which brings life to the body is the soul. Incidentally, it is worth noting the parenthetical claim of 105d1 that 'this is always so'. We observed earlier (p. 139) that in general the 'more subtle' causes, while they may perhaps be sufficient conditions of their effects, are not necessary conditions. It is not true that all odd-numbered things are trios, or that all cold things are occupied by snow. However it does happen to be true, Plato thinks, that all living things are occupied by souls: having a soul in one is both a sufficient condition for being alive and a necessary condition too. It follows that the argument (if successful) will prove that *all* living things have immortal souls, not only those which are capable of thinking and reasoning, but also (e.g.) aphids, jellyfish, and (presumably) cabbages. In other words, this argument will give us no reason to connect the soul with consciousness in particular: what is relevant is that it causes life—any kind of life, and not just the rather special kind of life that humans have.

The next step is to claim that since the soul brings life to the body, it must be alive itself, and cannot admit the opposite of life, namely death (105d6–12). In this context we need not fuss about the fact that life and death are not properly viewed as opposites (p. 52), as it will do no harm to understand 'dead' as simply meaning 'not alive'. The claim is that the soul must be alive, and cannot be not alive. The ground for this claim is simply what I called Plato's principle of causation, that the proper cause of a thing's being P must itself be P and must be incapable of being not-P, so long as it exists. I have already argued that this principle is wholly mistaken (pp. 153–6), and it does not help to point out that there are *some* examples of causes—for instance, fire, snow, three—which seem to satisfy it. For equally there may be others which do not. Moreover, even if we were to grant Plato that all *proper* causes should satisfy it, there is still a gap in the argument here, for it now needs to be shown that the soul is a *proper* cause of life, and not just a cause in the everyday sense in which, say, the wind causes the windmill to revolve. (This is not because the wind is itself revolving.) However one looks at it, this step in the proof is clearly unwarranted.

But suppose for the sake of argument that we accept that what causes life must itself be living. Perhaps life is after all a special case to which Plato's principle does apply. Suppose indeed we accept that the soul, as cause of life, cannot admit death in just the same way that fire, as cause of heat, cannot admit cold, and snow, as cause of cold, cannot admit heat. What would follow from this? Well, it does not of course follow that you cannot apply heat to a piece of snow. The only thing that follows is that, when you do, you do not end up with a piece of hot snow. Either you still have some snow, in which case you have failed to heat it, or you succeed in heating it, but then what you have left is not snow. The case will be exactly similar with the soul. When you try to bring death to a soul, you will not end up with a dead soul; there cannot be such a thing as a dead soul any more than there can be hot snow, cold fire, or an even three. But that is not say that you cannot successfully bring death to a soul, in just the way that you can successfully bring heat to snow. It is just that, when you do, what you have left—if anything—is no longer a soul. Our premiss states that being alive is an essential property of souls, which is to say that a soul must always be alive *so long as it exists*. But it does not follow that souls always do exist, just as it does not follow that snow always does remain snow. In other words, even if we grant all Plato's premisses so far, the most we can conclude is

(i) Souls cannot die and still exist.

From this it does *not* follow that

(ii) Souls cannot die.

Which of these does Socrates mean when he argues at 105d13–e9 that it now follows that the soul is immortal?

Of course the word 'immortal' (more literally 'deathless', ἀθάνατος) *usually* means (ii). But equally, it might be said, the word 'unheatable' (ἄθερμος, 106a3) would *usually* mean what could not be heated *at all*, and the word 'uncoolable' (ἄψυκτος, 106a8) would *usually* mean what could not be cooled *at all*. So, in their usual senses it would not be true to say that snow was unheatable or that fire was uncoolable. Since Socrates does feel quite prepared to say these, he is perhaps aware that he is not using these words in quite their usual sense. In that case, he may also be aware that he is not using the word 'immortal' in quite the usual sense either. Perhaps, then, his claim that the soul is immortal is only meant to claim (i), that souls cannot both die and still exist, which is what his argument would entitle him to. Indeed, he at once develops the idea that there is something more to prove, namely that the soul is also imperishable (105e10–106d1), which seems to show very clearly that he is not using the word 'immortal' in its usual sense. For in the usual sense it is surely obvious at once that a living thing which is immortal—i.e. cannot ever die—must also be imperishable and indestructible.

But unfortunately when we turn to see what further argument Socrates will provide, we find that there simply is no further argument. Socrates says 'if it's granted us that the immortal must also be imperishable, then the soul, besides being immortal, would be imperishable too. But if not, another argument would be needed.' And Cebes' disappointing reply to this is 'But there's no need of one, on that score at least.' Cebes takes it to be just *obvious* that whatever is immortal will also be imperishable; no further argument is needed. As I have just said, that *is* obvious if the word 'immortal' is taken in its *usual* sense, and Cebes plainly is taking the word in its usual sense. This confirmed by the next line, where he adds that the immortal, 'being everlasting', will surely not admit destruction. That is, he simply takes it for granted that the immortal is everlasting. But if we bear in mind what the word 'immortal' *ought* to be meaning in this argument, 'cannot die *and still exist*' then there is no reason to suppose that the immortal is everlasting. I conclude that Plato has not in fact seen that further argument is required, because he too is taking the word 'immortal' in its usual sense.

Since this is extremely disappointing, commentators have endeavoured to find a further argument in this closing section at 106d2–9. The text perhaps suggests an argument on these lines. The first premiss is:

If there is anything that is indestructible, then what what is immortal is indestructible (d2–4).

The second premiss is:

But there is something indestructible, namely God and the form of life (d5–7).

And from these we draw the required conclusion that what is immortal is indestructible. But (*a*) this would be a completely unconvincing argument, for there would be no reason whatever to agree to its first premiss. And (*b*) it is anyway obvious that Plato is not trying to argue. When he slips into the first premiss the phrase 'the immortal, *being everlasting*', he shows that he has not seen the problem, and similarly when he slips into the second premiss that God, and the form of life, '*and anything else immortal*' is certainly indestructible. Thus the statement of each of these alleged premisses in fact includes, as an aside, a presumption of the conclusion they are supposed to be establishing. They cannot, then, be intended as premisses from which that conclusion will follow, and the truth must be that Plato has not seen that further argument genuinely is needed.

The long final argument, then, turns out in the end to be something of an anticlimax. We have laboured through a lengthy, and often perplexing, discussion of causation which attempts to substantiate the principle that the true cause of a thing's being *P* must itself have the property of being *P*, and must have it essentially. But even if this principle is granted, and it is granted also that the soul is the true cause of life, still the desired conclusion will not follow. For to say that life is an essential property of the soul is just to say that the soul must be alive so long as it exists, and if we regard this as claiming that the soul is 'immortal' ('deathless'), then certainly the word 'immortal' is being used in an unusual sense. But Plato has failed to notice this. Taking it for granted that the word is being used in its usual sense, he thinks it must obviously follow that the soul exists for ever. And I am afraid that this is simply a mistake which we can do nothing to put right.

I add one last comment on this final argument. When you succeed in heating up a piece of snow you do of course have something left, namely some water. The snow ceases to exist—since, for snow; to exist is to be snow—but it does so by changing into something else that is no longer snow. But what would be left if you succeeded in bringing death to a soul? Since it seems obvious that an immaterial soul could not change into any kind of material thing, we seem to need the idea that when a living soul dies it changes into a non-living but still immaterial thing—an inert and lifeless 'soul-corpse'. But this seems a very weird idea indeed: we have no conception of a non-living and immaterial thing. Another suggestion might be that the soul is a composite object, and at death it dissolves into a number of separated parts—immaterial soul-fragments, still living perhaps, but wandering desolately in isolation, until they are recombined into new wholes. But on reflection this can seem just as weird an idea as the last: we can only conceive of an immaterial being as a centre of consciousness, and we cannot really picture a soul as made up of *several* centres of consciousness, *each* capable of existing in isolation from the others. So in the end one is likely to be driven to the conclusion that, if an immaterial soul dies, it will just vanish altogether, and there will be nothing of it that remains. Yet this infringes the ancient principle that nothing can be destroyed into nothing, just as nothing can be created from nothing, and it may well seem rather difficult just to declare that that principle does not hold for immaterial things.

Putting all these points together, one can see how Plato may quite rightly have felt that there was something very funny about the idea of a dead soul, and so have tried to build an argument around the thesis that dead souls are impossible. As we have seen, the argument that he constructed did not in the end work out too well, but one might have some sympathy with the underlying idea.

X

THE THEORY OF FORMS

SOCRATES concludes his arguments for immortality by saying that to make further progress we need to examine the 'initial hypotheses' more closely (107b4–6). I shall accordingly end this book with a brief attempt to do this, at least for the chief hypothesis that there are forms. Obviously a full commentary on Plato's theory of forms would be a major work in itself, and I do not set out to do anything so ambitious. I shall be concerned only with those issues that arise fairly directly out of what the *Phaedo* has to say on the topic. It will be useful to begin with a brisk recapitulation.

A. FORMS IN THE *PHAEDO*

We are first introduced to forms in the course of Socrates' Defence at 65d–66a. As always in Plato's dialogues, the topic is introduced as a familiar one, and Simmias agrees without hesitation that there are forms of justice, beauty, goodness, and so on. He similarly agrees at once that they are not to be grasped by the senses, but by the intellect alone, as if this were nothing controversial. As all 'wisdom' is taken to lie in the understanding of forms, this explains why the true philosopher will pay no attention to the senses: what they can tell us about is not what he wants to know.

We learn more of the nature of forms from the Affinity Argument (78c–79e). We are told there that they are incomposite and of one form only (μονοειδές, 78d5), and for that reason they are not liable to change, and are eternal. It can be inferred from this that they exist independently of their embodiment in perceptible things, which is at least part of what Aristotle means when he says it was Plato's idea to 'separate' the forms (sc. from particulars. *Metaphysics* M4, 1078b30–2). For presumably there might come a time, or there might have been a time, when no just men existed; but that would not affect the existence of the form of justice in any way. (Compare *Symposium* 211b, where we are told that the form of beauty is in no way affected by the various things that participate in it.) The Affinity Argument does not explain why a form should be regarded as incomposite and 'of one form only'. Nor does it explain why the various things that participate in it should be said to be 'named after it' (78e2). But these points become clearer if we look into the role that forms have to play in the two serious arguments which invoke them: the Recollection Argument and the Final Argument.

In both it emerges that it is a crucial point about the form of *P*–hood that it is *unambiguously P*, which is to say that it is *P* and is not also in any way not–*P*. It is this characteristic of forms that entitles them to be regarded as causes in the Final Argument, and as 'the missing paradigms' in the Recollection Argument. For the form is contrasted with the perceptible objects that are *P*, on the ground that they always combine being *P* with being not–*P*, which is why they are said to fall short of it. So they are never 'of one form only', but combine two opposite forms, which it does not. Moreover, Plato thinks that our grasp of the notion of *P*–hood depends upon our having met an unambiguous example of this kind, and hence our employment of the word '*P*' can be said to derive from this original acquaintance. That is no doubt why he thinks of the word '*P*' as applying primarily to the form, and only derivatively to the things that participate in it.

It is true that much of the Recollection Argument is in fact independent of this—or any other—view of forms. The main claims of that argument can be stated simply as the claims that we do understand our language, and that the only source of knowledge available in this life, perception, cannot account for this. To substantiate the latter claim one needs the point that perceptible things which are *P* are also not–*P*, but one does not yet need to suppose that there must therefore be something else which is *P* without being not–*P*. (It is enough to point to the obvious fact that the word '*P*' means being *P* and does not mean being not–*P*). However, from these premises one can at best infer that the relevant knowledge was with us when we came into this world, not that it was acquired *before* then. It is to make this last step plausible that we must call upon Plato's positive view of how we do come to understand the word '*P*'.

The Final Argument relies on forms even less directly. The crucial claim of that argument is that the cause of a thing's being *P* must itself be *P* and cannot be not–*P*, and in fact Plato never does argue directly for this principle. His tactic seems to be to recommend it in the first place on the ground that forms are the most obviously satisfactory causes, because they clearly do have the full generality that he desires, and forms at any rate do satisfy the principle. He then goes on to show that the principle is satisfied in other cases of causation too, namely his 'more subtle' causes, and this part of the argument has little to do with forms, except insofar as one of his examples is again a form. (And notice that here too he is presuming that the form of *P*–hood is itself *P*. The form of threeness compels the trios that it occupies to be odd-numbered because it is *itself* odd-numbered, and that is presumably because it is *itself* a trio.) We may say, then, that this characteristic of forms is helpful in recommending the needed principle about causation, but it does not provide a direct argument for the principle, and in fact no direct argument is ever given.

This roughly summarizes the part that forms in fact play in the arguments of the *Phaedo*. I now wish to raise two questions about forms on which the *Phaedo* is somewhat reticent. First, what forms are there? Second, what is the relation between the forms and the particulars that are called after them?

(i) *What forms are there?*

The *Phaedo* gives us no clear answer to this question. As prominent examples of forms we have justice, beauty, goodness, and holiness (65d, 75e, 100b), and again largeness, smallness, and of course equality (75c, 100b). We also hear of health and strength (65d), and during the course of the final argument of hotness and coldness (103e), odd-numberedness and even-numberedness (104a–c), and life and death (105d, 106d). Indeed the final argument would appear to treat *all* opposites as forms. It incidentally adds to the list of those specifically mentioned the opposite of health, namely illness (105c4), and perhaps also musicalness and unmusicalness (105d17). But at the same time it makes clear that not all forms are opposites. The forms of one and of two have been mentioned at 101c, and from 104a–c it is clear that there is a form for each number, and these are not opposites. Apart from this list, we have very little to guide us on the general question, and are mostly left to speculate.

On the one hand it is perhaps relevant that Socrates never shows any hesitation in claiming something to be a form, as if some alleged cases might be doubtful, and this may well suggest that there will be a form for whatever you care to mention. The suggestion seems to be strongly confirmed by the way that he treats the formula '*x* is *P* by participating in *P*–hood'. He evidently takes this formula to mention a form, but he also regards it as entirely 'safe', which apparently implies that it is always safe to assume the existence of a form.[1] Again, on one way of reading the obscure definition of the more subtle causes at 104d1–3, it is explictly implied that anything occupied by a subtle cause will have 'its own form' (p. 186).

However, there are at least two points to be made on the other side. First, the one *reason* that we have for positing forms is to provide adequate paradigms where ordinary perceptible paradigms are missing, and one would not have supposed that perceptible paradigms always are missing. We know that Plato did think they are missing for the numbers (*Republic* vii, 524d–526a), and for such forms as justice, beauty, and goodness, and of course for equality. We can add that he also thought they were missing for such pairs of opposites as large and small, double and half, light and heavy (*Republic* v. 479b), and again thick and thin, hard and soft (*Republic* vii. 523c–524d). This accounts for a good number of the examples on our list, and would account for them all if we supposed that Plato had allowed himself to generalize from these opposites to all opposites. (But, if he did, the generalization was too hasty. The *Phaedo* itself admits—perhaps without noticing it— that there are adeqate perceptible paradigms for hot and cold, namely fire and snow, and it gives us no reason to expect a difficulty with paradigms for living and dead.) Second, there is the general consideration that forms are supposed to be the philosopher's special concern, and are to be studied without the help of the senses. This is also the suggestion of the one place in the *Phaedo* where a general characterization of forms is hinted at: at 75d Socrates says that he means to include 'everything on which we set this seal, *What it is itself*, in the questions we ask and the answers we give'. The questions and answers in point here are presumably those that *philosophers* address to one another. One would not suppose that philosophers do conduct dialectical enquiries into the true natures of sticks and stones, or hope to discover this by pure thought. Perception would seem to be an

---

[1] But see p. 159, note 4.

adequate guide here, as it appears to be on the question 'what is a finger?' (*Republic* vii, 523c–d).

We must say, then, that so far as the *Phaedo* is concerned the evidence on this question is somewhat inconclusive, but we do get more positive guidance from later dialogues. The bulk of the *Republic* would be quite consistent with the view that the range of forms is fairly limited: the only new category that is clearly added to the examples of the *Phaedo* is that of geometrical figures, e.g. 'the square itself' (*Republic* vi. 510d). But in the last book, which is a kind of appendix to the main work, we find Socrates announcing that he is accustomed to posit a single form for *any* set of many things that are all called by the same name (*Republic* x. 596a). He at once goes on to introduce forms of beds, tables, and bridles, and similarly in the *Cratylus* we have forms of shuttles and awls (389a–c). One role which these forms have is that they provide a pattern or guide for the craftsman, who fixes his eye on the form when deciding how to make these various artefacts. In the *Timaeus* the same line of thought is extended to natural objects, e.g. fire and man, where the Craftsman in question is now the creator of the world. But it is not clear whether we should regard this as a ground for supposing that there must be such forms: to judge from the announcement of *Republic* x the mere existence of a common name is by itself an adequate ground.[2] At a later date, then, Plato evidently believed in a very wide range of forms indeed, but of course it by no means follows that he also held that view when he wrote the *Phaedo*. Before resuming discussion of this question, let us first turn to the other.

(ii) *How are forms and particulars related?*

If forms are conceived of as unambiguous paradigms—the really adequate examples of things that *P*, because they are *P* without also being not–*P*—then the correct thing to say about the relationship between forms and particulars seems to be that the particulars *resemble* the form, but also fall short of it. We have already noted (p. 91) that in the *Phaedo* Plato seems strangely coy about asserting this resemblance outright, though he certainly hints at it, and he asserts it clearly enough elsewhere. In the

---

[2] At a later date again, we learn that some names do not after all correspond to forms, because they do not really indicate a common characteristic, e.g. βάρβαρος, which just means 'not Greek' (*Statesman*, 262)

Republic, Phaedrus, and *Timaeus,* particulars are constantly called images or copies of forms, and said to 'imitate' them or 'reflect' them. But on this view it is not a very natural turn of phrase to speak of particulars as *sharing* in forms, and it is quite distinctly wrong to say that particulars have forms *in* them. What is in a particular may perhaps be a (partial) resemblance to the form, but it cannot be the form itself.

The standard terminology of the *Phaedo* seems to be the sharing terminology. The words usually translated 'participate in' (μετέχειν, 100c5 and 101c3–6) and 'partake of' (μεταλαμβάνειν, 102b2) could equally well be translated 'share in'. They carry the suggestion that each participant will share by taking or possessing its own share of whatever is in question, as you and I may share in a cake by each having a piece of it, but by themselves they do not force that interpretation. Socrates' other suggestions at 100d5–6 'whether by the presence of the form, or its communion,[3] or in whatever way the form attaches to it' are equally somewhat vague, and are evidently meant to be so. In fact he says that he is deliberately not committing himself to any definite account of this relationship. Nevertheless the terminology is, as I say, not quite what one would expect if the relationship is actually that of a defective example of something to a better example of the same thing.

It later looks very much as though Socrates is indeed thinking of sharing pretty much as in sharing a cake. When he proceeds at 102b–e to distinguish the form of largeness from the largeness in this or that thing, it is difficult to find any interpretation of the passage that does not adopt the picture of each particular large thing having its own piece of largeness in it. Perhaps it is unfair to press this too far, for certainly the text is not very explicit about it, but at least this much can surely be said: Plato sees nothing specially odd or inappropriate about saying that forms are *present in* the particulars that are called after them. But this surely is notably odd and inappropriate if forms are unambiguous examples. In fact much of the terminology is very much better suited to the idea that the form is not so much an example of something which is *P* but is rather the property of being *P*. The property can quite naturally be said to be in things, or present to them, or shared by

---

[3] κοινωνία: there is no satisfactory English equivalent just because the Greek word covers such a variety of relationships.

them, though none of these can be reasonably be said of an example of a *P* thing.

There are two other points which strongly suggest the same conclusion, one of them again a matter of vocabulary. Plato often refers to forms by using the peculiarly Greek idiom 'the equal itself' or 'the large itself', where it may be said that the correct English translation is uncertain. He also uses some other peculiar phrases of his own devising, which it is not easy to understand. But as well as these he is also quite willing to use explicit abstract nouns, 'equality' or 'largeness', to refer to forms, and these are much more naturally taken to refer to the property of being equal, or the property of being large, rather than to any examples of large or equal things. Another consideration is this. Plato always takes it to be obvious that there is just *one* form of each kind (explicit at *Republic* x 597c, but implicit throughout), and this is indeed obvious if forms are properties. There cannot be more than one property which is the property of being *P*. But it is by no means obvious that there can be only one unambiguous example of a thing that is *P*: on the contrary, if there can be one then there seems no reason why there should not be others too, each just like the first one.

To sum up, we can find in the *Phaedo* traces of two quite different views of what the forms are: on one view they are unambiguous examples of properties, and on the other view they are the properties themselves. (The same two views can also be found side by side elsewhere, e.g. in the *Republic*). This may perhaps be connected with the fact that we also seem to find two different views on what forms there are. In so far as forms are examples of *P*-hood, examples which illustrate what it really is to be *P*, it is quite natural to find them restricted to those properties which do not already have satisfactory perceptible examples. And it is, of course, just such properties which do tend to interest philosophers. But in so far as forms are not examples of properties but the properties themselves, there seems no special point in such a restriction. Whenever we can single out certain things as the things that are *P*, it seems automatic that there must be a property they all share, namely the property of being *P*. And there is no call to say that some of those properties are forms but others not. In sum, the *Phaedo* seems to contain two quite different theories side by side: one is a theory of missing paradigms, and the other is a theory of properties. But they are not distinguished from one another, and both are regarded as the same theory, the theory of *forms*.

B. PLATO'S OWN CRITICISM OF FORMS (*Parmenides* 129–135)

Plato's early dialogues are by and large tentative, questioning, and critical. The middle dialogues, from the *Phaedo* (and *Symposium*) onwards, are altogether more positive and confident. But there comes a reaction: the *Parmenides* and the *Theaetetus* are both critical dialogues once more, and now it seems to be the theories of Plato's own middle period that are being subjected to criticism. At any rate, it is clearly Plato's own theory of forms that is being criticized in the *Parmenides*, at 129–35, and this criticism is well worth looking at. In this dialogue Socrates is portrayed as a young man, talking to the much older and more famous philosopher Parmenides of Elea. He has been led to propound the theory of forms in 129–130a, and Parmenides then proceeds to question him on it.

Parmenides begins by asking what forms there are (130b–e). Socrates had already mentioned forms of likeness and unlikeness, and of oneness and manyness, in his initial statement, and he now confirms that indeed he does believe in these forms as things separate and apart from the particulars that share in them. He then accepts without hesitation that there are also forms of justice, beauty, goodness, and so on. But Parmenides next asks him whether there are forms of man, fire, and water, to which he replies: 'I have often been puzzled about these, not knowing whether to say that the same holds of them as well.' Finally, Parmenides asks whether there are forms of such lowly and undignified things as hair, mud, and dirt, and Socrates says: 'In no way. With these things they are just what we see, and it would be altogether too absurd to suppose that they have a form. And yet it has sometimes troubled me whether to say that the same thing holds in all cases. But when I am in that position I turn and fly, fearing to fall into a pit of nonsense and so perish.' On this Parmenides comments that it is because Socrates is young, and still pays too much attention to what the world will think of him. When he has had more experience of philosophy he will despise none of these things.

We can certainly infer from this little episode that Plato had now come to see the possibility of a wider and a narrower theory of forms. The narrower theory would admit only certain forms, and it is plausible to hold that they would be the forms where perceptible and unambiguous paradigms were missing. At any rate he has just made the point that this applies to the forms likeness and unlikeness, and oneness and manyness (129a–d), and he has often in the past made it of justice, beauty, goodness, and so on. He has also now seen that if there is a form of man, and of fire and of water (as the wider theory requires), then there is also a form of mud. The implication of our passage seems to be that one ought to accept these latter forms too. At any rate, it seems to be the wider theory that is under discussion in the rest of the *Parmenides*, for a little later on Socrates agrees that his reason for supposing there to be a single form of largeness is just that the many things that are each large must share in some one form (132a1–5). This would evidently apply just as well to the many things that are each men, or the many things that are each mud. It seems to be exactly the position of *Republic* x, that there is a form for every set of things called by the same name. But it is tempting to suppose that Plato has now recognized that he was not always committed to the wider doctrine, and that it makes 'a pit of nonsense' of some of the things he was wont to say about forms. In particular, it would be absurd both to hold the wider doctrine and to hold the view of the *Phaedo* that forms are the special concern of the philosopher, and can only be studied by ignoring what we can see. From the perspective of the *Phaedo*, mud is 'just what we see', and there is no form of mud.

Parmenides next turns his attention to the relationship between a form and the particulars that share in it, and are called after it (130e5). Taking it for granted that particulars share in forms by having forms in them, he first asks whether each particular has as its share the whole of the form or merely a part of it, and he tries to convince Socrates that both these alternatives are impossible (131a–e). Socrates does not wish to allow that forms can properly be said to have parts at all (131c9–11), but is reluctantly forced to agree that if a thing is spread over several different places it must, strictly speaking, be only a part of it that is in each place. (The unstated premiss here, which ought to be rejected, is that a form is something that occupies space in its own right.) Once it is admitted that a particular has only a part of the form in it, Parmenides turns specifically to the forms largeness, smallness, and equality, and professes to deduce numerous absurdities. For example, the parts of largeness will be *smaller* than the whole, smallness itself will be *larger* than its parts, and a part of the equal which is *not equal* (to the whole) will be what makes a particular *be equal*. Socrates agrees with him that these results are absurd.

Clearly the Socrates of the *Phaedo* would have to agree that these results are absurd. If accepted, they would show that the hypothesis of forms meets with just the same 'contradictions' as were taken on rule out other hypotheses on causation. From the point of view of the *Phaedo*, we cannot allow that the largeness in Simmias is a (spatial) part of largeness itself, for if it were it would not be incapable of being small (i.e. smaller than something), and so could not be something that causes Simmias to be large. Unless we abandon the principle of causation, it thus appears that the largeness in Simmias must be the whole of largeness itself, in which case the two are after all not different things. But so long as we can maintain the view that it is the whole of largeness itself that is in Simmias, we may—so far as this argument goes—continue to claim that largeness itself is always large and never small. But Parmenides' next argument calls that claim too into question.

This next argument (132a) is perhaps the most famous of all arguments against the theory of forms, and has become known as the argument of 'the third man'.[4] Parmenides opens with the suggestion that Socrates thinks there is a single form of largeness because he sees that many things are all large. But then, he asks, what happens if we now consider the form itself together with all these other large things? Will there not appear yet *another* 'large' by which all of them are large? As well as the original form of largeness, then, and the things that participate in it, there will be a further form of largeness, and then for all these yet *another*, by which they in turn are all large, and so on indefinitely. But there was supposed to be only *one* form of largeness.

It is clear at once that one of the premises to this argument is the assumption that the form of largeness is itself large, and that

---

[4] As Plato presents it, the argument is designed to show that besides ordinary large things, and the form of largeness, there must also be a *third* largeness. For reasons which need not concern us here, the argument was very soon rephrased as an argument about ordinary men, the form of man, and a *third* man.

the argument reaches an absurd conclusion. But must we conclude that it is *this* premiss that should be blamed for the absurd result? Let us look at the argument more carefully. One premiss is evidently this:

(i)　For any set of things which are all P, there is a form 'by which' they are all P.

(This seems to be pretty well the principle of *Republic* x.) Another premiss is:

(ii)　A form 'by which' various things are P must itself be P.

At a first glance, these are the only premisses. But the first glance is mistaken, for these premisses by themselves give rise to no awkward regress. Certainly, when we consider the set of ordinary P things, then from premiss (i) it will follow that there is a form 'by which' they are all P, and by premiss (ii) it will also be P. So we now have another set of things which are all P, and by premiss (i) again there will be a form 'by which' all of them are P. But why must this be *another* form? Why should it not be the *same* form as the one we began with? In that case, the form we began with, by which ordinary things are P, also has a form 'by which' it is P, but that form is simply *itself*. The form of P things is P 'by' itself. If this alternative is to be ruled out, then we must add a third premiss:

(iii)　The form 'by which' any P things are P cannot itself be one of those things.

If this premiss is added, then we do get a properly valid argument giving rise to a regress. In fact, granted that there is a form of *all P* things, premisses (ii) and (iii) yield an outright contradiction: by premiss (ii) this form is one of the P things, and by premiss (iii) it cannot be. So one of the premisses must certainly be rejected. But which one?

The right answer is that it depends upon what we are taking forms to be. If forms are supposed to be something like standard examples, so that other things are P *by resembling* the form, then premiss (ii) is correct and premiss (iii) is false. For example, if things are one metre long because they *resemble* the standard metre in Paris (in the relevant respect), then it too is one metre long because it *resembles itself*. That is, the set of all things which are one metre long are so because they all have the appropriate resemblance to something which is itself a member of the set. But of course one ought also to observe that, so far as most properties are concerned, premiss (i) looks very dubious in this interpretation. It is not very plausible to say that the set of things which are men are so because they all resemble some 'standard man' (whether the 'standard man' is supposed to be in this world or in another). On the other hand premiss (i) looks safe enough if a form is just a property, and the various *P* things are *P by having* that property (and not *by resembling* it). But on this interpretation we (nearly always)[5] find that premiss (ii) is false and premiss (iii) is true. For example the property of being a man, *by having* which the various men are men, is not itself a man.

The true moral to be drawn from this argument, then, is that we must choose whether to say that forms are properties which things *have* (participate in) or that they are standard examples which things *resemble* (but perhaps also fall short of). For the argument makes it very clear that we cannot say *both*. Of course there is nothing against holding that there are both properties and standard examples. Without any logical error, one could suppose that for each property there is a standard example, and that we come to grasp that property only by meeting the standard example. This may not, on reflection, be very plausible, but it involves no contradiction. The contradiction arises only if we carelessly suppose that the property *is* the standard example, and it must be admitted that the *Phaedo* does seem to be careless in just this way.

Although this is the true moral to be drawn from the argument, I do not think it very likely that Plato himself saw the matter in quite this way. This is partly because his own presentation in the *Parmenides* does not bring out premiss (iii) very clearly, but makes it look as though the contradiction arose from premisses (i) and (ii) alone. So he probably did not see that it was possible to retain premiss (ii) and avoid the contradiction by denying premiss (iii) instead. Moreover, a little further on Socrates explicitly suggests that the relation between forms and particulars *is* one of resemblance, and Parmenides argues that it cannot be, by an

---

[5] There do appear to be *some* properties which are properties of themselves. For example, it seems that being a property which has more than one instance is itself a property which has more than one instance. But there are deep problems here which I cannot go into. (Consider the property—which most properties apparently have—of not being properties of themselves, and apply the reasoning of p. 170.)

argument which is very closely similar to the one we have just been discussing (132d–133a). Parmenides argues that if two or more things resemble one another, then that can only be because they all share some one form, and again he tacitly assumes that the form they all share will not itself be one of the things that share it. Given this tacit assumption, then again a similar regress follows. But once more the assumption remains unstated, and Plato does not point it out to us, so probably had not noticed that he was using it. I think, then, that in Plato's own opinion the second of these regress arguments showed directly that the relation between forms and particulars could not be resemblance, and the first showed that it was wrong to say that the form by which the various *P* things are *P* was itself *P*. This is of course the right conclusion to draw if forms are properties, but premiss (i) by itself does not show that forms are properties.

Parmenides brings two further arguments in our passage, which I shall briefly mention but not examine in detail. In between the two regress arguments at 132a and 132d–133a Socrates has suggested that perhaps these difficulties could be avoided if forms are just thoughts, and exist only in our minds. So far as we know, this is not a suggestion that Plato himself had ever endorsed, and Parmenides soon disposes of it (132b–c). I shall say more about it later (pp. 209–11). Finally, Parmenides offers an extremely sophistical argument that is meant to show that even if there were forms we could not know them (133b–134e). This argument is so riddled with fallacy that it is hard to believe that Plato could ever have taken it seriously, and it seems to me more likely that he included it mainly as an example of the kind of muddle one can get into by thinking of forms as perfect examples inhabiting another world. But it is perhaps worth noting that Socrates makes no attempt to reply with the doctrine of recollection. *Perhaps* Plato was now feeling that this doctrine was altogether too extravagant a solution of the problems that led to it.

The passage ends with Parmenides saying that despite all these difficulties there must *be* forms, if coherent thought is to be possible (135a–c).

After all this criticism, what remains of the theory of forms as we find it in the *Phaedo*? It seems to me[6] that Plato himself

---

[6] I should point out that this view is controversial, but it would take me too far afield to argue for it now.

henceforth abandoned the whole notion of forms as standard examples, as things which exemplify unambiguously the properties which perceptible things can have only ambiguously. He does not stop talking about forms, but this way of thinking of them does not recur in any of his writings after the *Parmenides*. (Nor does the doctrine of recollection.) But whether or not this was Plato's own reaction, it is surely the right reaction. I have already criticized what appear to be the two main sources of this approach to forms, a genuine puzzle about how we understand our language (and particularly its evaluative terms), and a muddle about causation (pp. 101–10, 153–6). Besides, the result to which it leads is evidently absurd when one considers it more closely:[7] whatever property being *P* may be, there could not be a thing whose whole nature it is to be *P*, and which therefore has no other property than that of being *P*. This view of forms should, then, be rejected.

But this view was the crucial view so far as the arguments of the *Phaedo* are concerned. It seems to me, then, that Plato himself eventually abandoned the 'initial hypotheses' of our dialogue, and anyway they ought to be abandoned. If, as most of us would now think, the only defensible view of forms is one that simply identifies forms with properties, then the hypothesis that there are forms lends no support whatever to the arguments of the *Phaedo*. Nevertheless it is still of some interest to ask whether even this 'safe' hypothesis is actually correct. Are there really such things as properties? I end with some brief and inconclusive remarks on this question.

C. FORMS AS PROPERTIES

In traditional terminology, properties are *universals* rather than *particulars*, the idea being that a universal is something in which many particulars may participate. Our question, then, could be phrased as the question whether there are such things as universals. But as I see no advantage in this terminology I shall

---

[7] Note (*a*) that Plato himself accepts this result: it is what he means when he says that the form is of just one character (μονοειδές), and it is why he says that forms could not partake of *any* opposite characteristics (*Parmenides*, 129c–130a). Also (*b*) it is what his theory of language–learning requires: if a standard example of *P*–hood *also* had the property of being *Q*, then, when faced with it, I might take it as an example of *Q*–hood rather than of *P*–hood. In that case, my acquaintance with it would not explain how I understand the word '*P*'.

continue to speak of properties. (The same considerations would equally apply to relations, but we need not fuss over that.)

As I first introduced the notion (p. 44), a property is supposed to be what is predicated of a subject in a simple subject–predicate statement. Thus in the statement 'Socrates is wise' a certain property is predicated of Socrates, the property of being wise. So when we ask 'are there really such things as properties?' we are asking, *inter alia*, whether there is such a thing as being wise. To this the answer seems at first sight to be perfectly obvious: 'yes, of course'. But it is important to be clear that we do not mean by this question to ask whether there are any people (or other things) that are wise. Even if nothing is wise, still the Platonic view of properties insists that there is such a thing as the property of being wise (or 'wisdom itself', as Plato would say). Properties are supposed to exist independently of whether or not anything *has* them. For example, the statement 'the animal over there is a unicorn' is one which attributes to a certain designated object the property of being a unicorn. Even if such a statement is always false, nevertheless it has a perfectly good *meaning*, and that is enough to show—according to the view in question—that the property of being a unicorn is a perfectly good property.

To build a little more on this connection between properties and meanings, we rely on considerations of meaning to provide *criteria of identity* for properties. The property of being *P* and the property of being *Q* are counted as the same property if and only if to say of something that it is *P* is the same as to say of it that it is *Q*, which in turn will be the case if and only if the words 'is *P*' and 'is *Q*' have the same meaning. In a sense, then, properties just are meanings, but we must be careful to understand this in the right way. For one thing, the meaning of a word may evidently change over time, but (as the Platonic theory has it) properties never change. If some word does change its meaning, as e.g. the word 'spinster' now means an unmarried woman but used simply to mean one who spins, then the correct thing to say (according to this theory) is that the word used to mean (or signify, or connote, or whatever) one property, and now means (etc.) another. Those two properties were there all along, and neither has altered in any way; the change is in the language we use to speak of them, and not in them.

This brings out a further point, that just as properties exist independently of whether or not anything has them, so equally they exist independently of whether or not we ever think of them, or have any words for them. For example the Greeks had no word for a gas-cooker, or electricity, or an antibiotic, and no thought of them either. But this does not mean that the property of being a gas-cooker did not exist until modern times. On the contrary, properties exist timelessly, and no property ever comes into existence or goes out of existence. Consequently we should recognize too that there also exist many properties which *we* never think of and *we* have no words for, and which perhaps no one will ever think of or speak of. If one likes to look at it this way, properties can be thought of as 'possible meanings', but they would still exist even if there never had been any human beings, or any language to have those meanings.

That is the rough outline of a Platonic theory of properties. It does little more than apply to properties the clearly Platonic doctrines that forms are unchanging and eternal, and to contrast this with the everchanging nature of the physical world, including human thought and language. It would nowadays be called a 'realist' theory of properties, and it is quite possible to adopt 'realist' theories of other kinds of abstract objects too (for example numbers, or propositions), but we need not explore that now. Is it an acceptable theory? Well, there have been, and still are, many philosophers who are perfectly content with it, but also there have been, and still are, many who are not. Traditionally, the 'realist' has two main rivals, namely the 'conceptualist' and the 'nominalist'. I shall briefly outline each of these positions.

The conceptualist position broadly takes the line 'forms are thoughts'. It recommends us to cease believing in properties in the Platonic sense, and to speak in terms of concepts instead. Concepts are then to be construed as 'in our minds', and they are neither unchanging nor eternal. To put the position in terms of meanings, the idea is that it is a mistake to think of meanings as eternal objects somehow waiting for us to invent words for them. Rather, meanings are created by us, and owe their existence entirely to human thought. To believe in Platonic properties is, on this view, to make a mistake about what kind of things meanings are.

This is so far somewhat vague, and I shall not attempt to formulate any properly worked out conceptualist position. But it is worth drawing attention to one point that shows that a proper formulation is not entirely straightforward. We could put the issue in this way: the Platonist will of course be very happy to agree that there are infinitely many properties, but will the conceptualist wish to say that there are infinitely many concepts?

On the one hand, it seems that he is bound to. For example there is the concept of one grain of sand, and the concept of two grains of sand, and the concept of three grains of sand, and so on infinitely. There is no conceivable ground for breaking off this series at any point. We can go on up to the concept of one billion and thirty-two grains of sand, and then of one billion and thirty-three, and so on and on without end. But on the other hand if concepts are actual thoughts, or any actual states or occurrences in human minds, it seems absurd to suppose that there can literally be infinitely many of them. Our mental activity is limited, if only by the fact that it takes time to think and we live only for a finite time.

Faced with this dilemma, the conceptualist must, I think, retreat to saying that concepts do not have to be actual thinkings, or any other actual goings-on in the mind, but should rather be thought of as mental *abilities*. So we shall say that I 'have' the concept of so and so provided that I *could* think of so and so, whether or not I actually do. But then, if I may put the position crudely, concepts have turned out to be merely possible thinkings, apparently in much the same way as we said that the Platonist could view properties as 'possible meanings'. Is there, then, any important difference between them? Certainly, there is still a difference. The Platonist is thinking of what it is *logically* possible for some person (or some language) to mean, and that does not at all depend upon what people actually do think, or what languages in fact exist. By contrast the conceptualist is thinking of what it is *in practice* possible for a given person to think at a given time, taking his mental capacities as they are at that time, and not permitting any further experience or instruction. Doubtless this will depend to a fair extent on the thoughts he has actually had up to that time, and the language that he speaks. But still, given this way of looking at the debate, with both sides invoking the notion of possibility in one or another way, it may well seem that the dispute between them is more a matter of taste than a fundamental disagreement on what there is.

This is, however, rather a modern perspective, and is certainly not how the dispute at first appeared. It had seemed that the one side claimed that 'forms' (properties) existed independently of human thought and language, inhabiting a changeless and eternal realm of their own, while the other side claimed that 'forms' (concepts) were human creations, located in human minds, and just as subject to change and decay as any other piece of human handiwork. In a word, 'forms are just thoughts'. Seen in these terms, the relevant argument appears to be exactly the one that Plato himself gives in the *Parmenides* (132b–c).

Forms, Parmenides argues, cannot just be thoughts, because a thought must be a thought *of* something, and though the thought will be in a mind, what the thought is a thought of will not be. To put this in terms of concepts, the concept of being a unicorn is no doubt to be found in various minds, but what it is a concept *of*, namely *being a unicorn*, is not in anyone's mind (nor in any other place either). The argument may perhaps be strengthened a little by raising the question of *which* minds this concept is in. The answer must no doubt be that it is in several minds: I have the concept of a unicorn, and so have you, though some others may not. But we now have to explain how the *same* thing can be in many minds. In one sense, of course, a thought in my mind must be a different thing from any thought in your mind, just because one is mine and the other is yours. But in another sense we wish to say that you and I can have the same thought (the same concept). How so? Well, one naturally says that they are the same in that they are both thoughts (concepts) *of the same thing*, namely being a unicorn. But how can we say that, if we do not admit the existence of the thing that the thought is a thought of?

I shall not try to assess this argument, which—in one form or another—is still somewhat controversial. The realist (or Platonist) will find it convincing, and the conceptualist will not. Instead, let us turn briefly to the nominalist. He would agree with the realist that when we talk of 'forms' (properties) we are not intending to talk of our own thoughts, but, he would say, we are not trying to talk of Platonically eternal and changeless objects either. The truth is that we are not trying to talk of any objects at all, and it only appears that we are because of an illusion fostered by the grammar of our language. To put his position *very* crudely, it is that forms are mere *names*. To put it a little better, we have expressions in our language which look as though they are names for certain peculiar things called forms (or properties, etc). But when you examine them more closely, you see that these expressions are not really names at all, and are not meant to designate objects of any kind.

To illustrate this idea, consider the (controversial) statement 'beauty is in the eye of the beholder'. On the surface, this appears to be a statement about a certain object, beauty, and seems to be saying where that object is. But clearly what the statement means is something like 'there is no objectively right answer to the question whether this or that thing is beautiful; all one can say is that it looks beautiful to some people, but not to others'. In this paraphrase we no longer even appear to be mentioning a peculiar object called 'beauty', and certainly we are not describing its location. Again, a statement such as 'age brings wisdom' appears on the surface to be mentioning an object called 'wisdom', but in fact it merely means something like 'those who are older are (on the whole) wiser'. Similarly, 'justice prevailed' simply means 'in the end they acted justly', and so on. The general idea is that our language contains a number of idioms which use abstract nouns ('beauty', 'wisdom', 'justice'), or more complex abstract noun-phrases, *as if* they named objects. But in context we can always paraphrase these expressions so as to eliminate the abstract nouns. Moreover, the language of the paraphrase is the 'more basic' language, and the abstract nouns are introduced simply for brevity, or for style, or for some other similar reason which is of no genuine importance to the meaning of what is said. In a word, we do indeed use abstract nouns, but it is a sheer mistake to suppose that they function as names of 'abstract things'. There are no 'abstract things'; there are only concrete things, and it is concrete things that we are talking of—though in a roundabout way—when we use abstract nouns.

This approach clearly has its attractions, but the difficulty has always been to see how it can be systematically carried through. The examples I chose were perhaps especially favourable to the nominalist, and by themselves they do not go very far towards showing that abstract nouns can *always* be paraphrased away. Of course the nominalist need not promise to provide a suitable paraphrase for absolutely *all* uses of abstract nouns, including the philosophical statements made by his realist or conceptualist opponents. He would be entitled to say that the statement 'there is such a thing as wisdom itself' has no suitable paraphrase, and does not really have any proper sense, but is simply a philosophical muddle. The most that he will allow is that there is such a *word* as 'wisdom'. However, it is hardly a controversial and philosophical thesis to say 'not only is there such a word as "wisdom"; it also has a *meaning*'. Indeed we can quite sensibly ask whether the meaning of this word is or is not the same as the meaning of Plato's word φρόνησις, and there is nothing especially philosophical about such an enquiry. The nominalist, then, must provide some account of our usual talk about meanings, and how can he do this if he will not admit that there are such things as meanings? Well, in rough outline he will hope to show that all our talk about meanings can be paraphrased in terms of the two notions of being significant (having a meaning) and being synonymous with (having the same meaning), and that these two notions can be grasped and understood without supposing that there are such things as meanings. But I shall not further enquire whether, in the end, this plan can be made to work. (If it can, then perhaps the nominalist can also find a place for those 'possible meanings' that seem to lie behind the Platonist's claims.)

I shall go no further with this metaphysical debate on what there is, and in particular on whether there are such things as Plato took forms to be. It was Plato who first raised the question, and the answer that he himself gave to it is one that many philosophers still believe to be correct (once we have discarded the unfortunate muddle about perfect paradigms). But Plato also has his opponents, as well as his supporters, and the debate is still with us.

SUGGESTIONS FOR FURTHER READING

THERE are many English translations of the *Phaedo* available. I mention here just the more recent ones that include a commentary or extensive notes on the dialogue

[1] R. S. Bluck, *Plato's Phaedo* (London, 1955).

[2] R. Hackforth, *Plato's Phaedo* (Cambridge, 1955).

[3] D. Gallop, *Plato: Phaedo* (Oxford, 1975).

Gallop's notes are extremely useful, but can be over-difficult. The commentaries by Bluck and Hackforth are both more straightforward, but overlook some important difficulties.

Among many general books on Plato it is worth mentioning

[4] I. M. Crombie, *An Examination of Plato's Doctrines* (2 vols., London, 1963).

This contains stimulating discussions of all Plato's important works (though often at some distance from Plato's own text). Useful studies of special topics particularly relevant to the *Phaedo* include

[5] W. D. Ross, *Plato's Theory of Ideas* (Oxford, 1951).

[6] R. Robinson, *Plato's Earlier Dialectic* (Oxford, 1953).

[7] T. M. Robinson, *Plato's Psychology* (Toronto, 1970).

Chapter 1 : Introduction

Readers who would like more detail on Plato's life and writings may consult the succinct account in

[4] Crombie, vol. i, ch. 1.

A rather different impression is given by

[8] *Encyclopaedia of Philosophy*, ed. P. Edwards (New York and London), 1967, s.v. 'Plato' (by G. Ryle).

It is difficult to suggest anything which will fill out the background on Socrates without including far too much that is not very relevant to the *Phaedo*, but the energetic reader might try

[9] W. K. C. Guthrie, *History of Greek Philosophy* (Cambridge, 1969), vol. iii, part 2.

For more on the Pythagoreans one can confidently recommend

[10] J. Barnes, *The Pre-Socratic Philosophers* (London, 2nd edn., 1982), ch. 6 (and possibly chs. 18 and 22).

Chapter 2 : The Soul and Immortality

Some of the main problems with Plato's conception of the soul are nicely introduced in a general way by

[4] Crombie, vol. 1, ch. 3, § 1.

Crombie turns to the *Phaedo* in his following § 3, but here it might be better to look instead at

[7] T. M. Robinson, ch. 2.

For a brief account which surveys all Plato's dialogues on this topic (and sees very little change in his views), see

[11] W. K. C. Guthrie, 'Plato's Views on the Nature of the Soul', in G. Vlastos (ed.), *Plato: A Collection of Crictical Essays* (New York, 1971), vol. ii, pp. 230–43.

The reader who wishes to reflect further on the consequences drawn for morality in 68c–69d might begin with

[12] T. Irwin, *Plato's Moral Theory* (Oxford, 1977), ch. 6, § 11,

where he will find a view rather different from mine.
The problem of personal identity (and hence of the possibility of personal immortality) is still much debated. All modern discussions are heavily indebted to

[13] J. Locke, *Essay Concerning Human Understanding* (many editions), book ii, ch. 27.

For a modern discussion of Locke's theory, see

[14] J. L. Mackie, *Problems from Locke* (Oxford, 1976), ch. 6.

A number of important contributions to the debate (including Locke's) are usefully reprinted in

[15] J. Perry (ed.), *Personal Identity* (Berkeley and Los Angeles, 1975).
But Perry's *Further Reading* should be expanded to include

[16] R. G. Swinburne, 'Personal Identity', *Proceedings of the Aristotelian Society*, 74 (1973–4), 231–47.

Chapter 3 : The Cyclical Argument

For a view of the argument that is rather different from mine (and from Gallop's) see

[17] J. Barnes, 'Critical Notice of Gallop: *Plato's Phaedo*', *Canadian Journal of Philosophy*, 8 (1978), 397–419.

Barnes takes the view that the 'principle of opposites' does not apply to cases of coming into existence. There is a reply in

[18] D. Gallop, 'Plato's Cyclical Argument Recycled', *Phronesis* 27 (1982), 207–22.

There is a fascinating investigation of what happens if you deny that existence is a property in

[19] C. J. F. Williams, 'On Dying', *Philosophy*, 44 (1969), 217–30.

But the argument is somewhat convoluted, and may confuse a beginner in philosophy.

Chapter 4 : The Recollection Argument

Two very readable articles on the *Phaedo*'s recollection argument are

[20] J. L. Ackrill, '*Anamnesis* in the *Phaedo*: Remarks on 73c–75c', in E. N. Lee, A. P. D. Mourelatos, and R. Rorty (eds.), *Exegesis and Argument* (Assen, 1974), pp. 177–95.
[21] J. C. B. Gosling, 'Similarity in Phaedo 73 seq', *Phronesis* 10 (1965), 151–61.

Ackrill pays more attention to the premisses on being reminded than I do; Gosling puts forward a version of what I call the 'simple' interpretation of the argument (pp. 88 ff.). To these one might add, on the *Meno*,

[22] G. Vlastos, '*Anamnesis* in the *Meno*', *Dialogue* 4 (1965), 143–67.

The problems arising from 74b7–c6 have been hotly debated, but the debate nearly always presupposes a knowledge of Greek. For those who do have this knowledge one could recommend the brief but wide-ranging discussion in

[23] J. M. Rist, 'Equals and Intermediates in Plato', *Phronesis* 9 (1964), 27–37.

or the much fuller treatment in

[24] K. W. Mills, 'Plato's *Phaedo* 74b7–c6', *Phronesis* 2 (1957), 128–47, 3 (1958), 40–58.

For those without Greek there is a discussion in

[4] Crombie, vol. ii, ch. 3, § C(ii)*e*, esp. pp. 295–303.

This is often suggestive, but not very rigorous.

The basic question raised by the *Phaedo*'s recollection argument is the question of how meanings are learnt, or how concepts are formed. There is a vigorous attack on the traditional doctrine of 'abstraction' in

[26] P. T. Geach, *Mental Acts* (London, 1957), §§ 5–11.

This should certainly set one thinking. One reaction to the problems with 'abstractionism' has been to pay more attention to the meaning of whole sentences rather than individual words. A relatively early theory of this kind is

[27] A J. Ayer, *Language, Truth and Logic* (London, 1936), Intro. and ch. 1.

Ayer's theory is now known to involve many difficulties, but more recent work on the topic is too difficult to be mentioned here.

Chapter 5 : The Affinity Argument

No further reading should be needed on this chapter, but some readers may like to consider the speculations in

[28] K. Dorter, 'Plato's Image of Immortality', *Philosophical Quarterly* 26 (1976), 295–304.

Chapter 6 : The Soul as a Harmony

There is a nice discussion of what it means to say that the soul is a harmony (or attunement) in

[10] Barnes, ch. 22, §§ (*c*) and (*d*).

(Barnes defends the view that the theory is due to Philolaus).

Modern debate on the question whether the soul is an immaterial thing takes its start from

[29] R. Descartes, *Meditations on the First Philosophy* (many editions), esp. Meditations II and VI.

There is a vigorous attack on Descartes' position in

[30] G. Ryle, *The Concept of Mind* (London, 1949), ch. 1.

For a more general discussion of the question one might consult

[31] K. Campbell, *Body and Mind* (New York, 1970), esp. chs. 3 and 4.

Chapter 7 : Causes, Reasons, & Explanations

A stimulating paper on this topic is

[32] G. Vlastos, 'Reasons and Causes in the *Phaedo*', *Philosophical Review* 78 (1969), 291–325.

This paper requires careful reading, but is worth the effort. (It will be seen that Vlastos and I are not always in agreement) Of many other discussions one might perhaps mention

[33] E. L. Burge, 'The ideas as *Aitiai* in the *Phaedo*', *Phronesis* 16 (1971), 1–13.

This makes some useful points, especially in its first three sections, but it will be difficult for those without knowledge of Greek. Aristotle's fourfold classification of reasons (or causes) is to be found in his *Physics*, book ii, ch. 3 (and cf. ch. 7), while his views on teleology in nature are defended in ch. 8 of that book. A convenient translation and commentary is

[34] W. Charlton, *Aristotle's Physics. Books I and II* (Oxford, 1970).

A somewhat imaginative account of Plato's views on teleology in nature may be found in

[1] Crombie, vol. ii, ch. 2, §§ 1–2.

Modern discussions of causation are heavily influenced by Hume's treatment of the topic, for which see

[35] D. Hume, *Enquiry Concerning Human Understanding* (many editions), §§ 4–7,

and for a commentary on Hume's account

[36] B. Stroud, *Hume* (London, 1977), chs 3 and 4.

However, Hume introduces several issues not very germane to the *Phaedo*, and the reader may be satisfied with the simpler introduction in

[37] J. Hospers, 'What is Explanation?', revised in A. Flew (ed.), *Essays in Conceptual Analysis* (London, 1966).

A useful collection of modern contributions to the topic is

[38] E. Sosa (ed.), *Causation and Conditionals* (Oxford, 1975).

But several of these articles will be too difficult for the beginner. An influential discussion of the relation between a person's reasons for acting and the causes of his action is

[39] D. Davidson, 'Actions, Reasons and Causes', *Journal of Philosophy* 60 (1963), pp. 685–700.

Chapter 8 : The Method of Hypothesis

Important reading on Plato's method of hypothesis is

[6] R. Robinson, chs. 7–9.

This may be complemented by

[1] Bluck, appendix 6,

who argues for a rather different view.

To make a start on the difficult problem of what can be known a priori one might begin with

[27] Ayer, ch. 4,

who argues that all a priori knowledge has a linguistic foundation, and against him

[40] W. and M. Kneale, *The Development of Logic* (Oxford, 1962), ch. 10, § 5.

The more adventurous reader might try

[41] W. V. Quine, 'Two Dogmas of Empiricism', in id. *From a Logical Point of View* (2nd edn., Harvard, 1961),

perhaps with the reply by

[42] H. P. Grice and P. F. Strawson, 'In defense of a Dogma', *Philosophical Review* 65 (1965), 141–58.

In effect, Quine argues that *no* knowledge is a priori.

Chapter 9 : The Final Argument

A brief diagnosis of the faults in the final argument may be found in

[43] D. Keyt, 'The Fallacies in Phaedo 102a–107b', *Phronesis* 8 (1963), 167–72.

His interpretation is disputed by

[44] J. Schiller, '*Phaedo* 104–105: Is the Soul a Form?', *Phronesis* 12 (1967), 50–58.

However, Keyt may be rather difficult for those without knowledge of Greek. Better on this score are the fuller accounts in

[45] D. O'Brien, 'The Last Argument of Plato's *Phaedo*', *Classical Quarterly*, 2nd ser., 17 (1967), 198–231, 18 (1968), 95–106.

and

[46] D. Frede, 'The Final Proof of the Immortality of the Soul in Plato's *Phaedo* 102a–107a', *Phronesis* 23 (1978), 24–41.

Both these are rather friendly to the argument.

Chapter 10 : The Theory of Forms

A succinct general account of Plato's theory of forms may be found in

[47] A. Wedberg, *Plato's Philosophy of Mathematics* (Stockholm, 1955). ch. 3.

For a fuller treatment, consult

[5] Ross, up to p. 92 (the discussion of the *Parmenides*).

The most influential paper on the 'Third Man' argument in the *Parmenides* is

[48] G. Vlastos, 'The Third Man Argument in the Parmenides', *Philosophical Review* 63 (1954), 319–49.

But see also

[49] C. Strang, 'Plato and the Third Man', *Proceedings of the Aristotelian Society*, supplementary vol. 37 (1963), 147–64.

On the question of Realism (or Platonism) *v.* Conceptualism *v.* Nominalism one might make a start with

[50] B. Russell, *The Problems of Philosophy* (Oxford, 1912), ch. 9

and

[51] W. V. Quine, 'On What There is', in id. *From a Logical Point of View* (2nd edn., Harvard, 1961).

GENERAL INDEX

The index does not include works cited only in the suggestion for further reading

INDEX LOCORUM

This index records the passages cited from Plato's dialogues other than the *Phaedo*

Printed in the United Kingdom
by Lightning Source UK Ltd.
131797UK00001B/127-129/A